GOD: THE COVENANT MAKER
Genesis 9:1-17

"God's Covenant with His People" is the title for our study of the next three months. The covenant idea surfaces again and again through the Bible, and these thirteen lessons begin with Noah in Genesis and end with the covenant of God being fulfilled in the New Jerusalem of the book of Revelation. So, this is another way of doing a panoramic study of the Bible, following one of its key concepts. As the account unfolds, we will be focusing each Sunday on some Bible personality and his relationship to God's covenant. At the same time we will be discovering how Christians are related to God and to one another through the "new covenant" of the life, death, and resurrection of Christ. Naturally, this session deals with the Bible's first reference to covenant—with Noah.

The Bible Lesson

GENESIS 9:

8 And God spake unto Noah, and to his sons with him, saying,

9 And I, behold, I establish my covenant with you, and with your seed after you;

10 And with every living creature that is with you, of the fowl, of the cattle, and of every beast of the earth with you; from all that go out of the ark, to every beast of the earth.

11 And I will establish my covenant with you; neither shall all flesh be cut off any more by the waters of a flood; neither shall there any more be a flood to destroy the earth.

12 And God said, This is the token of the covenant which I make between me and you and every living creature that is with you, for perpetual generations:

13 I do set my bow in the cloud, and it shall be for a token of a covenant between me and the earth.

14 And it shall come to pass, when I bring a cloud over the earth, that the bow shall be seen in the cloud:

15 And I will remember my covenant, which is between me and you and every living creature of all flesh; and the waters shall no more become a flood to destroy all flesh.

16 And the bow shall be in the cloud; and I will look upon it, that I

may remember the everlasting covenant between God and every living creature of all flesh that is upon the earth.

17 And God said unto Noah, This is the token of the covenant, which I have established between me and all flesh that is upon the earth.

The Lesson Explained

A NEW BEGINNING FOR MANKIND (9:1-7)

The pride and disobedience of Adam and Eve had shown that persons with free will would not always be loyal to their Maker. Then jealous Cain killed his brother Abel, showing how he despised God's handiwork. As population increased, even the imagination of mankind "was only evil continually" (6:5). Apparently convinced that conditions were beyond reclaiming, God decided to start over. In Noah he found assurance that the creation of mankind, however, had not been a mistake. After giving him instructions for preserving Noah's family and representatives of the animal kingdom, God promised to make a covenant with him (6:18).

When the rains came and the waters rose, the huge boat carried its living cargo safely for months. Finally the earth was dry enough for persons and animals, and after the ark was emptied, Noah built an altar and offered sacrifices to the Lord. In response, the Lord promised never to punish the earth again because of man's sin but to maintain a dependable pattern of seasons.

Then God blessed Noah and gave him special instructions about replenishing the earth and respecting human life. His commission was almost the same as the one given to Adam because this was a new beginning for the human race. A major change was in the permission to eat flesh, in addition to the "green herb" (v. 3). That strengthened the dominion of mankind over the rest of creation, but it also added to man's responsibility. Because blood was seen as the principle of life, persons must not eat the blood of animals. Also, murder must be punished because it violates the image of God.

A COVENANT WITH HIS CREATURES (9:8-11)

But God's most significant message to Noah and his sons was the voluntary covenant he made with them and their descendants. We may overlook in verse 10 that the covenant extended also to all living creatures. It was God's promise, with no obligation on man's part, that never again would a flood destroy the earth. Without God's promise, mankind would lose confidence in the reliability of nature and in the providence of God. This covenant grew out of God's decision in 8:22.

A REMINDER OF THE PROMISE (9:12-17)

As a visible sign of God's promise or covenant, he caused a bow of color to appear in the sky. People who used bows for hunting and warfare would recognize it as a bow at rest. Although we generally think of it as an assurance to mankind, God said, "I will look upon it, that I may remember the everlasting covenant." Three times the writer referred to "the bow in the cloud," and that is the customary way that the rainbow appears. While the cloud in that day might make the people fear another flood, God used the rainbow to reassure them that no matter how hard the storm, he would remember his promise. This covenant was made with all mankind—not just the chosen people—and with all creation. God would not destroy the earth by flood even if it spurned his original purpose in creation.

Truths to Live By

The Bible reveals a God who communicates with persons.—That is true from the first chapter of Genesis and extends throughout the Bible. We are so used to the idea that we may take it for granted that all religions portray their gods in that way. But the records of ancient peoples—some of Israel's neighbors—don't reveal it so. While the Hebrews thought of God in anthropomorphic terms, having manlike features and feelings, they also saw him as exalted and completely different from man. Still, he was concerned for his creation and communicated with persons. He talked with the patriarchs, the prophets, and many others. Christians today believe that he inspires, guides, encourages, and rebukes them through his Holy Spirit. Because he communicates, they are led to pray and praise.

God has provided a dependable universe.—Those who have experienced a flood that lasted a week or two know how it damaged property, upset community activities, and threatened life. We cannot imagine the effects of one that lasted for months—from one season through another. God said that would never happen again, but days and seasons would follow their usual patterns. Thus, the earth revolves to give day and night so precisely that time can be measured in seconds. Movements of the stars and eclipses of the sun and moon can be predicted years in advance. After noting for generations the nature and actions of gases and chemicals, scientists can deal with them successfully because of their dependability. Scientific law is not something proposed and enacted by scientists; it is a statement of what they have observed happening over and over again. The universe is dependable.

God believes in his creation.—Several years ago a popular movie portrayed God as saying that he did not know why some persons did not believe in him; after all, he believed in *them*. This lesson about Noah and the flood shows that. To be sure, he was grieved because most people rejected the kind of life he meant for them to live. But the fact that Noah was different proved that creating mankind was not a failure. If *one* man could be righteous in such a wicked atmosphere, it could happen again, and that possibility made it worthwhile. God still believes in persons, and he sent his Son to make it possible for believers to be at home in the family of God, accepting his pattern for their life-style.

A Verse to Remember

And I will remember my covenant, which is between me and you and every living creature of all flesh.—Genesis 9:15.

Daily Bible Readings

Sept.   1—Sin Grieves God. Gen. 6:5-13
Sept.   2—God's Plan for Safety. Gen. 6:14-22
Sept.   3—Safety in the Flood. Gen. 7:1-5,17-23
Sept.   4—Thanking God for Safety. Gen. 8:6-12,20-22
Sept.   5—Living with God's Blessing. Gen. 9:1-7
Sept.   6—The Covenant of the Rainbow. Gen. 9:8-17
Sept.   7—The Majesty of God. Ps. 8

GOD'S COVENANT AND ABRAHAM
Genesis 12:1-7; 17:1-21

The Hebrew word used most frequently for covenant was *berith*, which originally meant probably a fetter or bond. So a covenant was a binding agreement between two parties. Covenants or treaties between nations were known long before Abraham's time. Frequently they were proposed by a powerful ruler and accepted by heads of smaller realms, but they usually contained promises on both sides to control relationships. So, the covenant idea was known in Abraham's world. Beginning with the covenant we study in this session, it became a key concept for describing the basic relationship of God with his people in the Old Testament. Then Jesus focused attention on it when he said at the Supper, "This is my blood of the covenant, which is poured out for many" (Mark 14:24, RSV). God's covenant shows his love and grace.

The Bible Lesson

GENESIS 12:
1 Now the Lord had said unto Abram, Get thee out of thy country, and from thy kindred, and from thy father's house, unto a land that I will shew thee:
2 And I will make of thee a great nation, and I will bless thee, and make thy name great; and thou shalt be a blessing:
3 And I will bless them that bless thee, and curse him that curseth thee: and in thee shall all families of the earth be blessed.
4 So Abram departed, as the Lord had spoken unto him.
GENESIS 17:
1 And when Abram was ninety years old and nine, the Lord appeared to Abram, and said unto him, I am the Almighty God; walk before me, and be thou perfect.
2 And I will make my covenant between me and thee, and will multiply thee exceedingly.
3 And Abram fell on his face: and God talked with him, saying,
4 As for me, behold, my covenant is with thee, and thou shalt be a father of many nations.
5 Neither shall thy name any more be called Abram, but thy

name shall be Abraham; for a father of many nations have I made thee.

6 And I will make thee exceeding frutiful, and I will make nations of thee, and kings shall come out of thee.

7 And I will establish my covenant between me and thee and thy seed after thee in their generations for an everlasting covenant, to be a God unto thee, and to thy seed after thee.

8 And I will give unto thee, and to thy seed after thee, the land wherein thou art a stranger, all the land of Canaan, for an everlasting possession; and I will be their God.

The Lesson Explained

RESPONDING TO GOD'S CALL (12:1-4)

Chapters 10—11 list many descendants of Noah's sons, and finally in the closing verses of chapter 11 the family of Terah comes to the fore. He lived in Ur of the Chaldees and took his family, including Abram his son, to Haran. Abram's wife was Sarai and she had no children.

Within a context of moon worship, Abram heard the Lord calling him to leave his clan—his "father's house"—for an unknown country. He had to give up comfort, safety, and family ties to answer God's call. Although Sarai seemed to be barren, God promised that Abram would father a nation. Having many sons and grandsons would make him famous. But even more, Abram would "be a blessing." The blessing of God had a purpose; Abram and his descendants would be the channel for God's will in the world. "All families of the earth" would include everybody. So, from the first patriarch of the Hebrews, the intent of God was for them to influence and bless the world. Abram did not know what God had in mind, but his faith did not require that to answer God's call with action.

WORSHIPING IN A FAR COUNTRY (12:5-7)

At seventy-five years of age Abram took Sarai, his nephew Lot, and all their possessions out of Haran to find the land of Canaan. The phrase "the souls they had gotten" may refer to slaves, workers, or followers. The caravan finally reached its goal and camped at Shechem, in the valley between Mount Ebal and Mount Gerizim. The Lord appeared to Abram there and promised to give that land to his descendants. Abram responded by building an altar to Yahweh and worshiping

14

him. In a land of many local gods and rank heathenism, he erected a symbol to his faith in the God who had called him in Haran and was still with him in Canaan.

GOD OFFERS HIS COVENANT (17:1-8)

The intervening chapters tell of several major events in the life of Abram, and this one begins with the announcement that he had reached his ninety-ninth year. The Lord appeared to him again. Calling himself *El Shaddai,* "the Almighty God," Yahweh said that if Abram would measure his conduct in God's presence and by his standard, God would agree to enlarge Abram's family and line. God took the initiative in making the covenant; it was an offer of grace based on God's choice rather than Abram's merit.

To underscore the significance of his promise to Abram, God changed his name to Abraham—from "exalted father" to "father of a multitude." Even kings and nations would eventually come from his line—all of which seemed unthinkable to a man in his old age. In selecting Abraham as a channel for his purposes, God also selected a family, a clan, a nation. The covenant would provide a living relationship in which God would show his standards of righteousness and the scope of his compassion in his dealings with the Hebrews and in their witness to other nations. Canaan would be their home, and Yahweh would be their God.

Truths to Live By

Responding to God with faith usually calls for action.— That is a recurring theme of the Bible. It is not a collection of just wise sayings or mystical speculations. It is a rather complicated story of living people responding to God's challenge to live by his pattern. They had faith in him, and that faith was not something they hoarded or bragged about, but they acted on it. By faith Abram left home for a country he had never seen. By faith Moses later challenged Pharaoh and led a host of slaves out of Egypt. By faith Paul and Barnabas left Antioch to tell Jews and Gentiles about Jesus the risen Christ. By faith Martin Luther took a stand against the evil practices of the Roman Catholic Church. By faith William Carey went from England to India to preach the gospel while some of his fellow ministers believed that God did not need human help for that purpose.

God's chosen people must be a blessing to others.—Being chosen by God does not guarantee one's health, wealth, or popularity. Abraham's descendants did eventually gain Canaan, but the Hebrews never became a "world power." God had something else in mind. It is the same today; the gross national product and world influence do not prove God's selection. His chosen people live by his standards and show his compassion. They are chosen more to be a blessing than to get one. They are not limited by nationality, geography, or language. They are not intended to be exclusive but to yearn for the widest possible fellowship.

In our covenants with God we respond to his grace with our obedience.—Although the covenant with Noah made no requirements of him, the covenant with Abraham said, "If you will do this, I will do that." Often the people were so pleased with the second part that they overlooked the first. Moses and the prophets had to remind them of their obligations to God. He offered the covenant voluntarily, and its rewards were greater than its demands. As Christians we accepted God's covenant of salvation by his grace. But no one can be a real Christian without living by Christ's pattern. While no believer can live a sinless life, true fellowship with Christ will lead us away from selfishness and pride.

A Verse to Remember

I will establish my covenant between me and thee and thy seed after thee in their generations for an everlasting covenant, to be a God unto thee, and to thy seed after thee.—Genesis 17:7.

Daily Bible Readings

Sept.   8—Going Out in Faith. Gen. 12:1-9
Sept.   9—Fear Causes Failure. Gen. 12:10-20
Sept. 10—A Parting and a Promise. Gen. 13:1-16
Sept. 11—Counted Righteous. Gen. 15:1-6
Sept. 12—Father of Many Nations. Gen. 17:1-8
Sept. 13—Promise of a Son. Gen. 17:9-21
Sept. 14—Righteousness Based on Faith. Rom. 10:5-13

September 21, 1980

GOD'S COVENANT AND MOSES
Exodus 2:23 to 3:14; 19:1-9

God's covenant in Noah's time was a promise that he made to the whole world. Last Sunday we studied the covenant between the Lord and Abraham, who would be the father of several nations. It was repeated in God's dealings with Isaac and Jacob, still a covenant between God and individuals. In this session God spoke to Moses, but the covenant was to be between God and the people of Israel. For generations they had lived in Egypt and much of the time had been slaves. Although they acknowledged the God of the patriarchs and accepted Moses and Aaron as his messengers, their concept of his uniqueness and power may have been limited. Their self-image was also limited. The covenant with the Lord would speak to both of these problems and provide a new sense of purpose for them as a nation.

The Bible Lesson

EXODUS 19:

1 In the third month, when the children of Israel were gone forth out of the land of Egypt, the same day came they into the wilderness of Sinai.

2 For they were departed from Rephidim, and were come to the desert of Sinai, and had pitched in the wilderness; and there Israel camped before the mount.

3 And Moses went up unto God, and the Lord called unto him out of the mountain, saying, Thus shalt thou say to the house of Jacob, and tell the children of Israel;

4 Ye have seen what I did unto the Egyptians, and how I bare you on eagles' wings, and brought you unto myself.

5 Now therefore, if ye will obey my voice indeed, and keep my covenant, then ye shall be a peculiar treasure unto me above all people: for all the earth is mine:

6 And ye shall be unto me a kingdom of priests, and an holy nation. These are the words which thou shalt speak unto the children of Israel.

7 And Moses came and called for the elders of the people, and

laid before their faces all these words which the Lord commanded him.

8 And all the people answered together, and said, All that the Lord hath spoken we will do. And Moses returned the words of the people unto the Lord.

The Lesson Explained

GOD SELECTS A LEADER (3:4-7,10)

While marveling at the miraculous bush, many readers of this chapter miss other important things in Moses' unexpected encounter with God. For instance, although Moses had been reared in Pharaoh's palace, he was a fugitive from Egyptian justice. Also, he was surprised to meet God in the desert; he probably thought he was limited to a certain place. Further, God identified himself with the patriarchs to show his continued concern for his people. "I know their sorrows," he told Moses, "And I am come down to deliver them" (vv. 7-8).

Just when Moses felt relieved by that news and wondered how God would deal with Egyptian power, he heard God say, "Come now therefore, and I will send thee unto Pharaoh." God always uses persons to accomplish his will in the world. When Moses was reluctant (4:1-16), God rebuked his fearfulness. But God did not change his mind. Moses might need a speaker to help him, but God knew that he had selected the right leader for his people.

GOD DELIVERS HIS PEOPLE (19:1-4)

Between chapters 3 and 19 the role of Moses grew to national importance as the children of Israel did actually leave Egypt and journey to the wilderness of Sinai. After three months on the trail, they had finally reached the place that God had set as their first goal. "When thou hast brought forth the people out of Egypt," God had said, "ye shall serve God upon this mountain" (Ex. 3:12). Moses went up into Mount Horeb (usually identified today as Jebel Musa) in the southern mountains of the Peninsula of Sinai to receive God's instructions. He began by reminding Moses of the miraculous deliverance from Egypt and his continuing providence. God had done it.

GOD PROPOSES A COVENANT (19:5-8)

On the basis of what he had done, God then proposed a

covenant between himself and the nation. In Egypt the people had been oppressed, probably unified mostly in their suffering. In the wilderness they were a newly freed people, growing in self-awareness but not yet sure of their directions. They still needed to make a commitment to the delivering God and to his purpose for them. They should be reminded that they owed their freedom to him; he was far more powerful than Pharaoh.

God's condition for the covenant was that the people "obey my voice indeed, and keep my covenant." His voice sounded loud and clear in declaring the Ten Commandments (20:1-17). They required single-minded devotion to God and justice in all human relationships. Those laws were like the stipulations of the political treaties (called covenants) of that day. They combined into a pattern of conduct that would make the Israelites distinctive among the heathen nations of that time.

Although the whole earth belonged to God, those who committed themselves to this covenant would be his "own possession among all peoples" (RSV). As a nation dedicated to him, in their loyalty to God they would be a whole nation of priests. They could worship directly and mediate for one another. The requirements were high, and so were the benefits. When Moses told the people what the Lord had said, they answered: "All that the Lord hath spoken we will do."

Truths to Live By

God uses men and women as his deliverers.—Americans believe that God used George Washington to deliver the Colonies from the oppression of King George III. Many black Americans believe that God used Martin Luther King to free them from community practices that prevented their being accepted as persons. But oppression can be found in the town as well as in the nation. God needs men and women to be deliverers in their own communities. Some children need tutoring to escape the oppression of ignorance. Others have been scarred by the divorce of their parents and need some understanding friends. Some young people need a knowledgeable adult to help them avoid drug enslavement. Some adults need friends to overcome loneliness. God is calling such deliverers.

19

Responding to God's covenant brings his kind of reward.—Although God had promised the Israelites a homeland in Canaan, his covenant provisions did not mention wealth or power. Instead, they would become a distinctive nation among the peoples of the world. Their religious sensitivity combined with high morality would reveal them as a consecrated nation. Their reward was to be a witness. It is the same today. Our covenant of faith with God in Christ does not promise fame or wealth. Instead, it offers resources for becoming a mature person, guidance in dealing with life's problems, and concern for others who need what God in Christ can give. The true rewards from God for being Christian are not a good reputation and a nice home but satisfaction in living by Christ's pattern and courage to do it in face of opposition.

A high goal can challenge the best in persons.—Beware of taking the Ten Commandments for granted. They may show some similarities to the Code of Hammurabi, but they surpassed all patterns of human conduct for their day. So, the covenant offered by the Lord was far beyond the standards of the Israelites. Our daily news papers show they are still more than many people can live up to. Christians have an even higher pattern to follow in the life of Christ. Low goals never inspired great living. Christians look to the Holy Spirit for guidance and support in living beyond themselves for Christ's sake.

Verses to Remember

If ye will obey my voice indeed, and keep my covenant, then ye shall be a peculiar treasure unto me above all people: ... And ye shall be unto me a kingdom of priests, and an holy nation.—Exodus 19:5-6.

Daily Bible Readings

Sept. 15—Drawn from the Water. Ex. 2:1-10
Sept. 16—Running from Danger. Ex. 2:11-25
Sept. 17—Hearing God's Call. Ex. 3:1-10
Sept. 18—Protest and Promise. Ex. 3:11-22
Sept. 19—The Song of Victory. Ex. 15:1-13
Sept. 20—Promising to Obey God. Ex. 19:1-8
Sept. 21—Learning God's Way. Ex. 33:9-19

GOD'S COVENANT AND JOSHUA
Joshua 24:1-31; Judges 2

Since the first eight sessions of this quarter's study of "God's Covenant with His People" are based on the Old Testament, we need some historical perspective. In the apparent repetition of the covenant we must not think that we are dealing with the same people. The nation is the same, but the generations are different. So, we need to peg these prominent persons in their time. Abraham's era is really unknown, but it may have been about 1700 B.C. The Exodus under Moses occurred about 1250 B.C. Joshua's challenge to the people in this lesson could have been about fifty years later, after the doubters had died off in the wilderness and Israel had invaded Canaan sucessfully.

The Bible Lesson

JOSHUA 24:

14 Now therefore fear the Lord, and serve him in sincerity and in truth: and put away the gods which your fathers served on the other side of the flood, and in Egypt; and serve ye the Lord.

15 And if it seem evil unto you to serve the Lord, choose you this day whom ye will serve; whether the gods which your fathers served on the other side of the flood, or the gods of the Amorites, in whose land ye dwell: but as for me and my house, we will serve the Lord.

16 And the people answered and said, God forbid that we should forsake the Lord, to serve other gods;

17 For the Lord our God, he it is that brought us up and our fathers out of the land of Egypt, from the house of bondage, and which did those great signs in our sight, and preserved us in all the way wherein we went, and among all the people through whom we passed:

18 And the Lord drave out from before us all the people, even the Amorites which dwelt in the land: therefore will we also serve the Lord; for he is our God.

19 And Joshua said unto the people, Ye cannot serve the Lord: for he is an holy God; he is a jealous God; he will not forgive your transgressions nor your sins.

20 If ye forsake the Lord, and serve strange gods, then he will turn and do you hurt, and consume you, after that he hath done you good.

21 And the people said unto Joshua, Nay; but we will serve the Lord.

22 And Joshua said unto the people, Ye are witnesses against yourselves that ye have chosen you the Lord, to serve him. And they said, We are witnesses.

23 Now therefore put away, said he, the strange gods which are among you, and incline your heart unto the Lord God of Israel.

24 And the people said unto Joshua, The Lord our God will we serve, and his voice will we obey.

25 So Joshua made a covenant with the people that day, and set them a statute and an ordinance in Shechem.

The Lesson Explained

A CALL FOR COMMITMENT (24:14-15)

This is an important chapter for understanding the religion of Israel because it pictures the act of covenant renewal. Having begun between God and Abraham, that relationship included the promise of God and the obligations of the people. When Joshua gathered the tribes at Shechem, it was for a religious purpose because they "presented themselves before God" (v. 1). Then Joshua spoke for "the Lord God of Israel" in recounting the great events in which God had guided and delivered the people: from Egypt, through the wilderness, and into Canaan.

Thus having tried to convince the Israelites that God cared for them and had in mind something great for them to do, Joshua came to the commitment part of the ceremony. He urged them to "fear the Lord, and serve him in sincerity and in truth." They could do that only by renouncing other gods, both the ones their fathers had worshiped beyond the Euphrates River (Abraham's homeland) and those they worshiped while in Egypt. If they were not willing to accept only the Lord as God, they should go the other way; but Joshua declared his own commitment to the Lord only.

TESTING THE PEOPLE'S RESPONSE (24:16-24)

The people's first response seemed to come easily in words like these: "We couldn't possibly forsake the Lord to serve other gods." And they repeated some of the things Joshua said that the Lord had done for them. But Joshua tested their answer by reminding them of Yahweh's holiness and his demand for single-minded loyalty. If they should violate their pledge, they could expect God's punishment. His love was balanced by his righteousness.

Although the people again declared their intention to serve the Lord, Joshua must have suspected that some of them were weak in loyalty or truthfulness. Judges 2 shows how right he was, at least as to the influence of parents on their children (vv. 7, 10). Joshua told his listeners that if they were sincere about their commitment to the Lord, they should "put away the strange gods" (24:23). Then the people professed their loyalty a third time.

A WRITTEN COVENANT AT SHECHEM (24:25-28)

It was then that Joshua took steps to help the people remember their commitment. First, he drew up a statement that acknowledged God's goodness and promised the people's obedience to "a statute and an ordinance," which were probably plural. That document was added to "the book of the law of God." Then he had a large stone raised to stand under an oak tree in the holy place of the Lord. He said that because the stone "hath heard all the words of the Lord," it would be a reminder of how the people had promised to serve the Lord.

It was at Shechem that Abraham built his first altar to the Lord in Canaan, and now the Israelites had renewed their covenant there in the homeland the Lord had given them. The federation of tribes was making itself at home while becoming a nation among pagan neighbors. It was time for a binding commitment with the Lord.

Truths to Live By

Each generation must make its own commitment to God.—Just because our forefathers sought religious freedom in the New World does not mean that we have made this a Christian nation. The religious surge during and just after World War II did not guarantee that our national goals would accord with God's will. Religious experience cannot be inherited. A father's devotion to God may influence his son for good, but to have a living relationship with God, the son must make his own commitment. However the "new times" may affect the wording of that commitment, it must be the son's own experience for God to lead him into becoming a real person.

Some tangible reminders are needed to keep believers on course.—So long as those reminders do not take the place of God's reality, they can be helpful. In Jeremiah's day the Temple meant more to the people than the Lord and his law. A crucifix and a statue of a saint may appear to have won the kind of reverence that only God should receive. But that does not mean that tangible reminders are all wrong. After all, the church building itself is a tangible reminder of faith and religious experience. A stained-glass window or an open Bible may say more than many words. Surely a cross is more appropriate on the church than a weather vane. Baptism is a tangible reminder of Christ's death and resurrection.

It is easier to profess faith than to practice it.—Because Joshua knew that some of the people still had idols in their homes, he questioned their glib agreement to serve the Lord. They were the liars in the crowd. But there were others with a different problem. They had given up the old idols, and they had learned the "right" answer when a leader was talking about Yahweh. "Sure, sure, we're with you," but they were hypocrites. But possibly the larger group was sincere when promising to serve the Lord. Some may have been as strong as Joshua, but others did not realize how persuasive and insidious the worshipers of Baal would be. We, too, have learned that it is easier to profess faith than to practice it.

A Verse to Remember

The Lord our God will we serve, and his voice will we obey.—Joshua 24:24.

Daily Bible Readings

Sept. 22—Joshua's Good Advice. Josh. 23:1-3,11-16
Sept. 23—Joshua Remembers God's Blessing. Josh. 24:1-8
Sept. 24—Joshua Gives an Example. Josh. 24:9-18
Sept. 25—The People Choose God. Josh. 24:19-31
Sept. 26—The People Forget God. Judg. 2:1-13
Sept. 27—Another Opportunity. Judg. 2:14-23
Sept. 28—God's Word to Joshua. Josh. 1:1-9

GOD'S COVENANT AND DAVID
2 Samuel 7; 1 Chronicles 16:1-36

After Joshua died about 1200 B.C., no one man was ready to lead the whole nation of Israel. In fact, as a confederation of tribes, the people were still seeking real unity. Strong personalities called "judges" became temporary and sometimes tribal leaders, usually as warring captains. The last and most notable was Samuel, but late in his career the people demanded a king for the whole nation. Tall and handsome, Saul was anointed in 1020 B.C. for that responsibility, but he was a disappointment. Then about 1000 B.C. young David succeeded him but not without a struggle. The northern tribes preferred Saul's son to the shepherd-singer from Judah. But David won them over and then captured Jerusalem—between the northern tribes and Judah—to be his capital. This was the beginning of Israel's golden age.

The Bible Lesson

2 SAMUEL 7:

8 Now therefore so shalt thou say unto my servant David, Thus saith the Lord of hosts, I took thee from the sheepcote, from following the sheep, to be ruler over my people, over Israel:

9 And I was with thee whithersoever thou wentest, and have cut off all thine enemies out of thy sight, and have made thee a great name, like unto the name of the great men that are in the earth.

10 Moreover I will appoint a place for my people Israel, and will plant them, that they may dwell in a place of their own, and move no more; neither shall the children of wickedness afflict them any more, as beforetime.

11 And as since the time that I commanded judges to be over my people Israel, and have caused thee to rest from all thine enemies. Also the Lord telleth thee that he will make thee an house.

12 And when thy days be fulfilled, and thou shalt sleep with thy fathers, I will set up thy seed after thee, which shall proceed out of thy bowels, and I will establish his kingdom.

13 He shall build an house for my name, and I will stablish the throne of his kindgom for ever.

14 I will be his father, and he shall be my son. If he commit

25

iniquity, I will chasten him with the rod of men, and with the stripes of the children of men:

15 But my mercy shall not depart away from him, as I took it from Saul, whom I put away before thee.

16 And thine house and thy kingdom shall be established for ever before thee: thy throne shall be established for ever.

The Lesson Explained

REMEMBERING GOD'S COVENANT (1 Chron. 16:1-17)

Finally in a time of peace when "the fame of David went out into all lands" (14:17), he built his palace in Jerusalem and pitched a tent for the ark of the Lord. Since it had been ignored during the reign of Saul, David wanted to have it in the capital as the symbol of the nation's faith. In a joyful procession, with the Levites singing and playing instruments, the ark was brought up to Jerusalem. Sacrifices were offered before the tent of the ark, and David appointed some Levites as its permanent choir and guard. To Asaph, the choir director, he gave a psalm, beginning with 16:8, and verses 8-22 are the same as Psalm 105:1-15.

That psalm of thanksgiving reminded the people of the Lord's "marvellous works . . . and the judgments of his mouth" (v. 12). It also urged them to remember his covenant that was to last forever. It began with Abraham and was renewed with Isaac and Jacob; it was an everlasting covenant with Israel. It seems that little had been said about it since the days of Joshua. But David saw it as a factor in unifying the people.

DECLINING DAVID'S OFFER (2 Sam. 7:4-11a)

Although we are using different Bible books, we are dealing with the same event. The Chronicles passage emphasized the worship aspect of the coming of the ark to Jerusalem and called attention to the ancient covenant. The account here in 2 Samuel refers to another covenant, a promise of God to David.

While he was enjoying some peacetime at home, David told Nathan the prophet that it did not seem right for the king to live in a "house of cedar" while the ark of God had only a tent. Nathan's first response was favorable to whatever David was thinking, but that night the prophet had another word from the

26

Lord. He was to tell David that ever since their deliverance from Egypt he had traveled with his people in the symbolism of a tent. He had never asked any of the leaders to build him a house, and the time for that still had not come. Instead, the Lord had been more concerned with finding a leader for his people. From being a shepherd, David had become king of his nation. With God's help, he would lead them into peace.

PROJECTING A ROYAL LINE (2 Sam. 7:11b-16)

Instead of David building a house for the Lord, the Lord would make him a house, or royal line, forever. After his death, David's son would succeed him and so on into the future. That first son would build the house of God that David wanted to build. The Lord would be like a father to that young king. If the son should sin, the Father would punish him, but his mercy would always be available. The king would never be forsaken to endure the kind of depression that Saul experienced. He would be the first of many descendants in the line of David to rule over the chosen people.

Nathan reported this latest revelation to David, and the rest of the chapter consists of David's prayer when he "sat before the Lord," perhaps in the tent that sheltered the ark of the Lord. This covenant with David in behalf of Israel provided a sense of continuity and destiny for the people, especially for Judah after the Northern Kingdom had come to an end. In New Testament times Jewish believers saw Jesus as continuing the Davidic line.

Truths to Live By

Recalling noble commitments of the past can help deal with problems in the present.—That is possibly what David hoped for in reminding the people of God's covenant with Abraham that was eventually renewed with the people of Israel. They had been disappointed by their first king, Saul, and his successor from Judah was seeking the support of the northern tribes. It was a crucial time for the nation. In times of marital tension, remembering their vows may help a husband and wife see how their blessings outweigh their irritations. Remembering his pledge to follow Christ's pattern for his life may help a man decide for honesty in politics or business.

Reviewing the high goals and principles of the Constitution may help American citizens support unpopular but right legislation for the disadvantaged.

Some church needs may be more important than a fine new building.—When God declined David's offer to build a temple, he gave no reason. The tent for the ark seemed acceptable, and perhaps other matters were more pressing. Just because a congregation might rally to a building program should not be the main reason for getting involved. Most churches have fellowship problems; believers need to learn to appreciate one another and help those who need friendship and tangible resources. Some churches need to get involved in varied witnessing activities—both traditional and innovative. Some churches need to make better use of their present facilities before taking on a huge debt for more room. When a new building is really needed, a congregation must face that challenge, but a building program does not meet all the needs of a church.

God chooses able and willing persons to achieve his purposes.—He saw in David not a perfect man or king but one who was competent and willing to follow the Lord's leading. God is not concerned with a person's present situation; he evaluates potential. That includes native ability, willingness to learn, interest in others, and commitment to worthy goals.

A Verse to Remember

And thine house and thy kingdom shall be established for ever before thee: thy throne shall be established for ever.— 2 Samuel 7:16.

Daily Bible Readings

Sept. 29—Desire to Honor God. 2 Sam. 7:1-7
Sept. 30—God Honors and Reassures His Own. 2 Sam. 8:8-17
Oct.   1—Right Response to God's Goodness. 2 Sam. 7:18-24
Oct.   2—A Plea for Blessing. 2 Sam. 7:25-29
Oct.   3—Gratitude in Worship. 1 Chron. 1:1-7
Oct.   4—A God of Love to Proclaim. 1 Chron. 1:23-24
Oct.   5—Honoring the Lord in Everything. Rom. 14:1-9

GOD'S COVENANT AND ISRAEL'S SIN

1 Kings 11:1-13,26-40; 12:25-33; 14

Except for God's covenant with Noah's family after the flood, his covenant always began with a condition: "If you will obey...." Then came the promised blessings and advantageous relationship between God and the people. It was vastly different from the religious dynamics of neighboring nations. But Israel never seemed to realize how difficult it would be to obey the Lord. Perhaps they thought he would be indulgent or that he was not really serious about his requirements. Especially after they reached the Promised Land did they find it difficult to ignore the gods of their neighbors. Why have only one God? What was wrong with having some images around? To guarantee a good harvest, why not make an offering to the god of fertility? Surely, they may have rationalized, the command against stealing did not mean that a rich farmer should not foreclose on a poor one.

The Bible Lesson

1 KINGS 11:

4 For it came to pass, when Solomon was old, that his wives turned away his heart after other gods: and his heart was not perfect with the Lord his God, as was the heart of David his father.

5 For Solomon went after Ashtoreth the goddess of the Zidonians, and after Milcom the abomination of the Ammonites.

6 And Solomon did evil in the sight of the Lord, and went not fully after the Lord, as did David his father.

7 Then did Solomon build an high place for Chemosh, the abomination of Moab, in the hill that is before Jerusalem, and for Molech, the abomination of the children of Ammon.

8 And likewise did he for all his strange wives, which burnt incense and sacrificed unto their gods.

9 And the Lord was angry with Solomon, because his heart was turned from the Lord God of Israel, which had appeared unto him twice,

10 And had commanded him concerning this thing, that he should not go after other gods: but he kept not that which the Lord commanded.

11 Wherefore the Lord said unto Solomon, Forasmuch as this is done of thee, and thou hast not kept my covenant and my statutes, which I have commanded thee, I will surely rend the kingdom from thee, and will give it to thy servant.

12 Notwithstanding in thy days I will not do it for David thy father's sake: but I will rend it out of the hand of thy son.

13 Howbeit I will not rend away all the kingdom; but will give one tribe to thy son for David my servant's sake, and for Jerusalem's sake which I have chosen.

The Lesson Explained

A FOOLISH OLD MAN (11:4-8)

This book began with the last days of David and the beginning of Solomon's reign about 962 B.C. Chapters 3—10 give a glowing account of Solomon's prayer for wisdom, his administrative skills, his wealth, his building the Temple, his prayer of dedication, and his international reputation. Between the lines we sense that much of this was achieved through heavy taxation and forced labor. Also foreign ideas and values were infiltrating the country.

Solomon was largely responsible for that through his harem. Although the Lord had forbidden intermarriage with their pagan neighbors, "Solomon loved many strange women" (11:1). According to the record, his first wife was a daughter of Pharaoh, and the marriage was related to a political alliance (3:1). In his later years his love for his many wives turned him toward their gods. Probably to maintain good relations with the nations they represented, Solomon had allowed them to bring their idols and set up shrines.

AN INEVITABLE JUDGMENT (11:9-13)

Scorning Yahweh on such a grand scale brought judgment even on the king. After all, God had appeared to Solomon (3:5) and answered his humble prayer for wisdom to reign; again the Lord appeared to him (9:2) after the Temple had been dedicated. Surely a man having had two such wonderful experiences would not turn against God. But even worse, Solomon had brazenly disobeyed the plain commandment of that second visitation. So, the Lord pronounced judgment against him: instead of the kingdom going to his son when Solomon died, it would go to one of his administrators. For David's sake,

God was angry with

this would not happen in Solomon's lifetime but after his son was on the throne. Furthermore, and again for David's sake, one tribe would remain loyal to the king in Jerusalem.

A PERMANENT DIVISION (12:25-32) *Solomon and this wife*

Among the people who gave Solomon trouble in his closing years *way* was Jeroboam, an Ephraimite whom Solomon had appointed as one of the bosses of forced labor (11:28). He sided with the northern tribes in asking Rehoboam (Solomon's son) about his policies. When the new king promised even worse treatment than under Solomon, the ten tribes rebelled and chose Jeroboam as their king. At first Rehoboam wanted to force their return, but the Lord forbade it (11:21-24).

Jeroboam chose Shechem, about thirty miles north of Jerusalem, as his capital and fortified it. When he remembered how the people would probably trek to Jerusalem for feasts and sacrifices, he feared that Rehoboam might win their loyalty. So he named two shrine cities: Bethel, about twenty miles to the south, and Dan, north of the Sea of Galilee. In each he set up a golden bull calf and, like Aaron, told the people these were the gods who delivered them from Egypt. He also selected "priests from families who were not of the tribe of Levi" (TEV), declared a feast for the eighth month similar to the one celebrated in Judah in the seventh month, and he personally offered sacrifices at Bethel. For these imitations and perversions Jeroboam would always be remembered as the king "who made Israel to sin" (14:16).

Truths to Live By

Older persons can be tempted to turn against God.— Because older people are rather prominent in most churches, and because they are often wise and devout, persons in the middle years assume that the older ones have no trouble in their religious and moral lives. But a pastor who had served once in a resort area was amazed at how many deacons and their wives from other sections refused church membership in their new town. Some people after twenty years of regular participation in church life seem to feel that they are due a vacation and practically disappear. Others become reactionary toward young people, the disadvantaged, and social problems in the community. Their idea of God gets smaller, and his pattern for life becomes exclusive, petty, and legalistic. Even without an idol in the house, older men and women can turn against the God of the Bible.

Along with his promises, God must also be true to his righteousness.—He promised Abraham, Jacob, and Moses some great things, but every one included one or more requirements. We can trust his promises, but we must expect him also to live up to his righteousness. He expects loyalty in the form of obedience, and disobedience carries its own punishment. Without that balance, the world would be an uncertain place in which to live.

False religion can lead a whole nation astray.—"In God we trust" is a good motto; it would be even better as a real affirmation of faith. Too often, however, the "god" we have trusted has been white supremacy that forced Indians onto barren reservations and refused to recognize the human rights of black people. Another false "god" has been the idea that we can exploit natural resources and even people to make as much money as possible. Another false "god" is the kind of nationalism that looks down on other nations and attempts to justify all American ambitions without concern for other nations. These are false religions.

A Verse to Remember

Thou shalt have no other gods before me.—Exodus 20:3.

Daily Bible Readings

Oct. 6—Dishonoring the Relationship with God. 1 Kings 11:1-8

Oct. 7—God's Reaction to Faithlessness. 1 Kings 11:9-13

Oct. 8—Preparation for Punishment. 1 Kings 11:26-33

Oct. 9—The Promise Given to Another. 1 Kings 11:34-40

Oct. 10—A Fatal Choice of Worldly Wisdom. 1 Kings 12:25-33

Oct. 11—Judgment on Willfulness. 1 Kings 14:1-10*a*

Oct. 12—The Faithful and Secure Way. Isa. 55:6-11

October 19, 1980

GOD'S COVENANT AND JEREMIAH
Jeremiah 31

With this lesson and the next one, you may feel that we are repeating some of the study for last quarter on "Judah's Later History." This lesson does include one of the Bible passages for July 20, and next Sunday's session will include a little from the one for August 17. But the reason is that the current study of "God's Covenant with His People" must deal with both Jeremiah and Ezra. Now let's check the historical setting. After the kingdom was divided about 922 B.C., with Jeroboam ruling Israel in the north and Rehoboam ruling Judah in the south, they continued until Israel was in 721 B.C. carried into captivity and oblivion. Then in 587 B.C. Jerusalem was captured and most of its people were exiled to Babylonia. Perhaps it was a few years after that traumatic event that Jeremiah wrote what is called the "book of consolation," chapters 30—33 in his prophecy.

The Bible Lesson

JEREMIAH 31:

1 At the same time, saith the Lord, will I be the God of all the families of Israel, and they shall be my people.

2 Thus saith the Lord, The people which were left of the sword found grace in the wilderness; even Israel, when I went to cause him to rest.

3 The Lord hath appeared of old unto me, saying, Yes, I have loved thee with an everlasting love: therefore with lovingkindness have I drawn thee.

29 In those days they shall say no more, The fathers have eaten a sour grape, and the children's teeth are set on edge.

30 But every one shall die for his own iniquity: every man that eateth the sour grape, his teeth shall be set on edge.

31 Behold, the days come, saith the Lord, that I will make a new covenant with the house of Israel, and with the house of Judah:

32 Not according to the covenant that I made with their fathers in the day that I took them by the hand to bring them out of the land of Egypt; which my covenant they brake, although I was an husband unto them, saith the Lord:

33

33 But this shall be the covenant that I shall make with the house of Israel; After those days, saith the Lord, I will put my law in their inward parts, and write it in their hearts; and will be their God, and they shall be my people.

34 And they shall teach no more every man his neighbour, and every man his brother, saying, Know the Lord: for they shall all know me, from the least of them unto the greatest of them, saith the Lord: for I will forgive their iniquity, and I will remember their sin no more.

The Lesson Explained

GOD'S EVERLASTING LOVE (31:1-3)

All through chapter 30 the Lord had been speaking to and through Jeremiah about the eventual end of the captivity of both Israel and Judah. Their punishment had been of the Lord's making, and he would see it concluded, as a father would treat an errant and repentant son.

In these three verses, especially the first one, we have a reminder of the old covenant language. The Lord would be the God of Israel, and they would be his people. When those who escaped death in the fall of Jerusalem still had to endure the wilderness of exile, they found God's grace. He answered their need for rest. Again the Lord declared his devotion: "I have dearly loved you from of old,/ and still I maintain my unfailing care for you" (NEB). All this came through the prophet who a few years before had predicted God's punishment on his people for their sins. Even then, however, the Lord was loving them.

RESTORATION AND RESPONSIBILITY (31:23-30)

This chapter continued to describe the joy, comfort, and reassurances that would come when the children of Israel returned to their homeland. Once again they would say a blessing for Jerusalem, "habitation of justice." Farmers and herdsmen would again be at home in the land, and God would meet the needs of weary and hungry people. He would also enlarge the families of man and beast—a sign of favor and wealth. The Israelites had probably felt that God was persistent in his judgment: "to break down, . . . and to destroy, and to afflict." Now he would show them that he was just as eager to "build, and to plant." He wanted very much to see them restored.

When that time came, the people would stop blaming their problems on their forebears. Although both the health and morality of children can be affected by their fathers, God does not hold the present generation responsible for the sins of the previous one. Only the person who eats the sour grape will have his teeth set on edge. Ezekiel used this saying as a text for an eloquent sermon (Ezek. 18).

A NEW COVENANT TO COME (31:31-34)

Here Jeremiah reached probably the peak of his whole writing as he described the Lord's intention to make a new covenant with both Israel and Judah. It would not be soon but as "the days come," whenever God willed it. The covenant with their forefathers suited the time when God "took them by the hand to bring them out of . . . Egypt." That covenant the people violated although the Lord continued faithful to them. This new covenant would be written on their hearts instead of on stone tablets, as were the Ten Commandments. It would be a spiritual relationship between God and his people.

Persons of the covenant would not need to teach one another about the Lord, from the wise man to the unlearned, because they would all know him, "from the least . . . unto the greatest." They would all know him through his forgiveness. Centuries later, Christian believers saw this as a foretelling of God's provision of salvation in Christ and also of the convicting and teaching ministry of the Holy Spirit. Together they would bring a spontaneous obedience within the new covenant that God had intended.

Truths to Live By

One's commitment to God affects all areas of life.—One problem with the people of Jeremiah's day was their attempt to compartmentalize religion. They wanted it to stay in the Temple, but the prophets insisted that it must be practiced in the marketplace. That is true especially of Judaism and Christianity, and today as much as in Bible times. The God of the Bible was worshiped by sacrifice and song on holy days, but he commanded honesty, fidelity, and compassion on the other days as well. When the Christian believer commits himself or herself to God in Christ, it is far more than a Sunday or religious act. Yielding to Christ as Lord must affect all of life.

Each person is responsible before God because each can know God for himself.—The old Negro spiritual said it right: "It ain't my brother nor my sister, but it's me, O Lord, standing in the need of prayer." Everybody wants to put the blame on somebody else: heredity, the stars, a dominant parent, poor coaching—anything but me. But the Lord helped Jeremiah see that the individual with the bitter taste in his mouth is the one who ate the bad grapes. He can know what God expects, and that makes him responsible for his actions. Of course, various factors influence our development and outlook, but God holds us responsible for what we know he requires within the range of our possibilities.

Inner motivations are the mark of the mature person.—The child must be constantly reminded of what Mommy said about sharing toys or not abusing the cat. Later, there are school rules, the Scout Law, or some other pattern for acceptable conduct. Also along the way there are approving words, a simple reward, and some kind of merit badge to reinforce a feeling of acceptance and achievement. But ultimately the mature person will act from inner motivations rather than with the hope of some reward. He or she will, as a follower of Christ, absorb his pattern for living so that it won't be a matter of rules and bargaining.

A Verse to Remember

I will put my law in their inward parts, and write it in their hearts; and will be their God, and they shall be my people.—Jeremiah 31:33.

Daily Bible Readings

Oct. 13—The Faithfulness of God. Jer. 31:1-6
Oct. 14—The Reward of the Faithful. Jer. 31:7-14
Oct. 15—Hope for the Future. Jer. 31:15-22
Oct. 16—Each One Is Responsible. Jer. 31:23-30
Oct. 17—A Covenant in the Heart. Jer. 31:31-40
Oct. 18—A Promise to the Faithful. Jer. 7:1-7
Oct. 19—Call to Repentance. Ezek. 18:25-32

GOD'S COVENANT AND EZRA
Nehemiah 8:2-3; 9:32-38

This is the last session of the quarter to deal with the covenant in the Old Testament. It really began with God's calling Abraham to leave his father and homeland to find a country he had never seen. There he would start a family that would become God's chosen people. There he would learn to trust the Lord beyond all other gods and would be his key witness among other nations. Again and again, that covenant was renewed with the children of Israel. But finally in 586 B.C. all seemed to be lost when Jerusalem and the Temple were destroyed, and many of the people were herded off to Babylon. Even after they were allowed to return, they had to be exhorted to rebuild the Temple; their commitment to Yahweh was weak. Then about 445 B.C. Nehemiah came to help them rebuild the city walls, and later Ezra rekindled their faith.

The Bible Lesson

NEHEMIAH 8:

2 And Ezra the priest brought the law before the congregation both of men and women, and all that could hear with understanding, upon the first day of the seventh month.

3 And he read therein before the street that was before the water gate from the morning until midday, before the men and the women, and those that could understand; and the ears of all the people were attentive unto the book of the law.

NEHEMIAH 9:

32 Now therefore, our God, the great, the mighty, and the terrible God, who keepest covenant and mercy, let not all the trouble seem little before thee, that hath come upon us, on our kings, on our princes, and on our priests, and on our prophets, and on our fathers, and on all thy people, since the times of the kings of Assyria unto this day.

33 Howbeit thou art just in all that is brought upon us; for thou hast done right, but we have done wickedly:

34 Neither have our kings, our princes, our priests, nor our fathers, kept thy law, nor hearkened unto thy commandments and thy testimonies, wherewith thou didst testify against them.

35 For they have not served thee in their kingdom, and in thy great goodness that thou gavest them, and in the large and fat land which thou gavest before them, neither turned they from their wicked works.

36 Behold, we are servants this day, and for the land that thou gavest unto our fathers to eat the fruit thereof and the good thereof, behold, we are servants in it:

37 And it yieldeth much increase unto the kings whom thou hast set over us because of our sins: also they have dominion over our bodies, and over our cattle, at their pleasure, and we are in great distress.

38 And because of all this we make a sure covenant, and write it; and our princes, Levites, and priests, seal unto it.

The Lesson Explained

READING THE LAW TO THE PEOPLE (8:1-3)

Since the books of Ezra and Nehemiah were once just one book, and since this is the first time that Ezra is named in the book of Nehemiah, some scholars have made an interesting suggestion. They suggest reading Nehemiah 8 between Ezra 8 and 9. That combination tells of Ezra leaving Babylon and arriving in Jerusalem, reading the law to the people, and then discussing the problem of intermarriage with the pagans. Whether that is the right order, we do know from Nehemiah 8 that Ezra had arrived and did read the law.

Ezra was a scribe and priest who had been allowed to bring some Jews from Babylon along with some money to buy sacrifices for worship in the Temple. He probably brought also a scroll of the Law (Pentateuch) and was asked to read it to the people. A large crowd of men and women, plus the children who were old enough to understand what was being read, gathered in the square before the water gate. From early morning until noon they listened attentively. Verse 7 mentions some men who helped the hearers understand what was read, perhaps translating the Hebrew into Aramaic.

RECOVERING A FESTIVAL (8:13-18)

That was the first day of the seventh month. On the next day the elders, priests, and Levites continued their study with Ezra. Since the proper date for the Feast of Booths (Tabernacles) was the fifteenth day of the seventh month, Ezra may have pointed that out, and they decided to celebrate it. The word went out to all the towns and in Jerusalem, and the people gathered all kinds of branches to build rustic shelters in streets, in courtyards, and even on rooftops. The observance reminded them of both the Exodus and the more recent deliverance from captivity. Not since the days of Joshua had the feast been kept in this way, and the people were very happy. The reading of the Law continued for the seven days of the feast.

RENEWING THEIR COVENANT (9:32-38)

Just two days after the feast the people convened again to confess their sins and worship the Lord (9:1-3). Apparently two groups of Levites led the service in a lengthy prayer recalling Israel's story from Abraham through the Exodus and the conquest of Canaan up to the Babylonian captivity (vv. 6-30). Despite Israel's infidelity and sin, the Lord did not forsake them (v. 31).

All of that was a preamble to these closing verses which begin with: "Now therefore, our God." Verses 32, 33, and 35 are reminiscent of the usual covenant structure that paid high tribute to God for his power, fidelity, and goodness. Then the same verses plus 34 also acknowledge the troubles and wickedness of Israel with the implied question: How could such a great and just God be concerned with such a disappointing nation? The sufferings at the hands of foreign rulers by all the people, including kings, priests, and prophets, were justified by their general disobedience. But now God's people were servants to a foreign power right in the middle of the Promised Land, and even their produce belonged to that foreign power. Because of all that, Israel volunteered to "make a sure covenant" with the Lord to live by his Law. They wanted it written down with the signatures of princes and religious leaders affixed.

Truths to Live By

All believers need to understand God's Word.—Both Judaism and Christianity assume their members are or will be readers. Of course the Bible can be recorded on tape or record, but it is primarily intended to be read. Since it is the record of God's revelation of himself, the message of salvation, and the guide for right living, it is required reading for all believers. But since it was written two thousand and more years ago, in two foreign languages, most readers need help in understanding it. They need to discover its portrait of God in the experience of the Hebrew people. They should see how he was mirrored in the life, work, and teachings of Jesus. It can show the devastating effect of sin and the deliverance of God's grace through faith in Christ. It can lead the believer into Christian prayer and practice.

Special times of worship help believers appreciate the past and deal with the present with God's help.—The Passover was instituted for yearly celebration to help Jews remember how God had delivered his people from bondage in Egypt. Of course the sabbath was a time for rest and also for worship, and the Lord's Day (first day of the week) took its place for early Christian believers. Although Thanksgiving Day is for many people an occasion for a big feed or big game, others let it remind them of God's generosity. Even such a national holiday can be oriented toward a religious experience.

God's mercy is available to all who seek it in spite of their past.—The prayer in Nehemiah 9 gloried in God's goodness to his chosen people, but it finally had to admit their shameful unfaithfulness. Without pinning that blame on anybody else, the people asked for a covenant with the Lord. He had a reputation for mercy to the penitent, and it still stands.

A Verse to Remember

So they read in the book in the law of God distinctly, and gave the sense, and caused them to understand the reading.—Nehemiah 8:8.

Daily Bible Readings

Oct. 20—Love for God's Word. Neh. 8:1-12
Oct. 21—Learning from God's Word. Neh. 8:13-18
Oct. 22—Confessing, a Part of Worship. Neh. 9:1-8
Oct. 23—Remembering God's Loving-kindness. Neh. 9:9-21
Oct. 24—God's Love and Patience. Neh. 9:22-31
Oct. 25—A Resolve to Be Faithful. Neh. 9:32-38
Oct. 26—"Thy Law Is My Delight." Ps. 119:169-176

GOD'S COVENANT AND JESUS CHRIST
Luke 4:16-30; John 13:31-35; Mark 14:22-25

For two months we have been looking at God's covenant as the Old Testament revealed it. At first it was a relationship between God and a person. Then it became a pledge of God's blessing and of his people's obedience. The covenant always began with God's grace with one generation after another. So it was a figure of God's love for his people. With today's session we turn to the idea of that covenant in the New Testament. Naturally we start with Jesus, who perfectly revealed God's love for all people. Although in the Gospels he never used the word for covenant until the night before his trial and crucifixion, he demonstrated the loving faithfulness of God in all his ministry even to the cross. In this lesson we see his view of his life's work.

The Bible Lesson

LUKE 4:

16 And he came to Nazareth, where he had been brought up: and, as his custom was, he went into the synagogue on the sabbath day, and stood up for to read.

17 And there was delivered unto him the book of the prophet Esaias. And when he had opened the book, he found the place where it was written,

18 The Spirit of the Lord is upon me, because he hath anointed me to preach the gospel to the poor; he hath sent me to heal the brokenhearted, to preach deliverance to the captives, and recovering of sight to the blind, to set at liberty them that are bruised,

19 To preach the acceptable year of the Lord.

20 And he closed the book, and he gave it again to the minister, and sat down. And the eyes of all them that were in the synagogue were fastened on him.

21 And he began to say unto them, This day is this scripture fulfilled in your ears.

MARK 14:

22 And as they did eat, Jesus took bread, and blessed, and break it, and gave to them, and said, Take, eat: this is my body.

23 And he took the cup, and when he had given thanks, he gave it

to them: and they all drank of it.

24 And he said unto them, This is my blood of the new testament, which is shed for many.

25 Verily I say unto you, I will drink no more of the fruit of the vine, until that day that I drink it new in the kingdom of God.

The Lesson Explained

RESPONDING TO AN ANCIENT CALL (Luke 4:16-21)

After a forty-day retreat in the wilderness while being tempted by the devil, Jesus returned to Galilee. Teaching in various synagogues, the young rabbi won much fame. Then he came to his hometown of Nazareth and went to the synagogue on the sabbath. When he stood up to read the Scriptures, he was handed the scroll of Isaiah and turned to what we know as 61:1-2, describing the prophet's ministry to the recently returned exiles to Jerusalem.

Based on the confidence that God's Spirit was moving him, the writer listed things he must do for the people in God's name. The poor should hear the good news. Those who grieve should be healed. Freedom was at hand for captives, and the blind could have their sight restored. Those who were oppressed should be liberated. In fact, he must declare that "the acceptable year of the Lord" had come; in other words, the messianic age was upon them.

When Jesus sat down (according to custom) to comment or preach on that text, he surprised everyone by saying that the prophet's words were being fulfilled in his own ministry. Jesus was concerned for the disadvantaged, both spiritually and materially. Thus, he was answering God's ancient call.

LOVING OTHERS AS A SIGN (John 13:31-35)

Before his betrayal and crucifixion, Jesus celebrated the Passover with his disciples and had a long talk with them. When Judas left the upper room, Jesus talked about being glorified and being separated from his disciples. He knew what the night held for him, and he wanted to prepare his followers for the shock of his death. Without him they might easily split up or return to their old ways. So he stressed "a new commandment." They were to love one another as he had loved them. It would not be an ordinary kind of love but an unselfish love, and that would prove they were followers of Jesus.

GIVING SELF TO SEAL A COVENANT (Mark 14:22-25)

As that Passover meal concluded, Jesus added what we call the Lord's Supper. He took a small loaf of bread, gave thanks for it, and then passed out pieces of it to his disciples. He told them to eat because it represented his body. As food offered as sacrifices was often eaten by the worshipers, his disciples would be partaking symbolically of the sacrifice of his body. In the same way Jesus picked up the cup and gave thanks for it. Then as he passed it around for each to drink from it, he explained, "This is my blood of the covenant, which is poured out for many" (RSV). While the wine was not really his blood, it symbolized the life he would pour out on Calvary's cross.

Jesus epitomized the new covenant described by Jeremiah (see lesson for October 19). In him God demonstrated his grace and love for all persons, making possible their right standing before God through the crucifixion. Victory over sin and death would be assured in his resurrection. Knowledge of and commitment to God's law would come through the work of the Spirit whom God would send to teach and support his followers.

Truths to Live By

Answering God's call includes practical service to the disadvantaged.—Although we have no record of the themes of Jesus' early teaching in the synagogues, we do know what he said at Nazareth. It was a declaration of purpose; instead of fitting the conquering hero kind of messiah that many were hoping for, he identified himself with the concerns of the prophet Isaiah. Instead of debating theological details, he was committed to helping the disadvantaged, the very people ignored by the religious leaders of Jesus' day. If it was right for the Master, it ought to be right for us. Black people have won many civil rights, but Christians—both black and white—need to be liberated from their prejudices and learn to be brothers. In advertising and entertainment sex is exploited to the undermining of morals and family; well-balanced Christian teachers and counselors are needed to help persons rejoice in God's gift and be freed from exploitation.

43

The Lord's Supper reminds us of God's new covenant in Christ.—It dramatizes a significant truth: that Jesus Christ gave himself to save sinners. As we eat the elements, we hear his instruction to do it to remember him. Celebrating the Supper with other believers reminds us of the wide Christian fellowship across the centuries and around the world. But most of all it represents the everlasting mercy and compassion of God available to all who will receive him in faith. Closely related is the realization that his forgiveness is desperately needed in our pride and sinfulness. So, the loving Father judges our infidelity and rebellion but at the same time offers his costly grace through the gift of the life of his Son for our salvation.

A loving church proves to the world its relationship to Christ.—A handsome church building may not prove anything to the world except that the congregation has the money and leadership to build. Numerical growth may mean to the world only that the church is aggressive, does a lot of visiting, or is located in a growing community. But the congregation that cares for the needy, that weathers some internal storm without loss, that maintains care and growth programs for both young and old, that develops the reputation of being a loving fellowship—that kind of church will show the world that it lives by Christ's new commandment.

A Verse to Remember

By this shall all men know that ye are my disciples, if ye have love one to another.—John 13:35.

Daily Bible Readings

Oct. 27—A Covenant Needed. Gen. 3:9-15
Oct. 28—A Renewed Covenant. Ex. 6:1-8
Oct. 29—The Covenant Is Secure. 2 Sam. 23:1-5
Oct. 30—God's Promise to His People. Ps. 147:1-11
Oct. 31—God's Son Is Confirmed. Mark 1:1-11
Nov. 1—The Living Covenant Is Coming. Isa. 61:1-3
Nov. 2—The Living Covenant. Luke 4:16-30

44

ar'- dent - passionate
intense, Hot **November 9, 1980** *burning*

GOD'S COVENANT AND PETER

Ar -- dent - energetic. *Acts 2:1 to 3:26*

All of Jesus' twelve disciples were Jews and all but one from Galilee. He himself was a Jew and based his message on the Jewish Scriptures. The Master and his men worshiped in the synagogues and knew the teachings of the Jewish faith. One of them was a Zealot, but perhaps because of Peter's housetop vision and visit with Cornelius, we may think of him as the most ardent Jew of the group. For that reason and because he was the early spokesman for the church, we are not surprised that he would be concerned to show how God's covenant with his people had been realized in Jesus as the Christ. In the early chapters of Acts we hear him preaching the gospel to Jews and leading a multitude of them to respond.

The Bible Lesson

ACTS 2:

14 But Peter, standing up with the eleven, lifted up his voice, and said unto them, Ye men of Judaea, and all ye that dwell at Jerusalem, be this known unto you, and hearken to my words:

15 For these are not drunken, as ye suppose, seeing it is but the third hour of the day.

16 But this is that which was spoken by the prophet Joel;

17 And it shall come to pass in the last days, saith God, I will pour out my Spirit upon all flesh: and your sons and your daughters shall prophesy, and your young men shall see visions, and your old men shall dream dreams:

ACTS 3:

18 But those things, which God before had shewed by the mouth of all his prophets, that Christ should suffer, he hath so fulfilled.

19 Repent ye therefore, and be converted, that your sins may be blotted out, when the times of refreshing shall come from the presence of the Lord;

20 And he shall send Jesus Christ, which before was preached unto you:

21 Whom the heaven must receive until the times of restitution of all things, which God hath spoken by the mouth of all his holy prophets since the world began.

45

22 For Moses truly said unto the fathers, A prophet shall the Lord your God raise up unto you of your brethren, like unto me; him shall ye hear in all things whatsoever he shall say unto you.

23 And it shall come to pass, that every soul, which will not hear that prophet, shall be destroyed from among the people.

24 Yea, and all the prophets from Samuel and those that follow after, as many as have spoken, have likewise foretold of these days.

25 Ye are the children of the prophets, and of the covenant which God made with our fathers, saying unto Abraham, And in thy seed shall all the kindreds of the earth be blessed.

26 Unto you first God, having raised up his Son Jesus, sent him to bless you, in turning away every one of you from his iniquities.

The Lesson Explained

GIFT OF THE SPIRIT (2:14-17)

On the fiftieth day after Passover came the Jewish festival of Pentecost. Because it was a time of thanksgiving, the Jewish believers had gathered in their usual place. Possibly while they were praying about nine o'clock in the morning, a noise came "from the sky which sounded like a strong wind blowing" (2:2, TEV). Then something like fire appeared in the room, and separating into tongues, it rested on the head of each believer. Suddenly possessed by the Spirit, they "began to speak in other tongues" (v. 4).

A crowd of Jews from various countries gathered outside, and the disciples were speaking clearly to all of them. When some made fun of the demonstration, Peter responded boldly. These believers were not drunk, he said. Really they were fulfilling a prophecy of Joel centuries before. The time had come for God to pour out his Spirit upon young and old, upon sons and daughters. No longer would just the prophet, priest, or judge be spiritually endowed. Others would be enabled by the Spirit to speak for God.

IDENTITY OF THE MESSIAH (2:22-24,36-39)

But the real focus of Peter's sermon was not the Spirit but Jesus of Nazareth. The marvelous things that Jesus did among the people showed that he was "approved of God," and Peter's hearers knew what he was talking about. Nevertheless, they had arrested Jesus and made it possible for the Romans to crucify him. That was bad enough. But even worse for them,

46

God had repudiated their deed by raising Jesus to life. He just could not be held by death.

In conclusion Peter declared that the Jesus whom they had killed was really God's promised Messiah. That was more than the Jews could stand, and they asked Peter what they should do. First, they must repent of that sin and of all others. Then, accepting Jesus the Christ as Savior, they should be baptized to symbolize that experience. Then they, too, would receive the gift of the Spirit because God's promise through Joel applied to them and their children.

CHILDREN OF THE COVENANT (3:18-26)

Some days after Pentecost Peter and John went to the Temple at prayer time. When they were accosted by a lame beggar at the gate, Peter healed him. Because the worshipers were amazed, Peter used the occasion to tell about Jesus, whom they had killed. But it was faith in that Jesus that had healed the lame man.

Because his hearers were ignorant of the real truth about the Messiah, Peter began to use the Scriptures to inform them. Verse 18 may reflect the experience of the disciples described in Luke 24:44-48 when Jesus used the Scriptures to show his followers how his ministry had been foretold. Instead of a national deliverer, the Messiah was the Suffering Servant. He had returned to heaven to await "the time for establishing all that God spoke by ... his holy prophets" (v. 21, RSV). Then Peter quoted Deuteronomy 18:15,19 to say that Moses was anticipating someone like himself to declare God's word, who must be heeded or else. Prophets from Samuel on looked ahead to "these days." As children of the covenant made with Abraham, they should remember God's promise in Genesis 22:18 and respond to Jesus as the fulfillment of that covenant. After all, he came to the Jews first.

Truths to Live By

The Old Testament helps us understand the person and work of Jesus.—A person need not know the Old Testament to accept Jesus as Savior and Lord. But for a growing comprehension of what he meant to the people of his day, especially those who wrote the New Testament, we need to study the Jewish Scriptures. They portray his God and Father. They tell of Yahweh's delivering his people from slavery and the laws he expected them to obey. They confess the sins of the people and preserve the preaching of the prophets. They describe the sacrificial lamb, the covenant of mutual responsibility, and the loving-kindness of the Lord. They are the source of many New Testament sayings.

The Holy Spirit works through old and young, men and women.—He is no respecter of persons, shows no partiality. Now and then, one group or another has claimed an exclusive access to the Spirit but with no biblical support. He looks only for a willing and committed channel for his purposes.

The message of Jesus is still intended for Jews.— Unfortunately, centuries of being forced by Christians to live in ghettoes in Europe and the continuing undercurrent of anti-Semitism in many countries have made Jews wary of Christian evangelism. But believers must still remember that Jesus was a Jew and that he preached to them first. Also, the thousands of believers in Jerusalem were Jews and committed themselves to Jesus as their longed-for Messiah. Perhaps in recent years more Jews than usual have been finding fulfillment in Christ. To prepare the way, Christians need to enlarge their appreciations and friendships, and to pray for integrity and wisdom in their witness.

A Verse to Remember

In the last days, saith God, I will pour out of my Spirit upon all flesh: and your sons and daughters shall prophesy.—Acts 2:17.

Daily Bible Readings

Nov. 3—Peter Encounters Jesus. John 1:35-42
Nov. 4—A True Confession. Matt. 16:13-19
Nov. 5—A Mountaintop Experience. Matt. 17:1-8
Nov. 6—A Promise to Be Broken. Mark 14:26-31
Nov. 7—A False Confession. Matt. 26:69-75
Nov. 8—Peter's Challenge. John 21:15-19
Nov. 9—Peter Proclaims. Acts 2:14-17

GOD'S COVENANT AND PAUL
Acts 13:13-52; 2 Corinthians 3:1-6

Even after the battles of Concord and Lexington in 1775, many prominent men of the Colonies were still hoping for a reconciliation with England. Then in January 1776, an eighty-page booklet was published in Philadelphia "written by an Englishman." It was a revolutionary message addressed to the American people, and 120,000 copies were sold within three months. And it began changing the minds of the great and small so that in July of that year the Continental Congress proclaimed the Declaration of Independence. The title of the booklet was *Common Sense* and its author was Thomas Paine. Out of a mass of feelings, resentments, and ideals, he condensed a reasonable argument and a fervent appeal for freedom. In somewhat the same way Paul, a Pharisee, brought to focus in his ministry the agelong concern of God for all persons.

The Bible Lesson

ACTS 13:
44 And the next sabbath day came almost the whole city together to hear the word of God.

45 But when the Jews saw the multitudes, they were filled with envy, and spake against those things which were spoken by Paul, contradicting and blaspheming.

46 Then Paul and Barnabas waxed bold, and said, It was necessary that the word of God should first have been spoken to you: but seeing ye put it from you, and judge yourselves unworthy of everlasting life, lo, we turn to the Gentiles.

47 For so hath the Lord commanded us, saying, I have set thee to be a light of the Gentiles, that thou shouldest be for salvation unto the ends of the earth.

48 And when the Gentiles heard this, they were glad, and glorified the word of the Lord: and as many as were ordained to eternal life believed.

49 And the word of the Lord was published throughout all the region.

50 But the Jews stirred up the devout and honourable women,

and the chief men of the city, and raised persecution against Paul and Barnabas, and expelled them out of their coasts.

51 But they shook off the dust of their feet against them, and came unto Iconium.

52 And the disciples were filled with joy, and with the Holy Ghost.

2 CORINTHIANS 3:

4 And such trust have we through Christ to God-ward:

5 Not that we are sufficient of ourselves to think any thing as of ourselves; but our sufficiency is of God;

6 Who also hath made us able ministers of the new testament; not of the letter, but of the spirit: for the letter killeth, but the spirit giveth life.

The Lesson Explained

Read

PAUL'S APPEAL TO JEWS (Acts 13:32-39)

Not too long after the resurrection of Jesus, a zealous young rabbi made a reputation for himself in hunting down Jewish Christians. But a remarkable experience on his way to Damascus turned him around, and Saul of Tarsus began to preach that Jesus was the Messiah and the Son of God. After working a year among Christians in Antioch, who were both Jews and Gentiles, he and Barnabas were commissioned by that church to go out as missionaries.

On that first journey Saul became known as Paul, and they arrived eventually at another Antioch, in Asia Minor. When they went to the synagogue on the sabbath, Paul accepted the invitation to preach. Eventually he mentioned Jesus as a son of David and described him as a Savior unto Israel. Although he was rejected and killed, God raised him up, and that was part of the glad tidings Paul had come to declare. Jesus was the fulfillment of God's ancient promise in their generation. Because of Christ's death and resurrection, forgiveness of sins was available to all believers—which the law could not do.

TURNING FROM JEWS TO GENTILES (Acts 13:44-52)

As Paul closed his sermon, he quoted Habakkuk 1:5 as a warning to those who might reject his message. As the people left, some asked Paul to preach again on the next sabbath. When the orthodox Jews saw the large crowd on that sabbath and noted how many Gentiles were there, they were jealous because their own message had not appealed to that many. So

50

they contradicted Paul as he spoke "and reviled him" (RSV). But Paul and Barnabas spoke above the noise.

They had felt it necessary to declare "the word of God" to the Jews first. Not only did Jews have the background to understand it, but God's promise had been given to their fathers. But if they did not feel worthy of "everlasting life," Paul and Barnabas would go to the Gentiles. After all, God had said through Isaiah (49:6) that Israel was to be "a light of the Gentiles" for salvation worldwide. So the once orthodox rabbi proclaimed the deeper meaning of Hebrew Scripture, and the Gentiles were glad as many believed. When the word spread through the countryside, the Jewish officials stirred up the people and forced the missionaries to leave the city. Although they protested, the disciples were filled with joy and the Holy Spirit. They saw God's covenant extending to other nations.

NEW COVENANT IN THE SPIRIT (2 Cor. 3:4-6)

Several years later, about A.D. 55, Paul wrote what we know as 2 Corinthians to a church that had problems. Here he said that neither he nor the church needed any letters of commendation because the church itself was a living letter. While the old covenant had been written on tablets of stone, God's new message was written by the Spirit on human hearts. Paul's trust and competence had come from God; the new covenant did not originate with him but with God. He had made Paul "capable of serving the new covenant" (v. 6, TEV). In the mood of Jeremiah (31:33) Paul explained that covenant as spiritual rather than tangible or literal. The written law of the old covenant had specified God's requirements and thus pointed to death in their disobedience. But the new covenant in Christ provides for a personal relationship and promises life eternal in the Spirit.

Truths to Live By

God's new covenant includes all people.—Some of the Hebrew prophets and psalmists realized that Israel was a chosen people for a larger purpose. They were to portray the truth of Yahweh so that other nations would accept him as their God. Many Jewish leaders missed that point, especially in their response to Jesus as Messiah. The basic problem is still with us.

51

God's new covenant in the message of Christ is for all people.

Faithfully proclaiming and living the gospel will provoke opposition.—The orthodox Jews of Paul's day were determined to protect their traditions. During the centuries, many had died to preserve them. Refusing to acknowledge Jesus as the Messiah, they vigorously opposed Paul's inviting Gentiles to accept Jesus as Lord without becoming Jews first. But Paul was convinced that both Gentiles and Jews would be set right by God's grace through their faith. Within the modern era some Christians have thought that converts needed to adopt Western dress or church patterns before they would be acceptable. Others have resisted cultural and economic changes based on real gospel truth about the worth of persons. Because the gospel is of God, it differs from human ideals.

Real life is in the Spirit, not in rigid legalism.—As soon as a law is passed, some people start looking for loopholes. And they usually find them either because the law is written to be evaded easily or because few laws can cover every possible application. But that attitude ought not to be true of Christians. They are committed to Christ and are led by his Spirit. So the Christian honestly tries to love others, that is, he or she practices active goodwill toward others. He or she can be trusted not just within the law but within the wider responsibilities under the Spirit.

A Verse to Remember

I have set thee to be a light of the Gentiles, that thou shouldst be for salvation unto the ends of the earth.—Acts 13:47.

Daily Bible Readings

Nov. 10—From Darkness to Light. Acts 9:1-9,19-22
Nov. 11—A Time for Living. Gal. 2:16-20
Nov. 12—A Time for Suffering. Rom. 8:12-18
Nov. 13—A Time for Standing Fast. Gal. 5:1-10
Nov. 14—A Time for Dying. Rom. 6:1-8
Nov. 15—A Time for Hope. 1 Thess. 4:13-18
Nov. 16—Sufficient in God. 2 Cor. 3:1-6

GOD'S COVENANT AND THE NEW ISRAEL
Ephesians 2; 1 Peter 2:4-10

When Jacob wrestled with a stranger on the night before he had to confront Esau, the stranger changed his name to Israel. Years later his sons buried Jacob in Canaan and returned to their families in Egypt. It was their children—the children of Israel—that were delivered from Egyptian bondage. That name stuck; it is used throughout the Bible far more than either *Hebrew* or *Jew*. The people of Israel were the people of God; they were the covenant people. But Jews who accepted Jesus as Christ (Messiah) saw him as the fulfillment of God's purpose for Israel. So, eventually both Jewish and Gentile Christians were seen as an extension of the people of God; together they made up the new Israel. Thus, the larger Old Testament concepts of Israel were applied to Christian believers without reference to race or ethnic background. The new Israel consists of those who trust the revelation of God's grace in Jesus Christ.

The Bible Lesson

1 PETER 2:

4 To whom coming, as unto a living stone, disallowed indeed of men, but chosen of God, and precious,

5 Ye also, as lively stones, are built up a spiritual house, an holy priesthood, to offer up spiritual sacrifices, acceptable to God by Jesus Christ.

6 Wherefore also it is contained in the scripture, Behold, I lay in Sion a chief corner stone, elect, precious: and he that believeth on him shall not be confounded.

7 Unto you therefore which believe he is precious: but unto them which be disobedient, the stone which the builders disallowed, the same is made the head of the corner,

8 And a stone of stumbling, and a rock of offence, even to them which stumble at the word, being disobedient: whereunto also they were appointed.

9 But ye are a chosen generation, a royal priesthood, an holy nation, a peculiar people; that ye should shew forth the praises of him who hath called you out of darkness into his marvellous light:

10 Which in time past were not a people, but are now the people of God: which had not obtained mercy, but now have obtained mercy. *Read first before going into the lesson.*

The Lesson Explained

BY GRACE THROUGH FAITH (Eph. 2:4-10)

After describing what his readers' life had been like in the past, Paul turned to the remarkable change that had come through Christ. In spite of their death-dealing sinfulness, and Paul's as well, God in his abounding mercy and love made them come alive again, just as he had raised Jesus. But even more, God had raised them for fellowship with Christ to demonstrate his grace through all time to come. It was that love and mercy that no one can never deserve that saved them. Grace is God's gift, accepted by faith. If salvation could be earned by obedience or good deeds, the successful ones would boast about it. But really "God has made us what we are, and in our union with Christ Jesus he has created us for a life of good deeds, which he has already prepared for us to do" (TEV). That is the one basis for both Jew and Gentile for taking part in the new Israel.

ALIGNED AS LIVING STONES (1 Pet. 2:4-8)

From various references in this epistle, scholars have decided that it was written as a sort of sermon with special concern for newly baptized converts and for believers who were being persecuted. Also from various passages, the readers appear to have been both Jewish and Gentile believers. Peter was concerned that they persist in their faith.

Then he urged all believers to come to the One who is the "living stone" that had been rejected by men but chosen by God. Back of that figure of speech were three verses that Jesus probably had in mind in Mark 12:10. In the first one that Peter quoted (Isa. 28:16) God promised to set up a cornerstone in Zion, a chosen and valuable person in whom believers could have complete confidence. The cornerstone served to anchor and align a structure. The second verse to be quoted (Ps. 118:22) appears in the second half of verse 7 and describes a stone that the builders rejected but became the cornerstone of the whole building. The third verse (Isa. 8:14) appears in verse 8 and refers to a stone that people stumbled over. Jesus was that living stone, rejected by the disobedient but loved and trusted by believers.

As "lively stones," they should join themselves to *the* living stone to form a spiritual house or temple in which they as holy priests could offer spiritual rather than physical sacrifices. So, Peter portrayed the growing relationship of believers with Christ in terms of the Temple but as a vibrant, worshiping fellowship. Ancient concepts were filled with new meanings.

A PEOPLE CHOSEN BY GOD (1 Pet. 2:9-10)

Peter's reference to "the scripture" in verse 6 probably appealed to his Jewish readers among the Christians; so would the four descriptive phrases in verse 9. They remind us of the way God spoke of his chosen people at the time of the Sinai covenant. Peter saw those who believed in Jesus as the Messiah (Christ) of God as a spiritual extension of the people God had chosen to fulfill his purpose. They had entered into that covenant of grace and faith. The purpose was the same: "to proclaim the wonderful acts of God" (TEV). In these two verses he may have been thinking primarily of Gentile believers. They had been called out of the darkness of paganism. Without earlier significance, they had become part of the people of God, being saved by his mercy.

Truths to Live By

All persons come to God by grace through faith.— Evangelical Christians take that truth for granted, at least when they are discussing theology. They may feel and act differently when asked to witness to the lost or accept a new convert with a "bad" reputation. Then they may want a person to do something to prove their conversion. Or the evangelical may doubt the reality of the religious experience of someone in the liturgical tradition. But the Bible makes it clear that the actual relation of any person with God is based on God's grace, that only his mercy and love can open the way into God's family of faith. The believer accepts that offer of reconciliation through his faith. When grace is offered and faith responds, a person yields to God's love, turns against his or her sin, and allows the Spirit to do his transforming work from the inside.

55

In acknowledging one Lord and Father, believers of all kinds become one people.—We have all been made by the same Creator; whatever our color, creed, or language, we are more alike than we are different. But pride, geography, traditions, and others factors have divided us through the centuries into races, nations, classes, and clans. Of course, there are differences and divisions, but God's will is that we treat others as brothers. But we won't do that until we accept him as Father and Lord. What about those who have done that already? Has it changed your attitude toward red and black Christians, toward Russian Christians, toward poor and rich Christians? Has our failure at that point handicapped the influence of Christ in our neighborhoods?

Being God's new people means giving him glory in good works.—Being Christian means more than wearing a cross on a golden chain, having one's name on a church roll, or reciting some creed or doctrinal statement without a single error. Beyond the experience of faith, it means discovering the meaning of God's love and practicing it in all relationships. In that way we give him the glory he seeks.

A Verse to Remember

But ye are a chosen generation, a royal priesthood, an holy nation, a peculiar people.—1 Peter 2:9.

Daily Bible Readings

Nov. 17—A New Direction. Luke 5:36-39
Nov. 18—A New Helper. Acts 1:6-14
Nov. 19—A New Challenge. Acts 10:9-15,28
Nov. 20—A New Openness. Acts 15:13-23
Nov. 21—A New Community. Eph. 1:11-23
Nov. 22—A New People. Eph. 2:11-22
Nov. 23—A New Israel. 1 Pet. 2:2-10

November 30, 1980

GOD'S COVENANT AND THE NEW JERUSALEM
Revelation 11:15-19; 21

For three months we have been studying the message of the Bible from the viewpoint of God's covenant. It is a remarkable concept—that God would approach a man, a family, or a nation to join a covenant with him. It started with God's promise to Noah after the flood. Many years later he called Abraham to find an unknown country and bless his neighbors by his obedience to Yahweh. That was the message through the centuries in the relation of God with the children of Israel. At the right time, the covenant was presented in the person and work of Jesus, and the covenant people came to include all who trusted him. From the beginning God's purpose was aimed at all persons. This lesson finds in the last book of the Bible a picture of the dramatic accomplishment of that purpose and covenant.

The Bible Lesson

REVELATION 11:

15 And the seventh angel sounded; and there were great voices in heaven, saying, The kingdoms of this world are become the kingdoms of our Lord, and of his Christ; and he shall reign for ever and ever.

16 And the four and twenty elders, which sat before God on their seats, fell upon their faces, and worshipped God,

17 Saying, We give thee thanks, O Lord God Almighty, which art, and wast, and art to come; because thou hast taken to thee thy great power, and hast reigned.

18 And the nations were angry, and thy wrath is come, and the time of the dead, that they should be judged, and that thou shouldest give reward unto thy servants the prophets, and to the saints, and them that fear thy name, small and great; and shouldest destroy them which destroy the earth.

19 And the temple of God was opened in heaven, and there was seen in his temple the ark of his testament: and there were lightnings, and voices, and thunderings, and an earthquake, and great hail.

REVELATION 21:

10 And he carried me away in the spirit to a great and high

mountain, and shewed me that great city, the holy Jerusalem, descending out of heaven from God,

11 Having the glory of God: and her light was like unto a stone most precious, even like a jasper stone, clear as crystal:

12 And had a wall great and high, and had twelve gates, and at the gates twelve angels, and names written thereon, which are the names of the twelve tribes of the children of Israel:

13 On the east three gates; on the north three gates; on the south three gates; and on the west three gates.

14 And the wall of the city had twelve foundations, and in them the names of the twelve apostles of the Lamb.

The Lesson Explained

GOD'S REIGN HAD BEGUN (11:15-19)

Last May we had three sessions on passages from the book of Revelation, and we discovered that it is not easy to understand. It is the kind of literature or writing that deals with the struggles between God and Satan, and it looks toward the time when God will conquer evil once for all. This passage concludes a section called "the seven trumpet visions" beginning with 8:2. As each angel would blow his trumpet, some catastrophe would occur showing God's power in nature.

Although the six trumpet visions seemed to be building up to an awful act of judgment, when the seventh trumpet sounded, a heavenly chorus declared the victory "of our Lord, and of his Christ." They acted as though his reign had already begun; that is the persistent confidence of Revelation. Really there has never been a time when God did not reign. Then the twenty-four elders, possibly representing the twelve tribes and twelve apostles, fell face downward to worship God. They thanked him for his rule that would bring judgment on the disobedient and reward to all "that fear thy name." Then John saw in his vision the temple of God in heaven and the ark of the covenant. The hidden symbol of God's presence from ancient history had been revealed to show his continuing presence.

A VISION OF THE PERFECT CITY (21:10-14)

The song of the heavenly multitude in 19:7 had already referred to the impending marriage of the Lamb and his bride, but she was not identified. Then after the judgment John saw in 21:1-2 "a new heaven and a new earth," and the new

Jerusalem, dressed like a bride, was descending from heaven. That bride was the church, the whole fellowship of the redeemed. In verse 10 John tells how he got a closer view of "that great city" from a high mountain. It glowed brightly with God's glory and reminded John of clear crystal. In its "great and high" wall were twelve gates, three in each of four sides, named for the twelve tribes of Israel. Verse 16 reveals that the city was a cube, measuring about 1,500 miles in each direction. Adding to all these symbols of perfection was the fact that the twelve foundations (supporting the walls) bore the names of the twelve apostles.

WITHOUT TEMPLE OR SUN (21:22-27)

After describing the magnificence of the city, John then noticed some deeper aspects of his vision. Since God's presence pervaded the whole city, there was no need for a temple in which to worship him. Because the glory of God and of the Lamb illuminated the total life of the city, there was no need of the sun or moon. Although the city had come down from heaven to earth, it was a different kind of earth. The phrase "of them which are saved" does not appear in the best sources, but we can assume from verse 27 that only the redeemed would be comfortable there. Note that Gentiles ("the nations") and "kings of the earth" are expected there along with believing Jews. Everyone whose name is "in the Lamb's book of life" would be gathered into that city to make up the bride of Christ.

Truths to Live By

In spite of human weakness and sin, the Bible portrays God's ultimate victory.—That may be easy for an affluent American to believe, but it is probably more difficult for Christians living under a cruel dictator, in a war-torn country, or where there isn't enough food to go around. They may never have known freedom, peace, or a full stomach. But the book of Revelation describes the radical differences between good and evil, and it promises that God will eventually overcome and destroy Satan. That doesn't mean that all God's people will be saved from suffering, but it does mean that they are on the winning side. Their loyalty to God, love, and righteousness will not be useless. God will have the last word.

The covenant idea is one key for understanding the unity of the Bible.—Many Bible readers are confused by the different books, the different literary styles, and the difficulty of following the story line through the books of prophecy. Then, of course, the very size of the Bible makes it hard for readers to discover the major ideas among all the details. Various themes appear here and there in its pages, but the call of Abraham and God's covenant with him is mentioned and recalled through the Old Testament. Then in the New Testament it takes on new meaning in the ministry of Jesus and his followers. In Revelation we see the people of the new covenant making up the new Jerusalem—the church, the bride of Christ.

Although the reign (kingdom) of God is open to all, actual participation awaits individual decision.—Again and again the Bible shows that God is willing to forgive if persons will repent, is willing to save if persons are willing to believe. He does not force his love and compassion on anyone. It is available to all, but it does not come automatically or without the desire to receive it. The "new Jerusalem" will not include the entire population of the world but those "which are written in the Lamb's book of life." Other passages in the Bible make it clear that this relationship comes about by accepting God's gift of loving grace through faith.

A Verse to Remember

The kingdoms of this world are become the kingdoms of our Lord, and of his Christ; and he shall reign for ever and ever.—Revelation 11:15.

Daily Bible Readings

Nov. 24—The Everlasting Kingdom. Rev. 11:15-19
Nov. 25—Proclamations of the Angels. Rev. 14:6-13
Nov. 26—Sing Praise to God. Rev. 15:1-6
Nov. 27—The Marriage of the Lamb. Rev. 19:6-10
Nov. 28—The Great Judgment. Rev. 20:11-15
Nov. 29—The New Creation. Rev. 21:1-8
Nov. 30—The New Jerusalem. Rev. 21:10-14

December 7, 1980

MATTHEW PRESENTS THE MESSIAH

Matthew 1:1-17; 5:17-20; 9:9; 13:51-52; 23:1-12

With this session we begin a twenty-two-week study of the Gospel of Matthew. This course fulfills a distinctive feature of the Uniform Series of the International Sunday School Lessons; that is, to study the life of Christ each year. Although Matthew is the first book in the New Testament and was long considered the First Gospel, it must have followed Mark, possibly being written after A.D. 70. Its author was well acquainted with the Old Testament and quoted from it more than sixty times. Matthew's major concern was to present Jesus as the Christ (Messiah) so that both Jewish and Gentile believers would see him as Lord.

The Bible Lesson

MATTHEW 1:

1 The book of the generation of Jesus Christ, the son of David, the son of Abraham.

. . . .

17 So all the generations from Abraham to David are fourteen generations; and from David until the carrying away into Babylon are fourteen generations; and from the carrying away into Babylon unto Christ are fourteen generations.

MATTHEW 5:

17 Think not that I am come to destroy the law, or the prophets: I am not come to destroy, but to fulfil.

18 For verily I say unto you, Till heaven and earth pass, one jot or one tittle shall in no wise pass from the law, till all be fulfilled.

19 Whosoever therefore shall break one of these least commandments, and shall teach men so, he shall be called the least in the kingdom of heaven: but whosoever shall do and teach them, the same shall be called great in the kingdom of heaven.

20 For I say unto you, That except your righteousness shall exceed the righteousness of the scribes and Pharisees, ye shall in no case enter into the kingdom of heaven.

MATTHEW 9:

9 And as Jesus passed forth from thence, he saw a man, named Matthew, sitting at the receipt of custom: and he saith unto him, Follow me. And he arose, and followed him.

MATTHEW 13:

51 Jesus saith unto them, Have ye understood all these things? They say unto him, Yea, Lord.

52 Then said he unto them, Therefore every scribe which is instructed unto the kingdom of heaven is like unto a man that is an householder, which bringeth forth out of his treasure things new and old.

The Lesson Explained

AN UNUSUAL DISCIPLE (9:9; 13:51-52)

Although this Gospel does not say that it was written by Matthew, the apostle, some Christian writers in the second century were convinced he was the author. Because most Bible readers accept that association, Matthew 9:9 has special interest. It tells of Jesus calling Matthew as a disciple. It happened in Capernaum. Matthew was sitting in the tax office, where he collected money for the Roman government. The Pharisees and others despised him because of his contact with his foreign employer and because he could collect more money than he had to report. But Jesus invited Matthew to become his disciple. The Gospels of Mark and Luke tell the same story but they say his name was Levi, and he invited his friends to a banquet for Jesus. The Pharisees complained about Jesus eating with such people (Mark 2:16; Luke 5:30).

Some New Testament scholars feel that Matthew revealed something about himself in 13:51-52. After a long session of teaching the multitude by parables, Jesus asked his disciples if they understood what he had been saying. When they said yes, he compared the Christian interpreter ("scribe who has been trained for the kingdom of heaven," RSV) with a householder. In caring for his family, he would draw on resources both old and new. So the Christian interpreter—like Matthew—would use both the truths of the Old Testament and the insights of Jesus.

HIS UNIQUE MASTER (1:1,17)

This first verse is really the superscription, like a title written before the book actually begins. In a few words it tells what the book is about. It declares that Jesus is the Messiah (Christ) and that he was descended from both Abraham and David. Then in verses 2-16 we have the genealogy of Jesus, from his legal

December 14, 1980

JOHN PREPARES THE WAY

Malachi 3:1-5; 4:5-6; Isaiah 40:1-11; Matthew 3:1-12;
11:7-15; 17:9-13

Except for about eighty years (141 to 63 B.C.) when the Maccabees maintained a free Jewish government, the chosen people had suffered centuries of foreign control. But they had survived by the conviction that the Lord (Yahweh) had called them for a distinctive purpose. Their sacred writings told the requirements of the Lord, and they strove to live by those laws even at the risk of death. They hoped that God would send a deliverer, the Messiah, but they looked for political rather than spiritual freedom. Whenever he might come, they knew he would have a familiar forerunner because Malachi had written: "Behold, I will send you Elijah the prophet before the coming of the great and dreadful day of the Lord" (4:5). All this is the context for this session dealing with John the Baptist as the forerunner of the Lord.

The Bible Lesson

MATTHEW 3:

1 In those days came John the Baptist, preaching in the wilderness of Judaea,

2 And saying, Repent ye: for the kingdom of heaven is at hand.

3 For this is he that was spoken of by the prophet Esaias, saying, The voice of one crying in the wilderness, Prepare ye the way of the Lord, make his paths straight.

4 And the same John had his raiment of camel's hair, and a leathern girdle about his loins; and his meat was locusts and wild honey.

5 Then went out to him Jerusalem, and all Judaea, and all the regions round about Jordan,

6 And were baptized of him in Jordan, confessing their sins.

7 But when he saw many of the Pharisees and Sadducees come to his baptism, he said unto them, O generation of vipers, who hath warned you to flee from the wrath to come?

8 Bring forth therefore fruits meet for repentance:

9 And think not to say within yourselves, We have Abraham to our father: for I say unto you, that God is able of these stones to raise up children unto Abraham.

10 And now also the axe is laid unto the root of the trees: therefore every tree which bringeth forth not good fruit is hewn down, and cast into the fire.

11 I indeed baptize you with water unto repentance: but he that cometh after me is mightier than I, whose shoes I am not worthy to bear; he shall baptize you with the Holy Ghost, and with fire:

12 Whose fan is in his hand, and he will throughly purge his floor, and gather his wheat into the garner; but he will burn up the chaff with unquenchable fire.

The Lesson Explained
WILDERNESS PREACHER (Matt. 3:1-4; Isa. 40:1-5)

Matthew assumed that his readers already knew about the Baptizer; he did not introduce him as Luke did. Not long before Jesus began his ministry, this simply dressed man attracted attention by his preaching and baptizing. For some time Jews had been baptizing Gentile converts, but John was baptizing Jews on confession of their sins. He was different also in appearance and daily fare. His garment was woven from camel's hair and was held at the waist by a simple leather belt. Leviticus 11:22 tells what kind of locusts the Hebrews could eat. John depended on the wilderness for his living.

His message was clear and forthright: "Turn away from your sins because the reign of God is about to begin." Everything about John reminded Matthew of the opening verses of Isaiah 40. There the prophet was talking about clearing the way for the people of the Lord as they returned from captivity in Babylon. But in the light of what happened later, Matthew saw another meaning. John was the forerunner of Jesus, who was acknowledged as Lord by his disciples. John's preaching repentance would prepare persons to seek forgiveness through the Master.

JUDGING RELIGIOUS LEADERS (Matt. 3:5-10; 17:11-13)

The blunt, Elijah-like preacher in the wilderness drew people from the whole region, even from the city of Jerusalem. Representatives of the Pharisees and Sadducees probably came out of curiosity or perhaps to check up on him. We cannot know how he recognized them, but it may have been a combination of dress, phylacteries, and facial expression. Although they differed among themselves in theology and politics, John knew they were alike in their pride and self-righteousness. Calling them "sons of snakes" shows that John was not trying to improve the "tone" of his congregation with prominent converts. Although they were religious leaders, they had as much to fear "from the wrath to come" as anyone else.

If they wanted to be baptized, John said they must prove their repentance by changed lives. No longer could they think they were acceptable before God merely because they had been born Jews. God could use the loose stones on the ground to increase Abraham's line. In another figure of speech, John said that the ax of God's judgment was ready to chop down every tree that did not bear "good fruit."

POINTING TO THE GREATER ONE (Matt. 3:11-12)

John's water baptism was a public symbol of an inner repentance, and remembering it might help the forgiven one to maintain a penitent attitude. The people were impressed with John's preaching, but the One who was still to come was "mightier than" he. John did not feel worthy of even carrying his sandals. That One would baptize believers with the Holy Spirit and with fire; they would be motivated and empowered by God's Spirit and would be cleansed of sin as by fire. So the baptism provided through Jesus would mean new life as well as forgiveness.

In verse 12 is another figure of judgment. As the farmer with his winnowing fork beats the stalks of ripe grain and throws them into the air to separate chaff and kernel, so the coming One would reveal the difference between good and evil persons. The grain would be gathered for food, but the chaff would be burned. John saw an awful finality in that judgment yet to come.

Truths to Live By

Repentance is essential to a redemptive relationship with Jesus.—All persons tend to defend their actions and attitudes as right and to justify the occasions when they do not measure up to certain standards. They may blame heredity, circumstances, or other people for their conduct. They may refuse to admit wrongdoing. Eventually, they may deny the validity of certain laws or standards and set up their own behavior as the norm. No one in this frame of mind can have a redemptive relationship with Jesus. He calls for repentance—a change of mind and life direction—before his view of life can be effective in any person. The repentant person recognizes his own self-centeredness and gives it up. He or she admits self-righteousness and wants to live by the righteousness revealed by God in Christ. The repentant person sees his own faults and wants help in changing.

Christians can help prepare the way for Christ today.—Of course he will not come again as he did when John announced him. But he still needs to come into the lives of many people. Our preparation can be done as we provide a caring and evangelistic ministry through the church. A new neighbor or unexpected visitor may be reached without planned or individual effort. But usually a way needs to be opened. The deacon care program may help a church member rediscover the warmth of Christian fellowship. An outreach leader may introduce a newcomer to the claims of Christ or may help that person reaffirm an earlier commitment. A class member may help a bereaved member avoid loneliness and bitterness through some ministry to others. All would be preparing the way for Christ as Redeemer and Healer.

Even religious leaders may need to change their minds or repent.—They were the people that John pointed out. Of course, he did not accuse all of them, but the Pharisees and Sadducees had a reputation for being proud of their religious attainments. In that pride they looked down on others, ignoring their real needs. That was the attitude John condemned.

A Verse to Remember

Prepare the way of the Lord, make his paths straight.—Matthew 3:3. Every believer has some skill for doing this.

Daily Bible Readings

Dec. 8—The Messenger of Good News. Mal. 3:1-5
Dec. 9—The Day of Hope Comes. Mal. 4:1-6
Dec. 10—The Voice in the Wilderness. Isa. 40:1-11
Dec. 11—A Song of Thanksgiving. Isa. 11:1-3
Dec. 12—The Roar of the Nations. Isa. 17:9-13
Dec. 13—Immanuel Promised. Isa. 7:10-15
Dec. 14—Prepare the Way. Matt. 3:1-12

December 21, 1980

GOD SENDS THE SAVIOR
Matthew 1:18 to 2:23

Last year a survey revealed that women had been spending a little less time in work around the home and that men were doing a little more than previously. Many factors could have influenced that condition, and it could have several good results. Although women will probably lead in the operation of homes, it is a good thing for men to become more involved there. Men ought to do more than bring in the money and cut the grass. In doing some household chores, a man can actually help his wife and can keep her from feeling like an unappreciated drudge.

Today's lesson focuses on Joseph rather than Mary in the Christmas story. Although he was not the father of Jesus, he accepted the responsibilities of fatherhood and must have been the right kind of man in the home for Jesus to respect in his growing up years.

The Bible Lesson

MATTHEW 1:

18 Now the birth of Jesus Christ was on this wise: When as his mother Mary was espoused to Joseph, before they came together, she was found of child by the Holy Ghost.

19 Then Joseph her husband, being a just man, and not willing to make her a publick example, was minded to put her away privily.

20 But while he thought on these things, behold, the angel of the Lord appeared unto him in a dream, saying, Joseph, thou son of David, fear not to take unto thee Mary thy wife: for that which is conceived in her is of the Holy Ghost.

21 And she shall bring forth a son, and thou shalt call his name JESUS: for he shall save his people from their sins.

22 Now all this was done, that it might be fulfilled which is spoken of the Lord by the prophet, saying,

23 Behold, a virgin shall be with child, and shall bring forth a son, and they shall call his name Emmanuel, which being interpreted is, God with us.

24 Then Joseph being raised from sleep did as the angel of the Lord had bidden him, and took unto him his wife:

25 And knew her not till she had brought forth her firstborn son: and he called his name JESUS.

The Lesson Explained

JOSEPH REASSURED BY AN ANGEL (1:18-21)

The first part of this chapter listed the forebears of Joseph, right on back to Abraham himself. So, the carpenter of Nazareth was definitely a son of the covenant, and the son he nurtured was legally in that same line. Joseph and Mary were promised to each other ("espoused"), and that fact was as binding as marriage. Before they began living together as husband and wife, it became apparent that Mary was pregnant. Joseph could only assume that she had violated her pledge to him; so the marriage plans must be stopped. The ancient law said he had that right, and he thought it was important to abide by the law. But he did not want to embarrass Mary or perhaps run the risk of her serious punishment (possibly even death) for infidelity.

While he was thinking about solving the problem quietly, Joseph had a dream. An angel told him to proceed with the marriage because Mary was pregnant through the power of the Holy Spirit. She would have a son, and Joseph was to name him Jesus. That name in Hebrew was Joshua, meaning "Yahweh is salvation." The name predicted the child's lifework in saving "his people from their sins." So Matthew tells how Joseph learned of Jesus' role as Luke tells how Mary learned of it (Luke 1:26-33).

BOTH EMMANUEL AND BABY JESUS (1:22-25)

Here we have an explanation by the Gospel writer as to how the virgin birth of Jesus paralleled the message in Isaiah 7:14. Matthew quoted from the Greek translation called the Septuagint. Although some scholars point out different meanings for the word translated "virgin" in the Hebrew and the Greek, Matthew's purpose is clear enough. Isaiah had written when King Ahaz was threatened on all sides, but the Lord had promised to deliver Judah, and a baby's name would celebrate his presence. Matthew was led to see the relationship of this passage to Jesus long after he came to realize who Jesus was. That ancient name fitted him perfectly; he was and is "God with us."

Then returning to his narrative, Matthew told how Joseph obeyed the angel. Without further hesitation, he married Mary and took her to his home, but he did not know her as his wife until after she had her baby. Again following the angel's instruction, Joseph named the son Jesus. One day he would be called Emmanuel, "God with us," but that night he was a tiny, helpless baby in rough surroundings but with loving parents treating him like other couples treat their firstborn.

FROM EGYPT TO GALILEE (2:13-15,19-23)

When the Wise Men said they were looking for the newborn "King of the Jews," King Herod determined to kill any rival. Before the slaughter of young boys began, Joseph was warned by an angel to seek refuge in Egypt. So the little family left Bethlehem at night. That reminded Matthew of another prophetic saying: "Out of Egypt have I called my son" (Hosea 11:1).

After Herod died, Joseph was given the news in a dream and was told to return home. But when he came near to Judea, he heard that the son of Herod was ruling there and feared he might be as cruel as his father. Again he was guided by God in a dream to settle in Galilee instead of Judea. That fact would keep many Jews from thinking later that Jesus could be the Messiah. The family settled in Nazareth, and Matthew said this fulfilled another message from the prophets. But the sentence, "He shall be called a Nazarene," does not appear in the Old Testament. Perhaps Matthew referred to a writing that has been lost. That the Messiah should come from a town like Nazareth is another evidence of the reality of the whole Christ-event.

Truths to Live By

God's purpose in Christ was to save people from their sins.—That was the reason given for his name; it was a continuing reminder of his role. Notice that the text says "his people." God was concerned for his chosen people; they had been given his law, and many had tried to live by it. But the angel said that they needed saving from *their* sins. The very people who were careful to observe the sabbath, to memorize the law, and to worship at the Temple—they needed saving from their sins. Evidently in God's sight, sinfulness went deeper than religious behavior. Later as Jesus talked about God's love and mercy and demonstrated them, even "good" people were revealed as sinners. Only through repentance, forgiveness, and faith in God could they be saved. And that is still true. As he came to save his people, Jesus came to save all people in the same way.

Many times we must look to God to clarify puzzling situations.—Joseph was surely surprised—and probably indignant and hurt—when he learned that Mary was pregnant. Since it was not fitting for her to defend herself, he needed God's help in meeting that situation. Later, when King Herod determined to destroy the child whom the Wise Men said would become king of the Jews, God's messenger told Joseph to leave the country. Although the narrative does not say that Joseph prayed for guidance, he was surely in a receptive mood.

Christmas reminds us of the importance of family in the safety and growth of persons.—God ran some risks when he entrusted Jesus to a village carpenter and his young wife. But Mary showed remarkable courage and maturity in her potentially dangerous role as a virgin mother. Joseph could have been only indignant, but because he wanted to protect Mary, he was ready to trust the word of the angel. When Jesus was born, Joseph did not hesitate to assume the role of father. And the baby needed both parents to grow through childhood toward his awesome responsibility. Every child needs that kind of protection, guidance, and understanding to become the person that God intended.

A Verse to Remember

Thou shalt call his name Jesus: for he shall save his people from their sins.—Matthew 1:21.

Daily Bible Readings

Dec. 15—Jesus' Birth Announced. Luke 1:26-38
Dec. 16—Mary Sings with Gladness. Luke 1:46-55
Dec. 17—Born in a Manger. Luke 2:1-7
Dec. 18—Angels and Shepherds Praise God. Luke 2:8-20
Dec. 19—Simeon Sees God's Salvation. Luke 2:22-23
Dec. 20—Wise Men Worship. Matt. 2:1-11
Dec. 21—God's Son—Prince of Peace. Isa. 9:2-7

JESUS BEGINS HIS MINISTRY
Matthew 3:13 to 4:25

With this session we close the first unit of our study having the title "Preparation for Ministry." So, the four December lessons lay the foundation for the study of "The Gospel of Matthew." They have made it clear that Jesus came into the world as a human being. He was not a god that sprang full-grown from anybody's forehead; nor was he a spiritual presence who appeared here and there. He came as a baby, grew through childhood and youth, and at last became a man. This lesson shows him getting started in his lifework in somewhat the same way as any man might do it. He was limited by time and space; he had to win followers; and he worked to fulfill his calling. The crowds saw him as a remarkable young teacher and healer.

The Bible Lesson

MATTHEW 3:

13 Then cometh Jesus from Galilee to Jordan unto John, to be baptized of him.

14 But John forbad him, saying, I have need to be baptized of thee, and comest thou to me?

15 And Jesus answering said unto him, Suffer it to be so now: for thus it becometh us to fulfil all righteousness. Then he suffered him.

16 And Jesus, when he was baptized, went up straightway out of the water: and, lo, the heavens were opened unto him, and he saw the Spirit of God descending like a dove, and lighting upon him:

17 And lo a voice from heaven, saying, This is my beloved Son, in whom I am well pleased.

MATTHEW 4:

17 From that time Jesus began to preach, and to say, Repent: for the kingdom of heaven is at hand.

18 And Jesus, walking by the sea of Galilee, saw two brethren, Simon called Peter, and Andrew his brother, casting a net into the sea: for they were fishers.

19 And he saith unto them, Follow me, and I will make you fishers of men.

20 And they straightway left their nets, and followed him.

21 And going on from thence, he saw other two brethren, James the son of Zebedee, and John his brother, in a ship with Zebedee their father, mending their nets; and he called them.

22 And they immediately left the ship and their father, and followed him.

23 And Jesus went about all Galilee, teaching in their synagogues, and preaching the gospel of the kingdom, and healing all manner of sickness and all manner of disease among the people.

24 And his fame went throughout all Syria: and they brought unto him all sick people that were taken with divers diseases and torments, and those which were possessed with devils, and those which were lunatick, and those that had the palsy; and he healed them.

25 And there followed him great multitudes of people from Gailee, and from Decapolis, and from Jerusalem, and from Judaea, and from beyond Jordan.

The Lesson Explained

BEING BAPTIZED BY JOHN (3:13-17)

We met John the Baptist in the lesson for December 14; he was the wilderness preacher who called on everyone to repent. Even Jews needed to be baptized to show their penitence. He condemned especially the religious leaders for their self-righteousness. At the same time, he announced the coming of One greater than himself.

Then one day Jesus arrived from Galilee and asked to be baptized in the Jordan. But John protested that it would be more appropriate for Jesus to baptize him. He felt unworthy, but Jesus insisted in order "to fulfil all righteousness." He wanted the people to know that he accepted John's message as coming from God. Although he had no sin to be forgiven, he showed his support of the need of repentance, symbolized by baptism. When he came up out of the water, Jesus saw a form descending out of heaven; like a dove, the Spirit of God came upon him. Then a heavenly voice declared: "This is my beloved Son, in whom I am well pleased." Jesus had committed himself to God's will for the Messiah.

CALLING HIS FIRST DISCIPLES (4:17-22)

After that commitment and divine approval, Jesus went into the wilderness for a forty-day retreat. While there, he was tempted by Satan to forsake God's way to achieve his life purpose. Then he went to live in Capernaum on the northern coast of the Sea of Galilee and began preaching.

His theme was: "Repent: for the kingdom of heaven is at hand," just what John had declared. Therefore, it seems natural that two disciples of John the Baptist—Peter and Andrew—would become followers of Jesus. Although they fished for a living, when Jesus called on them to follow him, they left their nets to do it. Being a disciple meant being a learner and friend of a teacher. A disciple in that day was someone who had accepted the viewpoint of the teacher and wanted to learn more. He would accompany the teacher from place to place as he sought to win other followers. He might be called on to defend the teacher and eventually to explain his teachings to others. Two more disciples were enlisted as Jesus walked along the shore, James and John. They left their father and his boat to go with Jesus.

TEACHING AND HEALING (4:23-25)

These three verses summarize the early ministry of Jesus, and every phrase is packed with meaning. Although no time span is mentioned, it is clear that Jesus was very busy. He walked from one Galilean town to another, accepting every invitation to teach in the synagogues. As he interpreted the Law and the Prophets, he also declared the good news of God's reign that was coming.

Along with his teaching Jesus showed compassion on the sick and distressed and began "healing all manner . . . of disease."

Truths to Live By

Baptism is a memorable symbol of commitment.—I've never forgotten my baptism, although I was not quite nine years of age and thirty-two others were baptized that night. It ought to be that way because baptism portrays the two major aspects of the conversion experience: the repentant rejection of the old life and the gift of resurrected life through faith in Christ. Of course, it also reminds believers of the death and resurrection of Christ as the dual event that makes salvation possible. As a symbol of commitment, it begins with a radical picture of death and burial intended for the self-centered life and concludes with a startling affirmation of the God-centered life that comes as though the believer had been raised from the dead.

All believers in Jesus are disciples first and throughout life.—Although twelve of Jesus' disciples became known as apostles, they were always disciples. He had many more than twelve disciples; they were all learners, men and women who saw God working in him and wanted to be identified with his way of life. Even the twelve best-known disciples did not learn everything about him in their approximately three-year companionship. They were still learning things about the Way long after he had returned to the Father. Modern disciples are no smarter or more spiritual. Adult Christians are perfectly willing to have children and young people to do much study as believers, but they sometimes reject the idea that adult believers must be learners, too. Perhaps it is because the Christian life is presented as no more than being a good citizen or service club member. But there's more to it than that, and Christians need to "learn" Christ for the rest of their lives.

Combining ministry with teaching is still the way of Christ to reach others for him.—We do not have his healing power to deal with the sicknesses of mankind, but we can be used by his Spirit to help others. Teaching and preaching are not enough when so many people are hurting.

A Verse to Remember

From that time Jesus began to preach, and to say, Repent: for the kingdom of heaven is at hand.—Matthew 4:17.

Daily Bible Readings

Dec. 22—Jesus Is the Son of God. John 1:29-34
Dec. 23—A Wedding Miracle. John 2:1-11
Dec. 24—Opposing Corrupt Practices. John 2:13-22
Dec. 25—Confidence in Jesus' Word. John 4:46-54
Dec. 26—Jesus Declares His Mission. Luke 4:16-21
Dec. 27—Preparing Fishers of Men. Luke 5:1-11
Dec. 28—Faithful Though Tempted. Matt. 4:11-11

LET YOUR LIGHT SHINE
Matthew 5:1-16,21-48

"It's better to light a candle than to curse the darkness" is a proverb that speaks to many difficult situations. A new year has just begun, but instead of approaching it with zest, many see it as only a lengthening of their anxiety, pain, or frustration. Breadwinners are having trouble making ends meet. Parents are worried about the aimlessness of their teenagers. Churches are confused by the disloyalty of many members and the disinterest of unbelievers. Citizens are wondering if any leaders have the integrity and ability to handle the nation's political, social, and economic problems. Darkness takes many shapes, and only light can dispel it. Even one candle in a room can change attitudes. Jesus calls on each believer to *be* a candle.

The Bible Lesson
MATTHEW 5:

1 And seeing the multitudes, he went up into a mountain: and when he was set, his disciples came unto him:

2 And he opened his mouth, and taught them, saying,

3 Blessed are the poor in spirit: for theirs is the kingdom of heaven.

4 Blessed are they that mourn: for they shall be comforted.

5 Blessed are the meek: for they shall inherit the earth.

6 Blessed are they which do hunger and thirst after righteousness: for they shall be filled.

7 Blessed are the merciful: for they shall obtain mercy.

8 Blessed are the pure in heart: for they shall see God.

9 Blessed are the peacemakers: for they shall be called the children of God.

10 Blessed are they which are persecuted for righteousness' sake: for theirs is the kingdom of heaven.

11 Blessed are ye, when men shall revile you, and persecute you, and shall say all manner of evil against you falsely, for my sake.

12 Rejoice, and be exceeding glad: for great is your reward in heaven: for so persecuted they the prophets which were before you.

13 Ye are the salt of the earth: but if the salt have lost his savour,

wherewith shall it be salted? it is thenceforth good for nothing, but to be cast out, and to be trodden under foot of men.

14 Ye are the light of the world. A city that is set on an hill cannot be hid.

15 Neither do men light a candle, and put it under a bushel, but on a candlestick; and it giveth light unto all that are in the house.

16 Let your light so shine before men, that they may see your good works, and glorify your Father which is in heaven.

The Lesson Explained

DESCRIBING THE INNER PERSON (5:1-6,8)

Of course, this is the beginning of the Sermon on the Mount; it continues through chapter 7. While it is described as a "sermon," the verb in verse 2 is "taught"; so it is a teaching discourse. The word *them* in the same verse may refer to the disciples, the multitudes, or both; but 7:28 shows that the crowd had listened. Verses 3-12 are known as the Beatitudes because the word *blessed* is *beatus* in Latin, the official translation of the church for so many centuries. The word can also be translated "happy."

So, in declaring the good news, Jesus described those he felt were happy or blessed, and we realize at once that his standards are quite different. First, those who recognized their spiritual poverty should not be embarrassed or blamed because they would be at home within the reign of God. As each Beatitude states what seems to be a contradiction in combining "happy" with an apparently unhappy condition, it promises a related gift from God. Thus, even those who grieve and share the grief of others can expect to be strengthened by God.

The fifth Beatitude is frequently misunderstood because of the connotation of "meek." It does not describe the "doormat" person but one who can trust and endure without arrogance. So, this person is like "the poor in spirit," and Jesus echoed an Old Testament promise in saying that the meek would inherit the earth. The "hunger and thirst" of the sixth Beatitude represent an overwhelming desire for righteousness, personal and social. Jesus said that a person who really wanted to see right win over wrong would eventually be satisfied. Also dealing with the inner person, the eighth Beatitude focuses on "the pure in heart," but it means more than clear of moral stain. This purity includes integrity, the opposite of double-mindedness. Since the heart represented both mind and emotions, this kind

78

of person was clean and dependable from the inside out—the kind who could have an intimate relationship with God.

DEALING WITH OTHERS (5:7,9-12)

Since being a Christian is not just an inner reality, Jesus included four Beatitudes that deal with Christian relations with others. Going back to verse 7, we hear him bless the merciful. Such a person is compassionate, willing to forgive, and anxious to help those in trouble. The mercy he receives from God is not a reward; it is the work of God's grace in the person capable of receiving it. The peacemakers of the seventh Beatitude were not just those who kept the peace but those who got involved in making it. They ran risks in trying to understand and bring enemies together. Such persons would be recognized as God's children.

Closely related to peacemaking is the experience of being "persecuted for righteousness' sake." Those who stand for the right will naturally arouse some opposition. Jesus knew what the religious establishment would do to him, and his loyal disciples could expect the same from various power groups. But they would thus be at home within the realm of God. Then in the last Beatitude he made that point more personal by speaking directly to his disciples. If they suffered for the Master's sake, they could be glad, having joined the fellowship of the prophets.

PEOPLE WHO MAKE A DIFFERENCE (5:13-16)

The kind of persons whom Jesus saw as blessed or happy in the preceding verses would be quite distinctive in any community, and he used salt and light to symbolize the difference they would make. Salt was used then as now for preserving food, and he was saying that Christians must be different in character so they could prevent corruption in society. If they lose their "saltiness," they cannot fulfill their purpose.

In somewhat the same way, light is radically different from darkness. Jesus' followers were to be lights in a dark world. The Christian wants his life in Christ to illuminate his community. Even more, Jesus commanded his disciples to let their distinctive lives bring glory to the Father.

Truths to Live By

The Beatitudes present an ideal pattern for Christian

discipleship.—Although they say little or nothing about faith or theology, they grow out of profound belief in God. Without trusting Christ for salvation and the Spirit for guidance, no one would dare try to live by them. Even with that support most believers have found the Beatitudes beyond their achievement. But that only stresses the perfect goodness of God, and the Beatitudes remain the ideal pattern that makes Christian discipleship worthwhile.

True happiness comes from an inner quality of life and real concern for others.—Whether we call it blessed or happy, the life Jesus described did not depend on outward circumstances. It is like the gyrocompass that retains its orientation toward the North Pole in all kinds of weather. It is like the home with Christian parents who nourish their children with love, respect, responsibility, and joy as well as with food and shelter. If the latter two run thin, the family lives and grows on the other resources. Being the right person inside and relating to others with generosity form the basis for real happiness.

Christian witnessing begins from within and makes itself clear to the world.—That's what this passage is telling us. Christians must be different people on the inside before they have anything to tell others. They cannot be boastful about their spirituality; nor can they be so happy that they cannot grieve with others. They must be really serious in wanting right to win over evil. With the inner person "on target," they must then let the world know by their deeds what a difference Christ has made in their lives. Those deeds won't gain human credit but will lead others to glorify God.

A Verse to Remember

Let your light so shine before men, that they may see your good works, and glorify your Father which is in heaven.— Matthew 5:16.

Daily Bible Readings

Dec. 29—God's Word Gives Light. Ps. 119:129-136
Dec. 30—Called from Darkness to Light. Eph. 5:3-14
Dec. 31—Christians—Light in the World. Phil. 2:12-18
Jan. 1—Living in Light Brings Freedom. John 3:16-21
Jan. 2—Walk in the Light. 1 John 1:5-10
Jan. 3—Love—Evidence of Walking in Light. 1 John 2:7-11
Jan. 4—A Shining Light to Others. Col. 3:5-17

January 11, 1981

BUILD ON THE SOLID ROCK

Matthew 6–7

The Sermon on the Mount got off to a rather quiet start as Jesus began to talk to both his disciples and the crowds that were following him. The Beatitudes picked out some common experiences and called them "happy" because of some marvelous results that could be expected. Then Jesus began to insist that his followers must live on a higher moral and spiritual level than the religious experts of that day. As he applied that principle to anger, marital fidelity, honesty, and personal relations, he finally declared: "Be ye therefore perfect, even as your Father which is in heaven is perfect" (5:48). Then he turned to the religious practices of almsgiving, prayer, and fasting, demanding sincerity in private as well as public devotion. So, the Sermon on the Mount must not be seen as a sentimental homily but as a divine standard that will always challenge believers to trust God's grace and strive toward his expectations.

The Bible Lesson

MATTHEW 7:

13 Enter ye in at the strait gate: for wide is the gate, and broad is the way, that leadeth to destruction, and many there be which go in thereat:

14 Because strait is the gate, and narrow is the way, which leadeth unto life, and few there be that find it.

15 Beware of false prophets, which come to you in sheep's clothing, but inwardly they are ravening wolves.

16 Ye shall know them by their fruits. Do men gather grapes of thorns, or figs of thistles?

17 Even so every good tree bringeth forth good fruit; but a corrupt tree bringeth forth evil fruit.

18 A good tree cannot bring forth evil fruit, neither can a corrupt tree bring forth good fruit.

19 Every tree that bringeth not forth good fruit is hewn down, and cast into the fire.

20 Wherefore by their fruits ye shall know them.

21 Not every one that saith unto me, Lord, Lord, shall enter into the kingdom of heaven; but he that doeth the will of my Father which is in heaven.

22 Many will say to me in that day, Lord, Lord, have we not prophesied in thy name? and in thy name have cast out devils? and in thy name done many wonderful works?

23 And then I will profess unto them, I never knew you: depart from me, ye that work iniquity.

24 Therefore whosoever heareth these sayings of mine, and doeth them, I will liken him unto a wise man, which built his house upon a rock:

25 And the rain descended, and the floods came, and the winds blew, and beat upon that house; and it fell not: for it was founded upon a rock.

26 And every one that heareth these sayings of mine, and doeth them not, shall be likened unto a foolish man, which built his house upon the sand:

27 And the rain descended, and the floods came, and the winds blew, and beat upon that house; and it fell; and great was the fall of it.

28 And it came to pass, when Jesus had ended these sayings, the people were astonished at his doctrine:

29 For he taught them as one having authority, and not as the scribes.

The Lesson Explained

TWO GATES AND TWO WAYS (7:13-14)

The Golden Rule in verse 12 is a principle by which Jesus' followers should measure their relations with others. To some extent it summarizes his teachings to this point, and it also catches the central ethical emphasis of the Scriptures.

This passage (vv. 13-14) begins the conclusion of the Sermon and stresses the demands of the Christian life. The idea of there being two ways—of life and of death—was not original with Jesus, but he used a familiar teaching to illustrate the difficulty in entering the kingdom. It is not a broad gate through which a person just drifts with the crowd. That well-paved highway leads eventually to destruction; it requires no choosing and makes no demands. But the gate that leads to life—the real thing—is narrow and hard to find. Most people don't find it or choose it because the restricted opening is not attractive or popular. Besides, the road or path beyond it is cramped and difficult. Jesus was looking for really committed followers to endure discipline toward God's reign.

TESTING FALSE PROPHETS (7:15-23)

Here Jesus seems to have been looking down the years of the

early church; he knew that some teachers and proclaimers would distort or dilute the gospel message. They would be "false prophets," and they would look and act all right, appearing to be a part of the flock. But if they aroused doubt or suspicion, the church should evalute them by their fruits. After all, any farmer uses that much common sense in his vineyard and orchard. In the same way, the believers must evaluate the prophet's life and words. If they were selfish or did not ring true, they revealed an inner corruption.

In the final judgment Jesus knew how he would treat that kind of person. Just because a person claimed to be a follower and spoke glibly about the Lord would not guarantee his relationship with Christ. Not even performing miracles in his name was enough for that. The key to the invisible relationship was doing "the will of my Father," Jesus said.

BUILDING LIFE ON SAND OR ROCK (7:24-29)

In verses 21-22 Jesus seems to have said that talk is cheap; anyone might call him Lord without being really committed. Here he was concerned with persons who listened but did not act. On the positive side were those who would do both. As hearers *and* doers, they were like a man who laid his foundations on a rock base. When the storm came with heavy rain and violent winds, the house founded on rock withstood it all. But persons who heard what Jesus said but did nothing about it were like a man who built his house straight up from the sand or earth. Heavy rains would come as a flash flood to loosen doorposts and wash out the siding. Soon it would come down upon his head. Jesus mentioned no differences in the houses except the way they were founded. The life that would last must include both hearing Jesus' teachings and then living by them.

Verses 28-29 comprise Matthew's conclusion for the Sermon on the Mount.

Truths to Live By

Jesus promised that the way to real life would be difficult.—That is what he said in describing the broad and narrow ways. While a person could just drift into the broad gate and way, he or she would have to look for the narrow gate. And once inside, the person would find the going rough and restricted. Entering the narrow gate requires repentance, which most people do not like. It also means accepting Christ as Lord instead of running things for oneself. The narrow way includes a discipline of study, stewardship, worship, and ministry; so it is not a casual stroll or a self-centered race.

Glib religious spokesmen must be judged by the ways they obey God.—Pious talk may cover mere personal ambition in a local church. The same may be true of the successful evangelist with a widespread radio or TV congregation. The Guyana tragedy of two years ago showed how hundreds of people can be fooled by a false prophet. Religious leaders must obey God in the use of their money, the way they treat disadvantaged people, and their witness as citizens.

Lasting life is based on both hearing and doing the words of Jesus.—Jesus said nothing in that final parable about education, heredity, or environment as crucial to the eternal quality of life. Both builders were described as having heard Jesus' teachings. Although hearing is essential, it is not everything. Many people become sermon-hardened or become so "familiar" with the Bible that they think just knowing it will save them. But Jesus said that living by his teachings is what really makes the difference.

A Verse to Remember

Wherefore by their fruits ye shall know them.—Matthew 7:20.

Daily Bible Readings

Jan. 5—Formula for Faith and Forgiveness. Matt. 6:1-15
Jan. 6—Treasures of the Heart in Heaven. Matt. 6:16-24
Jan. 7—Putting First Things First. Matt. 6:25-34
Jan. 8—Spiritual Nearsightedness. Matt. 7:1-6
Jan. 9—Giving Good Things. Matt. 7:7-12
Jan. 10—Way, Narrow, Hard. Matt. 7:13-23
Jan. 11—Hearing and Doing. Matt. 7:24-29

Pro- Clain -to announce aloud so in a public manner

PROCLAIM THE KINGDOM
Matthew 8—10

In England in the 1780s a village cobbler made a globe of the world out of pieces of leather and drew on it the continents and countries. William Carey, in his twenties, had learned a great deal about population, climate, vegetation, and religion around the world. To help him understand his Bible better he learned Hebrew and Greek, and then he added Dutch, Italian, and French to help him understand others. Although he was living at a time when almost everyone in Europe was a member of some state church, few believers seemed concerned for those who did not know Christ around the world. Even Carey's fellow Baptists were so convinced of predestination that he argued before his association that Christians of their day were as obligated to be missionaries as were Jesus' first disciples. And that was the beginning of the modern missionary movement.

The Bible Lesson
MATTHEW 9:

35 And Jesus went about all the cities and villages, teaching in their synagogues, and preaching the gospel of the kingdom, and healing every sickness and every disease among the people.

36 But when he saw the multitudes, he was moved with compassion on them, because they fainted, and were scattered abroad, as sheep having no shepherd.

37 Then saith he unto his disciples, The harvest truly is plenteous, but the labourers are few;

38 Pray ye therefore the Lord of the harvest, that he will send forth labourers into his harvest.

MATTHEW 10:

1 And when he had called unto him his twelve disciples, he gave them power against unclean spirits, to cast them out, and to heal all manner of sickness and all manner of disease.

. . . .

5 These twelve Jesus sent forth, and commanded them, saying, Go not into the way of the Gentiles, and into any city of the Samaritans enter ye not:

6 But go rather to the lost sheep of the house of Israel.

7 And as ye go, preach, saying, The kingdom of heaven is at hand.

8 Heal the sick, cleanse the lepers, raise the dead, cast out devils: freely ye have received, freely give.

9 Provide neither gold, nor silver, nor brass in your purses,

10 Nor scrip for your journey, neither two coats, neither shoes, nor yet staves: for the workman is worthy of his meat.

11 And into whatsoever city or town ye shall enter, inquire who in it is worthy; and there abide till ye go thence.

12 And when ye come into an house, salute it.

13 And if the house be worthy, let your peace come upon it: but if it be not worthy, let your peace return to you.

14 And whosoever shall not receive you, nor hear your words, when ye depart out of that house or city, shake off the dust of your feet.

15 Verily I say unto you, It shall be more tolerable for the land of Sodom and Gomorrha in the day of judgment, than for that city.

The Lesson Explained

COMPASSION FOR THE CROWDS (9:35-38)

Verse 35 is another summary (see 4:23) of Jesus' wide ranging ministry of teaching and healing. It hints at how busy he must have been and proves that the Gospels tell only a part of his activities. But the other verses tell of a particular time when Jesus showed his compassion for the crowds that were clustering around him. His figure of "sheep having no shepherd" reminds us of Micaiah's description in 1 Kings 22:17. That the people should be so "worried and helpless" seems contradictory in a land where religion was supposed to be vital.

COMMISSIONING THE TWELVE (10:1-6)

Here Jesus began to answer the prayer in the preceding verse. Who better than his own disciples could meet the need for harvesters? So, he "gave them authority" (RSV) to cast out unclean spirits and heal all kinds of disease and disability. As they preached the coming kingdom, they would need to show its power and goodness. Only in verse 2 does Matthew speak of the "apostles"; the word means those who are sent. The list in verses 2-4 is slightly different from those given in Mark, Luke, and Acts; but it is clear that these twelve disciples had a special relationship with the Master. Since they were the first he sent out, they were known as apostles; his giving them authority over evil led them into a prominent role in the church.

Jesus' first instruction sounds like a limited commission. The disciples were not to go among Gentiles or Samaritans but only "to the lost sheep of the house of Israel." That sounds strange in the light of the Great Commission at the end of this Gospel. But at this stage the disciples were not ready in spirit to deal with Gentiles and Samaritans, and the message of God's kingdom would be better understood by Jews.

SENT TO PREACH AND TO MINISTER (10:7-15)

The text of their preaching was the same as the one Jesus used (Matt. 4:17). It was anchored in the Old Testament but contained fresh meaning in the person of Christ. The disciples were to use their authority over pain and suffering freely (without pay) because they had received it as a gift. The effect of Christ's compassion would be multiplied at least sixfold through their ministry. While preaching his message, they could perform his kind of remarkable work, even raising the dead.

Verses 9-15 list specific instructions for that first missionary venture. By not carrying any money, the disciples would show that they were not trying to capitalize on their ministry. In verse 9 "brass" probably refers to copper coins. "Scrip" in verse 10 was a bag for carrying supplies. Mark 6:8-9 says they were to take only one staff and one pair of sandals. Not only should these walkers be free of excess baggage, but they would show their confidence in God's care. The people they helped would be glad to help them.

As they came to a town, they should discover who would be responsive to their message and look to him as host, without moving from house to house. If the household accepted the blessing of peace, all was well. If not, the blessing was rejected, and the disciples need not declare the message of the kingdom. Shaking off the dust was a sign of judgment. The real and final sentence would come "in the day of judgment."

Truths to Live By

Christians need to see the crowds through Jesus' eyes.—He saw them as persons and not as classes or faceless conglomerates. He would never have said, "They all look alike to me." Although we cannot deal individually with every person in a crowd, we must be willing to know some of them close-up.

Jesus still calls his followers to proclaim the kingdom.— Those disciples had not finished their training with him, but Jesus felt they were ready to tell what they knew and to be channels of God's power in helping others. Disciples today are called to a similar ministry. Some make it a life vocation at home or abroad. But for most disciples it is their "other vocation," as Elton Trueblood called it. So, they accept some cards and visit their neighbors to say a good word for Jesus Christ. Some talk with fellow workers at break-time or after a stint with the bowling team. Others get something extra into their neighborhood coaching efforts.

Missionaries need realistic preparation for their work.— First, those sent out by mission boards need education—in Bible, history, language, and the rest—but they also need to be prepared to meet opposition, discouragement, and loneliness. Second, "missionaries" in the local church also need preparation. They need to know the good news of Christ and be able to tell how it affected their own lives. But they need to discover how they can witness through their skills and friendliness. Their job is to demonstrate the spirit of Christ and help someone else to want it for himself or herself.

Verses to Remember

The harvest truly is plenteous, but the labourers are few; Pray ye therefore the Lord of the harvest, that he will send forth labourers into his harvest.—Matthew 9:37-38. Although it is "his harvest," the Lord looks to his laborers to bring it in.

Daily Bible Readings

Jan. 12—Action Based on Belief. Matt. 8:1-13
Jan. 13—Following in Faith. Matt. 8:14-27
Jan. 14—Time of Torment. Matt. 8:28-34
Jan. 15—Glorifying God. Matt. 9:1-13
Jan. 16—The Touch of Faith. Matt. 9:1-13
Jan. 17—Compassion and Commitment. Matt. 9:27-38
Jan. 18—The Call of the Kingdom. Matt. 10:1-15

January 25, 1981

LEARN FROM THE LORD

Matthew 11—12

Although the earliest mention of Jesus' ministry describes him as preaching, we read more often in the Gospels of his teaching. The first emphasized announcing or declaring while the second includes telling parables, explaining the law, answering questions, demonstrating a truth with some deed of mercy. Jesus used both to make clear the good news of God's grace. He was not worried about method—lecture, discussion or object lesson—but let the current need determine his approach. Because he was concerned with relationships—with God and with others—he majored on the application of God's law rather than its specific content. He was the Master Teacher because his life matched his words. hs death and resurrection gave eternal significance to his parables and declarations.

The Bible Lesson

MATTHEW 11:

2 Now when John had heard in the prison the works of Christ, he sent two of his disciples,

3 And said unto him, Art thou he that should come, or do we look for another?

4 Jesus answered and said unto them, Go and shew John again those things which ye do hear and see:

5 The blind receive their sight, and the lame walk, the lepers are cleansed, and the deaf hear, the dead are raised up, and the poor have the gospel preached to them.

6 And blessed is he, whosoever shall not be offended in me.

. . . .

25 At that time Jesus answered and said, I thank thee, O Father, Lord of heaven and earth, because thou hast hid these things from the wise and prudent, and hast revealed them unto babes.

26 Even so, Father: for so it seemed good in thy sight.

27 All things are delivered unto me of my Father: and no man knoweth the Son, but the Father; neither knoweth any man the Father, save the Son, and he to whomsoever the Son will reveal him.

28 Come unto me, all ye that labour and are heavy laden, and I will give you rest.

29 Take my yoke upon you, and learn of me; for I am meek and lowly in heart: and ye shall find rest unto your souls.

30 For my yoke is easy, and my burden is light.

The Lesson Explained

ANSWERING JOHN'S QUESTION (11:2-6)

When John the Baptist was imprisoned by Herod for criticizing Herod's adulterous marriage, Jesus went from Judea to Galilee (Matt. 4:12). After perhaps a year behind bars John was wondering what Jesus was doing. John had preached judgment and repentance in preparing the way of the Messiah. But judgment seemed slow for John's persecutors. No word came of Jesus leading any movement for deliverance of the people, which many expected the Messiah to do. So, his question brought by two of his disciples to Jesus was both honest and puzzled.

Jesus' answer was gentle and confident. John's disciples should report what they saw and heard. What John had heard about Christ's works was true; the hurting and disadvantaged people were having their needs met: the blind, the lame, the lepers, the deaf, and the dead. And contrary to the practice of the priests and Pharisees, the good news of God was being preached to the poor. Then he added a beatitude to reassure John: "How happy are those who have no doubts about me!" (v. 6, TEV). Although Jesus might not be doing what John had expected, he was fulfilling God's will.

CONTRASTING TWO APPROACHES (11:16-19)

In verses 7-14 Jesus gave high praise to John, even saying that John played the role of Elijah in heralding the Messiah as predicted in Malachi 4:5. So his greatness was affirmed. Then Jesus compared Jews of that day with children who cannot get their friends to join in either a happy or sad game. John had been so serious that he followed a restricted diet, and people said he was demon-possessed. Then Jesus came, willing to eat and drink with all and even going to dinner parties, and the people said he was "a glutton and a drunkard" (RSV). The closing sentence is not clear; "children" probably should be "works" although Luke uses "children." The point may be that in either approach the wisdom of God is justified by its results.

TAKING THE FITTED YOKE (11:25-30)

The people's contrary response to both John and Jesus may have led into the thought of verses 25-27. Jesus recognized the wisdom of his Father in making the revelation of himself available to ordinary folk who were open to truth. The well-educated people were so sure of their own views that they could not see what God was showing in Christ. The central truth was that God had given his Son a unique understanding of and participation in the Father's purpose. Thus, no mere human being could really *know* the Father or the Son. But the intention of the Son was to reveal the Father to persons—those whom he chose.

For careful readers verses 28-30 present a paradox. Jesus first invited all the overworked and burdened hearers to come to him for rest. Instead of physical fatigue, the probable emphasis was on the frustration of trying to live by the scribes' detailed interpretation of the Law. The "rest" that Jesus offered was pictured as taking a yoke—his yoke—and letting him be their teacher. So, instead of inactivity, this rest called for new commitment and active learning. Unlike the haughty and impatient instructors in the synagogues, Jesus would be humble and understanding. The yoke borne by oxen was heavy and sometimes galling, but the yoke Jesus pictured would be well-fitted ("easy") to individual needs. Yoked in learning with Christ as Teacher, the believer would find that living by Jesus' teachings would be a "burden" that was really light.

Truths to Live By

Jesus' ways of doing things sometimes differ from our expectations.—That was a problem for John the Baptist; he may have expected Jesus to pick up where he had left off in judging wickedness with dramatic vigor. But Jesus saw his role differently: healing, teaching, suffering, redeeming. This way he would accomplish both judgment and salvation. Some church members today identify Christianity with "law and order," but they overlook Jesus' concern for persons, his willingness to forgive the penitent, and his patience in teaching his disciples. Some church people are generous in giving for a handsome and comfortable building, but they hesitate to make it fully available for a diversified program of teaching and training toward Christian growth and enrichment. If Jesus were here in the flesh today, some people would be surprised—and perhaps embarrassed—about the time he would spend in the inner city and with the poor.

As our Teacher, Christ understands our needs and limitations.—That is suggested in the yoke being described as well-fitted. It is not a common yoke for all people. It is a yoke to symbolize the role of learner and it is individually designed. When we are born again, we do not immediately understand everything about the Christian life or know how to act as a Christian in every experience. We need to discover Christian principles and try to put them into practice in everyday living.

Being yoked with Christ leads to being yoked with others.—That is a conviction of Elton Trueblood, a Quaker professor who started the Yokefellow Movement in 1952. The familiar yoke is made for two animals, and that kind of pairing must have come to his hearers' minds when Jesus used this figure. The same Master who teaches us his way also teaches every other believer. No one has an advantage over another; everyone needs to learn. While some may study in neighborhood Bible groups, the basic community for worship, learning, and fellowship is the church.

A Verse to Remember

Take my yoke upon you, and learn of me; for I am meek and lowly in heart: and ye shall find rest unto your souls.— Matthew 11:29.

Daily Bible Readings

Jan. 19—Hear and See, Go and Tell. Matt. 11:1-11
Jan. 20—Accepting the Yoke. Matt. 11:12-30
Jan. 21—Lord of the Sabbath. Matt. 12:1-8
Jan. 22—Restoring to Wholeness. Matt. 12:9-21
Jan. 23—Standing United. Matt. 12:22-32
Jan. 24—Be Careful of Careless Words! Matt. 12:33-42
Jan. 25—When Evil Returns. Matt. 12:43-50

February 1, 1981

TRUST IN GOD'S VICTORY!
Matthew 13:1-50

Last Sunday's paper had eight pages of classified ads for help wanted—hundreds of job openings. Some of them offered to train applicants for specialized tasks, but most of them were looking for persons "with experience." The average employer wants someone who has already been trained for the job to be filled. Mere good looks, good health, and a few A's in high school or college won't make it. Whether it's typing or running a computer, selling real estate or repairing cars, the employee needs some training. Much the same thing can be said for Christian disciples. Just as they must be born again, they must also learn how to practice the Christian life. Lessons for February come from Matthew 13—18, and they focus on "Training for Service." As you study, be sure they speak to your own need.

The Bible Lesson
MATTHEW 13:

24 Another parable put he forth unto them, saying, The kingdom of heaven is likened unto a man which sowed good seed in his field:

25 But while men slept, his enemy came and sowed tares among the wheat, and went his way.

26 But when the blade was sprung up, and brought forth fruit, then appeared the tares also.

27 So the servants of the household came and said unto him, Sir, didst not thou sow good seed in thy field: from whence then hath it tares?

28 He said unto them, An enemy hath done this. The servants said unto him, Wilt thou then that we go and gather them up?

29 But he said, Nay; lest while ye gather up the tares, ye root up also the wheat with them.

30 Let both grow together until the harvest: and in the time of harvest I will say to the reapers, Gather ye together first the tares, and bind them in bundles to burn them: but gather the wheat into my barn.

31 Another parable put he forth unto them, saying. The kingdom of heaven is like to a grain of mustard seed, which a man took, and sowed in his field:

32 Which indeed is the least of all seeds: but when it is grown, it is the greatest among herbs, and becometh a tree, so that the birds of the air come and lodge in the branches thereof.

33 Another parable spake he unto them; The kingdom of heaven is like unto leaven, which a woman took and hid in three measures of meal, till the whole was leavened.

34 All these things spake Jesus unto the multitude in parables; and without a parable spake he not unto them:

35 That it might be fulfilled which was spoken by the prophet, saying, I will open my mouth in parables; I will uter things which have been kept secret from the foundation of the world.

The Lesson Explained

SAME SEED; DIFFERENT SOILS (13:18-23)

This thirteenth chapter of Matthew is rich with parables—eight in all. The first one is rather detailed, but several are only a sentence in length. The passage before us is Jesus' interpretation of that first one. Sitting in a boat a few feet out into the water, Jesus taught the crowd that lined the shore of Galilee. He had described a farmer scattering seed as he walked across a field, and he mentioned four kinds of soil that caught the seed. Some fell on the hardened path, and it represented those who hear "the word of the kingdom" but do not really receive it. Like a bird, the wicked one snatches it away. The shallow soil with rock under it was like those who receive the word enthusiastically but do not have endurance. The soil that was polluted with weed seed represented hearers who let other things choke out the word. But some seed fell into good soil, and those hearers understood it and let it bear fruit. Although the percentage of increase differed, such hearers and doers represented the good soil.

THE HARVEST AS JUDGMENT (13:24-30)

The "kingdom of heaven" means the reign of God; for Jesus it was both present and future. It was a living structure of relationships, and this parable is explained in verses 37-43. Jesus told of a farmer who "sowed good seed in his field," but when the plants first appeared something else came up also. Those "tares" were probably bearded darnel that resembles wheat. The farmer knew he had sowed good seed; so he surmised that an enemy had sowed the weed seed. Instead of

94

cleaning out the darnel during the early growing time, he chose to wait until the harvest. Then his workers could easily distinguish between the good and bad. One could be stored and the other destroyed.

MUCH FROM LITTLE (13:31-33)

Here Jesus used two simple comparisons to clarify a feature of the reign of God: that it begins in a small way but will have large results. First, he reminded his hearers of the tiny mustard seed, probably the smallest that farmers used at that time. But when it was planted, it grew into a shrub with branches like a tree, and birds could build their nests on them. For the second comparison, Jesus used an experience from the kitchen that his women hearers would appreciate. Three measures of meal would be probably more than our bushel, which would make a large quantity of dough. Into that mass Jesus pictured a woman hiding a little ball of fermented dough (probably saved from her last baking). Quietly and invisibly the leaven would work through all the dough.

GREAT TRUTH IN SIMPLE STORIES (13:34-35)

Jesus did not originate the parable, but he used it with great effectiveness. A parable may be a single sentence that compares one thing with another, or it can be a story of some imaginary people in a commonplace situation. Most parables try to make only one major point. Verse 34 may mean that some of his parables were not recorded. He knew the value of a story for explaining a principle or abstract truth, whether his hearers were learned or uneducated. Matthew saw this as a fulfillment of Psalm 78:2. In that case the psalmist was called a prophet. Compare the superscription of the psalm and 1 Chronicles 25:1.

Truths to Live By

God will ultimately triumph over evil.—That is a basic conviction of the whole Bible. No matter who wins the battles, he will win the war. At times evil seems to be invincible, but the Creator and Judge of the universe holds everything in his own balance. His "winning" may not meet our expectations, but he has the perspective of eternity. This confidence needs to be rekindled in our time with its ever-present nuclear threat, its spread of hunger and poverty, and its increase of crime and corruption. The parables of this lesson see God as in charge of the final separation of good and bad people, as responsible for the mysterious growth of his reign, and as the giver of good results when the seed of the Word is received by receptive hearers. This view does not ignore risk and struggle by persons, but it affirms the worth of all that in the outcome.

A good teacher interprets Christian truth in the language of the hearers.—If Jesus did not hesitate to use simple stories about farming and bread-making to explain the reign of God, we cannot afford to insist that there's only one language of Zion, that religious ideas must be phrased only in special religious words and concepts. Because the Christian faith deals with life and relationships, the Christian spokesman should use words and approaches that clarify rather than confuse.

God's reign among persons may start small and grow slowly.—A new convert was sincere in making his commitment to Christ, but it took him a while to realize that it affects more than his so-called religious life. He was serious about Bible study and regular worship, but it took several years before he would expand his giving beyond one dollar a Sunday. At first, he was fascinated by the diversity of people within the church on the corner, but some years later he discovered the wider fellowship of believers in countries around the world speaking many different languages. In Bible study and training groups he faced up to Christian standards in his vocation.

A Verse to Remember

The kingdom of heaven is like unto leaven, which a woman took, and hid in three measures of meal, till the whole was leavened.—Matthew 13:33.

Daily Bible Readings

Jan. 26—Responses to the Gospel. Matt. 13:1-9
Jan. 27—Reasons for Parables. Matt. 13:10-17
Jan. 28—Hearing and Understanding. Matt. 13:18-23
Jan. 29—The Growth of the Kingdom. Matt. 13:24-33
Jan. 30—The Time for Judgment. Matt. 13:34-43
Jan. 31—Discovery and Discernment. Matt. 13:44-50
Feb. 1—Judgment and Deliverance. Zeph. 3:8-13

HAVE COMPASSION
Matthew 13:53 to 15:39

Archibald Rutledge tells the story of the widow of a black preacher in his town. She spent much of her time and limited money in helping orphans and poor folk. Rutledge was so impressed and grateful that he built her a small house and furnished it. But soon after she moved in, he was shocked to learn that she had invited a disreputable woman to move in with her. So he visited the widow and asked: "How could you have such a woman in your lovely new home?" She replied softly, "Jesus would." And that is a vivid picture of compassion. It may seem unreasonable at one level, but deep down we know it is right. In training his disciples for service (our February emphasis), Jesus wanted them to see compassion as essential to the Christian way. Without it, their ministry would be barren. They might become religious leaders, but they would not reflect the Christ.

The Bible Lesson

MATTHEW 15:

29 And Jesus departed from thence, and came nigh unto the sea of Galilee; and went up into a mountain, and sat down there.

30 And great multitudes came unto him, having with them those that were lame, blind, dumb, maimed, and many others, and cast them down at Jesus' feet; and he healed them:

31 Insomuch that the multitude wondered, when they saw the dumb to speak, the maimed to be whole, the lame to walk, and the blind to see: and they glorified the God of Israel.

32 Then Jesus called his disciples unto him, and said, I have compassion on the multitude, because they continue with me now three days, and have nothing to eat: and I will not send them away fasting, lest they faint in the way.

33 And his disciples say unto him, Whence should we have so much bread in the wilderness, as to fill so great a multitude?

34 And Jesus saith unto them, How many loaves have ye? And they said, Seven, and a few little fishes.

35 And he commanded the multitude to sit down on the ground.

36 And he took the seven loaves and the fishes, and gave thanks,

and brake them, and gave to his disciples, and the disciples to the multitude.

37 And they did all eat, and were filled: and they took up of the broken meat that was left seven baskets full.

38 And they that did eat were four thousand men, besides women and children.

39 And he sent away the multitude, and took ship, and came into the coasts of Magdala.

The Lesson Explained

FOR A GENTILE WOMAN (15:21-28)

No reason is given for Jesus going into the area of Tyre and Sidon, but it may have been the hostility of the Pharisees from Jerusalem (15:1-12). A Phoenician woman called him "son of David" and asked his help for her demon-possessed daughter. When he did not respond, his disciples urged him to send her away because she kept crying out to them. Jesus said that his task was with "the lost sheep of the house of Israel"—a phrase he had used in sending out his disciples (10:6). Then the woman came again and knelt before him pleading for help. Jesus gave a strange answer. Was he testing her faith or setting the stage for a lesson to his disciples? Whatever was intended, she was willing to face any test if Jesus would help her suffering daughter. Then he said, "You are a woman of great faith! What you want will be done for you" (TEV). So a Gentile had faith in the Jewish Messiah who showed compassion on her.

FOR THOSE WHO SUFFERED (15:29-31)

Although verse 29 says Jesus returned to the region of the Sea of Galilee, we must look elsewhere for the actual place. When verse 31 says that the people "glorified the God of Israel," it suggests that these people would not normally worship that God. Then verse 39 says that Jesus went by boat to Magdala, which was on the western side of the lake. So we can assume that when he left Phoenicia, he traveled eastward and came down on the east side of the lake. That put him in Gentile territory and also safe from Herod's authority.

The news of the Healer got around, "and great multitudes" came to him in the hills, bringing persons with all kinds of disabilities and placing them at his feet. Although the crowd had come with hope and some faith, they were amazed to see all that he accomplished. Crippled persons were walking, and blind ones were seeing. So they "glorified the God of Israel." The young Jewish rabbi had compassion on Gentiles who suffered.

FOR THE HUNGRY CROWD (15:32-39)

The healing ministry lasted longer than the previous verses indicate; Jesus said three days. The people had probably brought some provisions, but they were exhausted. Because the place was "in the wilderness," Jesus did not want them to start for home without eating. When he declared his compassion, the disciples said they could not help.

But Jesus commanded that the crowd sit on the ground, perhaps in some orderly pattern. Then he took the seven loaves and "few little fishes," thanked God for them, and began breaking and passing them to the disciples. After everyone had eaten what he wanted, the disciples collected seven baskets of leftovers. Four thousand men, plus women and children, had been fed by the compassion and power of the Master. He had already shown great compassion on his own people; here he showed his concern for all mankind.

Some scholars feel that this account is a repetition of the narrative of feeding five thousand in Matthew 14:15-21, but there are a number of differences. All four Gospels mention that feeding, and Matthew and Mark refer to both (Matt. 16:9-10; Mark 8:19-20). Thus, Jesus showed compassion on both Jews and Gentiles.

Truths to Live By

Compassion has little meaning until someone is helped.— It is easy to feel sorry for someone, and just feeling that way makes some people feel better about themselves. But that is not compassion; compassion includes wanting to do something to help. And showing compassion means actually *doing* it. In his epistle James pictures some members of the church who need clothes and food. "What good is there in your saying to them, 'God bless you! Keep warm and eat well!'—if you don't give them the necessities of life?" (2:16, TEV). He understood the honesty and realism of Jesus. Some modern disciples enjoy feeling sorry for others but never get to the compassionate stage of sharing money, friendship, or life's necessities with others. If we "feel" without doing anything about it, we may lose the ability to feel.

God still multiplies the effect of a compassionate deed.— With his power, Christ could use a small supply of food to feed a crowd of hungry people. We don't have the power to do exactly that, but God can do more than we realize. The American Friends Service Committee refused to let World War II dry up its concern for hungry and cold people even behind enemy lines. The small beginnings of CARE packages became a major source of feeding and clothing war victims around the world. Elizabeth Fry, wife of a wealthy English Quaker, began about 1820 to befriend some women inmates of Newgate Prison, teaching them to read, to sew, and to keep their children and themselves clean. Her work led to some important prison reforms. Your deed of compassion could influence others.

Christian compassion seeks to help the whole person.— That was the approach of Jesus in teaching, healing, and feeding. He did not aim at meeting spiritual needs only; he did something about hunger and pain. Through the centuries Christians have made diverse contributions: hospitals, orphanages, schools, community service groups. Both home and foreign missions (better known as world missions) have reached people for Christ with a variety of ministries.

A Verse to Remember

And Jesus went forth, and saw a great multitude, and was moved with compassion toward them, and he healed their sick.—Matthew 14:14.

Daily Bible Readings

Feb. 2—Miracles that Did Not Happen. Matt. 13:53-58
Feb. 3—Dinner for Five Thousand. Matt. 14:14-21
Feb. 4—Walking on Water. Matt. 4:22-27
Feb. 5—The Higher Law. Matt. 15:1-11
Feb. 6—A Faith that Won. Matt. 15:21-28
Feb. 7—The Making of a Miracle. Matt. 15:29-39
Feb. 8—They Believed and Were Spared. Jonah 3:1-10

LIVE YOUR FAITH

Matthew 16:1-28; 17:10-27

Nearly three hundred years ago William Penn made a treaty with the Indians in establishing his colony that became known as Pennsylvania. The son of an admiral in the royal navy, Penn studied at Oxford for two years. His father rejected him temporarily when young Penn became a Quaker. Because that religious group criticized the formality and worldliness of the established church, and because they were pacifists and refused to take an oath, they were persecuted by civil authorities. By the time Penn was twenty-five years of age he was considered a leader in the Society of Friends. His most important book was *No Cross, No Crown*, emphasizing the need for living one's faith despite persecution. His colony in America was to be a Christian state allowing religious freedom to all. His life is a good illustration of the truth of this lesson.

The Bible Lesson

MATTHEW 16:

13 When Jesus came into the coasts of Caesarea Philippi, he asked his disciples saying, Whom do men say that I the Son of man am?

14 And they said, Some say that thou art John the Baptist: some, Elias; and others, Jeremias, or one of the prophets.

15 He saith unto them, But whom say ye that I am?

16 And Simon Peter answered and said, Thou art the Christ, the Son of the living God.

17 And Jesus answered and said unto him, Blessed are thou, Simon Bar-jona: for flesh and blood hath not revealed it unto thee, but my Father which is in heaven.

18 And I say also unto thee, That thou art Peter, and upon this rock I will build my church; and the gates of hell shall not prevail against it.

19 And I will give unto thee the keys of the kingdom of heaven: and whatsoever thou shalt bind on earth shall be bound in heaven; and whatsoever thou shalt loose on earth shall be loosed in heaven.

20 Then charged he his disciples that they should tell no man that he was Jesus the Christ.

21 From that time forth began Jesus to shew unto his disciples, how that he must go unto Jerusalem, and suffer many things of the elders and chief priests and scribes, and be killed, and be raised again the third day.

22 Then Peter took him, and began to rebuke him, saying, Be it far from thee, Lord: this shall not be unto thee.

23 But he turned, and said unto Peter, Get thee behind me, Satan: thou art an offence unto me: for thou savourest not the things that be of God, but those that be of men.

24 Then said Jesus unto his disciples, If any man will come after me, let him deny himself, and take up his cross, and follow me.

25 For whosoever will save his life shall lose it: and whosoever will lose his life for my sake shall find it.

26 For what is a man profited, if he shall gain the whole world, and lose his own soul? or what shall a man give in exchange for his soul?

The Lesson Explained

BASED ON CHRIST, SON OF GOD (16:13-19)

For possibly two years the disciples had been following Jesus. Now on a "retreat" about twenty miles north of Capernaum he asked those closest friends some pointed questions. Everyone knew him as Jesus of Nazareth, and only occasionally in Matthew do the disciples get a clue that he is more than that. His miracles and authoritatives teaching had made them wonder. They said that people in the crowds had been guessing that John the Baptist had come back from the dead or one of the prophets had returned.

But when he asked for the disciples' view, Peter answered, "Thou art the Christ, the Son of the Living God." Much more than a prophet, Jesus was the fulfillment of Jewish hope for the Messiah through the centuries. Jesus commended that answer, saying it had come by divine revelation instead of by human thought or reasoning. Roman Catholics have argued that verse 18 shows Peter to be head of the church. But Protestants have claimed that Peter's confession was the rock-like foundation of the church as the community of believers. Without the conviction and declaration that Jesus is Christ, Son of God, a person cannot be a Christian. This is the heart of the Christian faith.

THE SUFFERING SAVIOR (16:20-23)

Although verse 19 assured Peter that as a result of his confession he would be given authority in teaching, Jesus immediately insisted that the disciples tell no one that he was the Christ. The Hebrew word (Messiah) could mislead the Jews and excite the Romans. He probably did not want to be victimized by the popular misinterpretation of that role. Because his concept was so different Jesus knew it was time for the disciples to understand what he expected from the religious authorities whenever he went to Jerusalem. The very people who should respond to God's will would actually reject it. Instead of the Suffering Servant, they wanted a conquering hero. So Jesus would be executed but would be raised again in three days. This was more than Peter could stand; but when he rebuked Jesus, the Master accused him of acting like the evil one. What a reversal for the apostle who had just received a divine revelation.

REAL LIFE BY SELF-DENIAL (16:24-26)

The death which Jesus anticipated for himself would be more than an historical event; it would become a symbol for the life to which he called his disciples. A person who wants to commit himself to Jesus must deny himself (yield control of his life to another), take up his cross (willingly assume the risk of obedience to God), and follow him (learn from Jesus and act by his pattern). As some of those disciples proclaimed their faith in that alien world, they would actually lose their lives. Others would prove their self-denial in service for needy people for Jesus' sake. The person who is preoccupied with saving his life—his health, wealth, or social standing—will lose it, or his spiritual life. But he or she who is willing to risk the temporal aspects of life for Jesus' sake shall find *real* life. Somewhat the same idea appears in verse 26; in the Greek of both verses there is no distinction between "life" and "soul." But the way to real life is the way of self-denial.

Truths to Live By

Christian faith is focused on God in Christ.—That seems to be so obvious that someone may wonder why emphasize it. But in recent years some groups have appeared to stress the role of the Holy Spirit so much as to obscure the centrality of Christ. On the other hand, some seem so anxious to accord honor to him that they overlook his role as Son of God. That may be traced to a shallow understanding of the relation of the Old Testament to the New. But the major problem here may be with those who want the ethical emphases of Jesus' teachings without commitment to his unique message of salvation by grace through faith in him.

Christians are called to live their faith in community and not alone.—Of course that community is the church—on the corner and around the world. The first test of the reality of our faith may be in the home, but it must be practiced soon within the church with several score or several hundred other believers with varying ideas. Beyond the church on the corner there are tens of thousands around the world with different languages and cultures. Besides the challenge there is also the loving support and guidance that these communities can give us in ministry, worship, and stewardship. Jesus knew that believers would need the church.

Christians must be more concerned with giving than with getting.—After all, giving is an aspect of Christian ministry—giving money, time, helpfulness. Giving proves that one's profession of faith in Christ was real. So we give *through* the church to preach the gospel, support missions, enrich the lives of children, and other things. Real evangelism is more interested in giving than getting.

A Verse to Remember

If any man will come after me, let him deny himself, and take up his cross, and follow me.—Matthew 16:24.

Daily Bible Readings

Feb. 9—Blind to the Signs. Matt. 16:1-12
Feb. 10—The Great Promise. Matt. 16:13-20
Feb. 11—Losing and Finding Life. Matt. 16:21-26
Feb. 12—Blessing Out of the Past. Matt. 17:1-8
Feb. 13—The Way of the Cross. Matt. 17:9-13
Feb. 14—The Essential Faith. Matt. 17:14-23
Feb. 15—The Lord Will Answer. Isa. 58:8-12

IN MEMORY

OF

BERTHA MAE PEARL

Born June 27, 1896
Died August 2, 1973
Cincinnati, Ohio

PRAYER:

O gentlest Heart of Jesus, ever present in the Blessed Sacrament, ever consumed with burning love for the poor captive souls in Purgatory, have mercy on the soul of Thy servant **BERTHA MAE**, bring her from the shadows of exile to the bright home of Heaven, where, we trust, Thou and Thy Blessed Mother have woven for her a crown of unfading glory. Amen.

Our Father. Hail Mary.

Sweet Heart of Jesus, be my love.

—300 days indulgence.

Alba 13

PRINTED IN ITALY

1, Jesus before Pilate
And the whole multitude of
them arose, led him to Pilate
And they began to accuse him
And they were fierce, saying
He stirreth up the people teaching
thought all Judeas beginning
from Galilee to this place

Pilate sends Jesus to
Herod
When he questioned him in
many words
And the chief priests and
Scribes stood and violent accus
Herod send Jesus back
to Pilate; who seek to
release him.
Herod, with his men of
War treated him with
Contempt, mocked him and
Arrayed him in a gorgeous
robe. and sent him again
to Pilate
They were Friend
Pilate & Herod

on the Way to the
place of Crucifixion

Jesus is Crucified

An expressing Contempt or derision

The repentant
thief

Darkness from
the sixth to Ninth
hour Jesus dismissed
His Spirit

Jesus is buried

Repeat the Verses (twice) (2)
~~Hum~~ After All the Verses.

1. Got my religion. Got the
Lord on my side.

2. If the Lord don't help me
I can't stand the storm.

3. Please dont let this. let
this harvest Pass You by.

4. The Lord is my Shepherd
And I shall not want
~~to~~ envying one another
~~envying~~

See Wrath

Fruits of the
Spirit
Jn — 4 — 16

Roman 1 — 13

11 — 7 — 4

Gal 5 : 22

Eph 5 — 9

The fruit of the Spirit
is love, Joy, peace, long
suffering, gentleness, faith self
Control. meekness
Let us not be desirous of
Vainglory. Provoking one Another

February 22, 1981

LOVE AND FORGIVE

Matthew 18

Legendary feuds among mountain people and gang rivalries as in *West Side Story* make exciting drama but usually offer little help in getting along with other people. The animosity between the Capulets and Montagues is the essential context for Shakespeare's *Romeo and Juliet*, but it leads to the death of both characters. In all these cases pride led to an unforgiving spirit, and retaliation widened the gap between persons. Such conflict heightens dramatic effect, but in real life it causes pain and distorts personality. In real life someone must run a risk by injecting some good will into a bad situation. Love and forgiveness are sometimes costly because they are misunderstood, but they are needed to break the stalemate of pride. That is the theme of this lesson as we conclude the February unit.

The Bible Lesson

MATTHEW 18:

1 At the same time came the disciples unto Jesus, saying, Who is the greatest in the kingdom of heaven?

2 And Jesus called a little child unto him, and set him in the midst of them,

3 And said, Verily I say unto you, Except ye be converted, and become as little children, ye shall not enter into the kingdom of heaven.

4 Whosoever therefore shall humble himself as this little child, the same is greatest in the kingdom of heaven.

5 And whoso shall receive one such little child in my name receiveth me.

6 But whoso shall offend one of these little ones which believe in me, it were better for him that a millstone were hanged about his neck, and that he were drowned in the depth of the sea.

. . . .

15 Moreoever if thy brother shall trespass against thee, go and tell him his fault between him and thee alone: if he shall hear thee, thou hast gained thy brother.

16 But if he will not hear thee, then take with thee one or two

more, that in the mouth of two or three witnesses every word may be established.

17 And if he shall neglect to hear them, tell it unto the church: but if he neglect to hear the church, let him be unto thee as an heathen man and a publican.

18 Verily I say unto you, Whatsoever ye shall bind on earth shall be bound in heaven: and whatsoever ye shall loose on earth shall be loosed in heaven.

19 Again I say unto you, That if two of you shall agree on earth as touching any thing that they shall ask, it shall be done for them of my Father which is in heaven.

20 For where two or three are gathered together in my name, there am I in the midst of them.

21 Then came Peter to him, and said, Lord, how oft shall my brother sin against me, and I forgive him? till seven times?

22 Jesus saith unto him, I say not unto thee, Until seven times: but Until seventy times seven.

The Lesson Explained

A MODEL FOR THE KINGDOM (18:1-6)

One day while they were in Capernaum, the disciples came to Jesus with a question, as though to settle an argument: "Who is the greatest in the kingdom of heaven?" Without giving an answer, Jesus called a child to come to him. Then perhaps turning the child to face the men, he said that unless grown men radically changed their way of thinking and became like children, they could not even enter the kingdom. He was not commending childishness but childlikeness. The child is dependent, humble, and teachable. Humility measures greatness in God's reign, and that requires a real conversion.

RELATIONS WITHIN THE CHURCH (18:15-20)

This passage shows that Jesus was a realist; he was not going to be surprised if wrongs were done in the fellowship of believers. As human beings they could still sin, but as Christians they should deal with it in a creative way. He who was wronged should take the initiative in trying to make things right. Notice that Jesus did not suggest immediate forgiveness; the offender and his brother need first to see the offense together. If he listens and repents, then brotherhood has been repaired.

But if the offender won't listen, then the brother should take others with him to confirm the whole situation. If that does not work, report it to the church. If the offender rejects the church, then let him be rejected. He has shown that he does not want to be a part of the fellowship. Verse 18 shows that Jesus shared with the other disciples the authority he had given Peter in 16:19.

UNLIMITED FORGIVENESS (18:21-35)

Jesus' words in verse 15 had evidently set Peter to thinking. If he took the initiative in setting things right with an offending brother, how often should he do it to prove his Christian stance? Seven times sounded pretty generous, but Jesus countered with a fantastic proposal. Of course, he did not mean for anyone to keep account to 77 or 490. He meant that the true forgiving attitude would set no limit. So long as a person repented and asked for forgiveness, it should be granted.

To illustrate his principle, Jesus told a dramatic parable. A king decided to do a financial analysis, and he discovered a staff member who owed him an enormous sum of money. When the king demanded payment, the man begged for mercy. So the king cancelled the debt. But the man then confronted a fellow worker who owed him about twenty dollars, and he sent him to prison because he could not pay. When the king heard what had happened, he called the merciless one back into court and rescinded his previous action. Verse 35 tells what the parable means. In a thousand ways every person is indebted to God, but he responds when we ask for mercy. But how do persons act toward one another? Often they seem to think that God doesn't know about their refusal to forgive. Without the willingness and practice, no one is fit to receive God's forgiveness.

Truths to Live By

Humility is essential for one to be at home in God's family.—That is the point of Jesus' reference to the child. Humility is not the kind of mock meekness that Uriah Heep paraded. It is honest self-esteem that recognizes both one's limitations and abilities. But it is not boastful or proud. It acknowledges the strengths of others and does not criticize their weaknesses. Most people enjoy having an humble person around because he or she appreciates others. In God's family everyone accepts him as Father, lives because of his forgiveness, and identifies with others as their brothers and sisters. So, humility is essential.

Christians should be honest and persistent in dealing with personal problems in the church.—Although most Christians agree that they are not perfect, they seem to feel that personal problems in the church should be ignored. If two families in a church stop speaking to each other, the rest either choose sides or pretend there is no problem. Jesus gave some practical guidance for such problems in this lesson. His purpose was to safeguard both the alienated members and the whole fellowship. So long as all members act according to the spirit of Christ, it is better to deal with personal problems in the church than pretend they don't exist.

Unless a person forgives others, he will not be forgiven by God.—Of course, the relationship between a person and God cannot be known by another person; it is strictly between them. But Jesus shows us here a working principle. When a person repents and accepts Christ as Lord and Savior, God forgives his sin. In that experience he or she should become willing to forgive others. But if that spirit does not show up in the person, others may wonder about the reality of his or her salvation. Persisting in such an unforgiving attitude would leave a person under God's judgment. Forgiveness is a part of that humility which Jesus said was needed to enter the kingdom.

A Verse to Remember

Whosoever therefore shall humble himself as this little child, the same is greatest in the kingdom of heaven.— Matthew 18:4.

Daily Bible Readings

Feb. 16—Who Is Greatest? Matt. 18:1-6

Feb. 17—The Terrible Responsibility. Matt. 18:7-11

Feb. 18—Not One Shall Perish. Matt. 18:12-17

Feb. 19—The Power of the Fellowship. Matt. 18:18-22

Feb. 20—How to Forgive. Matt. 18:23-35

Feb. 21—Thanks for Your Partnership. Phil. 1:3-11

Feb. 22—Faith by the Power of God. 1 Cor. 1:26 to 2:5

March 1, 1981

RELATIONSHIPS IN THE KINGDOM
Matthew 19

As we continue our study of Matthew's Gospel, we focus now on five chapters under the theme "Affirmations of the Kingdom." Throughout March we will be examining some basic concepts of the reign of God in the lives of those committed to him. So that kingdom is more a pattern of relationships than a time or place. It is based on the fatherhood of God, with believers acknowledging themselves as his children. It recognizes Christ as Lord and Savior, with believers subject to his principles as taught in the New Testament and interpreted by the Spirit. So the relationship of believers to God in Christ shapes their relationships with one another. As God's children, they are also brothers and sisters in faith. This lesson deals with men, women, and children as Jesus saw them.

The Bible Lesson

MATTHEW 19:

1 And it came to pass, that when Jesus had finished these sayings, he departed from Galilee, and came into the coasts of Judaea beyond Jordan;

2 And great multitudes followed him; and he healed them there.

3 The Pharisees also came unto him, tempting him, and saying unto him, Is it lawful for a man to put away his wife for every cause?

4 And he answered and said unto them, Have ye not read, that he which made them at the beginning made them male and female,

5 And said, For this cause shall a man leave father and mother, and shall cleave to his wife: and they twain shall be one flesh?

6 Wherefore they are no more twain, but one flesh. What therefore God hath joined together, let not man put asunder.

7 They say unto him, Why did Moses then command to give a writing of divorcement, and to put her away?

8 He saith unto them, Moses because of the hardness of your hearts suffered you to put away your wives: but from the beginning it was not so.

9 And I say unto you, Whosoever shall put away his wife, except it be for fornication, and shall marry another, committeth adultery:

109

and whoso marrieth her which is put away doth commit adultery.

10 His disciples say unto him, If the case of the man be so with his wife, it is not good to marry.

11 But he said unto them, All men cannot receive this saying, save they to whom it is given.

12 For there are some eunuchs, which were so born from their mother's womb: and there are some eunuchs, which were made eunuchs of men: and there be eunuchs, which have made themselves eunuchs for the kingdom of heaven's sake. He that is able to receive it, let him receive it.

13 Then there were brought unto him little children, that he should put his hands on them, and pray: and the disciples rebuked them.

14 But Jesus said, Suffer little children, and forbid them not, to come unto me: for of such is the kingdom of heaven.

15 And he laid his hands on them, and departed thence.

The Lesson Explained

GOD'S PURPOSE IN MARRIAGE (19:1-6)

The teaching section referred to in verse 1 began with 17:22, and here we see Jesus starting out on his last trip to Jerusalem. As he left Galilee, he followed the usual route through Perea east of the Jordan. Even then a great crowd of people still followed him, and he healed along the way.

Some Pharisees—still trying to trap him—asked one of their favorite questions for debate. Two famous rabbis of that time took opposite positions as to legal justification for divorce. Shammai said that Deuteronomy 24:1 meant that a man could divorce his wife only if she were unfaithful, but Hillel argued that it gave a man the right to divorce for almost any reason. So Jesus' answer would have positionized him in a popular religious feud. But notice how wisely he responded: quoting Genesis 1:27 and 2:24, he asked whether the Pharisees had read those verses. God had created the sexual differences so that man and woman might complement each other. As they came together in marriage, they formed a new relationship, one so real and important that even the man was to separate himself from his original family to make a new one with his wife. Because their togetherness was God-given, no one should try to divide them. God sees them as one flesh.

DIVORCE: LESS THAN THE BEST (19:7-12)

But the Pharisees seemed to feel that such high idealism was not the real issue. They reminded Jesus that Moses had made room for divorce, and they lived by his code. Why would he allow it if it were not right? Jesus said it was because men were so hard to teach. Since so many stubbornly refused to abide by God's principle, Moses required a husband to give his divorced wife a certificate of divorce to prove that he had no legal claim to her. Thus both persons were protected to some extent. But that was not God's intention.

Jesus proceeded to show the effect of God's principle upon divorce as just an accommodation to man's selfishness. Any man who divorced his wife and marries another woman would be committing adultery because in God's sight he is still committed to his original wife. If the wife had been unfaithful, she had already violated the marriage vow.

JESUS' VIEW OF CHILDREN (19:13-15)

Although the Bible does not say who brought the children to Jesus, it was probably some mothers. The disciples were upset by the whole scene, perhaps feeling that what Jesus was doing was much too important to be interrupted by some women and children. But Jesus did not agree. He saw in children the kind of trust, zest, and teachableness that would be needed for any person to be at home under God's reign. This passage does not teach infant baptism or the kind of child evangelism that tries to get children into the church before they are ready. Jesus responded to the children as rabbis do today when parents ask for them to be blessed. He showed that he was interested in children and wanted them to have their part in God's goodness.

Truths to Live By

God sees marriage as a lifetime vocation of two self-sharing persons.—That is so different from the way most people seem to think and act today that even many church people might argue that it is unreasonable. The main problem with divorce is the casual attitude many people have toward marriage. But marriage is a calling to personal fulfillment for a man and a woman through sharing a lifetime together. In its physical and spiritual intimacy a new reality—"one flesh"—comes into being. Without giving up their own personalities, the husband and wife enrich each other in their oneness.

Although divorce is a last resort in broken marriages, Jesus still offers forgiveness and healing to those who are hurt.—Actually this Bible passage does not reveal that truth, but the whole teaching of Jesus shows that concern. And with such assurance some marriages have been reclaimed. Divorce is not the "unpardonable sin"; nor is it to be taken lightly. Even when children are not involved, two persons are distrustful, embittered, and one may be brokenhearted. For both parties Jesus offers understanding and forgiveness in repentance. In most cases, both must bear some blame. Even after the final break, friends with the Christian spirit can offer support that will lead to healing and acceptance.

Christians should treat all children as valued persons.—Jesus' words and action give guidance enough on this point, but we still hear harrowing stories of child abuse. Surely no Christian could be so cruel and insensitive. But some Christians do treat children strangely. A child is a growing person who must be allowed to develop his or her own personality, skills, and independence. Christian love will both protect and encourage a child.

A Verse to Remember

With men this is impossible; but with God all things are possible.—Matthew 19:26.

Daily Bible Readings

Feb.   23—Those Whom God Has Joined Together. Matt. 19:1-12

Feb.   24—Putting Christ First. Matt. 19:13-22

Feb.   25—Forsaking All to Follow Jesus. Matt. 19:23-30

Feb.   26—Living Together as Christians. Rom. 12:9-21

Feb.   27—Transformed Relationships. Col. 3:18-24

Feb.   28—"The Unity of the Spirit." Eph. 4:1-6

Mar.   1—Obedience to the Commandments. Deut. 30:15-20

GOD'S GENEROSITY
Matthew 20

"It just doesn't seem right," said Charlie when he heard of the conversion of a well-known "sinner" who had died a few days earlier. Old Jack had been on prayer lists for years, but he had ignored them while he wasted his life. But during his last illness a friend tried once more to reach him with the gospel. Facing ultimate realities at last, Jack had a genuine experience with Christ. But Charlie said, "It just does not seem right that he would receive eternal life after wasting so much here on earth. And Ed, over there, will have the same thing after being a Christian since he was a kid." Have you ever felt that way? Well, that is part of the problem that this lesson deals with. Open your mind for a fresh answer.

The Bible Lesson

MATTHEW 20:

1 For the kingdom of heaven is like unto a man that is an householder, which went out early in the morning to hire labourers into his vineyard.

2 And when he had agreed with the labourers for a penny a day, he sent them into his vineyard.

3 And he went out about the third hour, and saw others standing idle in the marketplace,

4 And said unto them; Go ye also into the vineyard, and whatsoever is right I will give you. And they went their way.

5 Again he went out about the sixth and ninth hour, and did likewise.

6 And about the eleventh hour he went out, and found others standing idle, and saith unto them, Why stand ye here all the day idle?

7 They say unto him. Because no man hath hired us. He saith unto them, Go ye also into the vineyard; and whatsoever is right, that shall ye receive.

8 So when even was come, the lord of the vineyard saith unto his steward, Call the labourers, and give them their hire, beginning from the last unto the first.

9 And when they came that were hired about the eleventh hour, they received every man a penny.

10 But when the first came, they supposed that they should have received more; and they likewise received every man a penny.

11 And when they had received it, they murmured against the goodman of the house,

12 Saying, These last have wrought but one hour, and thou hast made them equal unto us, which have borne the burden and heat of the day.

13 But he answered one of them, and said, Friend, I do thee no wrong: didst not thou agree with me for a penny?

14 Take that thine is, and go thy way: I will give unto this last, even as unto thee.

15 Is it not lawful for me to do what I will with mine own? Is thine eye evil, because I am good?

16 So the last shall be first, and the first last: for many be called, but few chosen.

The Lesson Explained

HIRING WORKERS THROUGH THE DAY (20:1-7)

This parable was so obviously intended to illustrate the proverb in 19:30 that the chapter division at that point is unfortunate. A rich young man had asked Jesus what he could do for eternal life, but Jesus' answer was more than he could take. When Jesus said it was hard for a rich man to enter the kingdom, the disciples were amazed and asked what they might expect since they had given up everything. Jesus concluded his answer with: "But many that are first shall be last; and the last shall be first."

Then he told the story of the vineyard owner who needed workers. About sunrise he went to the marketplace and hired some at the usual daily wage. The "penny" sounds cheap, but one writer says that four of them would pay for a lamb. At 9 AM he went to the marketplace again and enlisted more workers and said he would pay what was right. Again at noon and at 3 PM he employed more help. Even at 5 PM ("the eleventh hour") he found some men with no work to do, and he sent them into his vineyard. With the first workers he had made a definite agreement as to their pay, but with the others he had promised to be just. The best Greek manuscripts do not include that assurance to those who were hired last. They agreed to work without any promise of payment.

PAYING ALL THE SAME AMOUNT (20:8-12)

As the day ended (with sunset about 6 PM) the owner told his foreman to call the workers in from the vineyard and give them their pay. Deuteronomy 24:15 commanded that a worker should receive "his hire on the day he earns it, before the sun goes down" (RSV). Those who had been hired last were the first to be paid—to each one a denarius. That probably pleased those who had been hired first because they expected a proportionate increase for their whole day's work. But as other workers received their pay, the foreman continued paying one denarius per person. At last, the first hired received their wages, and they complained. They had worked the whole day, even during the hot hours. They really did not ask for more money, but they resented the fact that those who had worked only one hour had been made equal with them as to payment.

ANSWERING THE COMPLAINT (20:13-16)

The owner of the vineyard responded calmly that he had done no wrong to those who were hired first. They had accepted his offer of a day's wage, and he had paid it. The last hired had gone to work with no assurance of payment. But the owner must have felt that each one would need a day's wage to feed himself and family for that day. It was his vineyard and his money, and he had a right to deal with them as he thought best. Since all would have to agree with that argument, he asked whether the complainers were not begrudging his generosity to the other workers. At the end of the parable Jesus repeated the proverb or principle in 19:30.

Truths to Live By

Being at home under God's reign comes by his grace rather than our merit.—After all, that is what this parable is about. Peter and the other disciples were surprised that a rich man might not get into the kingdom. They thought his wealth was a sign of God's blessing. Peter wondered what the disciples would get for their own sacrifices. But Jesus said that people do not bargain their way into God's reign. Neither good deeds nor pious practices can open the way. But everything depends on God's grace and generosity, and they are equally available to all, and at all times. The disciple in the first century and the latest convert in your church are equally welcome in God's kingdom.

God's generosity is greater than we can expect.—Those who were hired last must have been overwhelmed with the generosity of the vineyard owner. All day they had looked for work and were wondering what their families would do when mealtime came that night. Then after only one hour of work they were paid for a whole day. Jesus was saying that God is like that, and Jesus dealt with all kinds of people with that assurance. The legalistically righteous people of his day were shocked by his friendship with prostitutes and collaborators with Gentile Rome in collecting taxes. But Jesus knew they needed the love and forgiveness that God was ready to give.

God has the right to reward persons as he sees fit.—This parable does not deal with economics; it pictures God as the vineyard owner with the right to do as he chooses. As the heart and source of justice and love, he can do no wrong. Legalists—whether Jewish or Christian—want to bargain with him as those first hired did. They recite the doctrines they believe word for word and count their religious deeds, expecting these to earn them a place in the kingdom. At the same time they resent the joy and freedom that other believers have discovered by accepting God's love by faith. God deals with both and rewards each one as he sees fit from the riches of his reign.

A Verse to Remember

The Son of man came not to be ministered unto, but to minister, and to give his life a ransom for many.—Matthew 20:28.

Daily Bible Readings

Mar. 2—Laborers in the Kingdom. Matt. 20:1-16
Mar. 3—Greatness in the Kingdom. Matt. 20:17-28
Mar. 4—God's Love in Our Hearts. Rom. 5:1-5
Mar. 5—Reconciliation Through Christ. Rom. 5:6-11
Mar. 6—The Free Gift. Rom. 5:12-21
Mar. 7—God's Gift to Believers. John 1:9-13
Mar. 8—A Separated People. Lev. 20:22-26

QUESTIONS OF PRIORITY
Matthew 21:45 to 22:46

A story is told about Dwight L. Moody, the famous evangelist of the nineteenth century, that when someone commented unfavorably about his faulty grammar, he answered something like this: "I'm using all the grammar I know for the kingdom of God; how are you using yours?" Although God has richly used many people with limited education, he has also had many brilliant men and women bearing his name and supporting his cause. Jesus has been their model and Master. He told stories so the common people could understand his teachings, but he also matched wits with Jewish scholars of his day and bested them. Luke tells of his visit to the Temple when he was twelve and was found sitting with the teachers, "both hearing them, and asking them questions" (2:46). This lesson reveals that same mind, sharpened in maturity, dealing expertly with one critic after another.

The Bible Lesson

MATTHEW 22:

15 Then went the Pharisees, and took counsel how they might entangle him in his talk.

16 And they sent out unto him their disciples with the Herodians, saying, Master, we know that thou art true, and teachest the way of God in truth, neither carest thou for any man: for thou regardest not the person of men.

17 Tell us therefore, What thinkest thou? Is it lawful to give tribute unto Caesar, or not?

18 But Jesus perceived their wickedness, and said, Why tempt ye me, ye hypocrites?

19 Shew me the tribute money. And they brought unto him a penny.

20 And he saith unto them, Whose is this image and superscription?

21 They say unto him, Caesar's. Then saith he unto them, Render therefore unto Caesar the things which are Caesar's; and unto God the things that are God's.

117

22 When they had heard these words, they marvelled, and left him, and went their way.

23 The same day came to him the Sadducees, which say that there is no resurrection, and asked him,

24 Saying, Master, Moses said, If a man die, having no children, his brother shall marry his wife, and raise up seed unto his brother.

25 Now there were with us seven brethren: and the first, when he had married a wife, deceased, and, having no issue, left his wife unto his brother:

26 Likewise the second also, and the third, unto the seventh.

27 And last of all the woman died also.

28 Therefore in the resurrection whose wife shall she be of the seven? for they all had her.

29 Jesus answered and said unto them, Ye do err, not knowing the scriptures, nor the power of God.

30 For in the resurrection they neither marry, nor are given in marriage, but are as the angels of God in heaven.

31 But as touching the resurrection of the dead, have ye not read that which was spoken unto you by God, saying,

32 I am the God of Abraham, and the God of Isaac, and the God of Jacob? God is not the God of the dead, but of the living.

The Lesson Explained

BETWEEN CAESAR AND GOD (22:15-22)

From 21:23 through 23:39 Matthew tells of Jesus in conversation with various groups in the Temple, mostly handling the questions and criticisms of his enemies. After the chief priests and elders had their turn, the Pharisees came with some Herodians. While the former were opposed to Roman rule, the latter favored the Herods under Rome. So their question to Jesus was tricky, and he called them hypocrites. But first they attempted to flatter him, saying things that were true but probably not representing their real opinion (v. 16).

Their question referred to a poll tax required by Rome of every person. When Jesus asked for the proper coin, someone handed him a denarius (the "penny" of last Sunday's lesson). They had to admit that its inscription and image were Caesar's. After all, the money minted for use in trade really belonged to the Roman Empire. So Jesus said they should pay Caesar what belonged to him. But immediately he declared another obligation: that persons should also give God what belongs to him.

GOD OF THE LIVING (22:23-33)

After the Pharisees and Herodians left, the Sadducees presented their test question. We must know basic Sadducee views to see what is involved here. Representing leadership in the priesthood, the Sadducees were more concerned with politics than religion. They affirmed Mosaic law but disagreed with the interpretations of the Pharisees. They did not believe in any resurrection. So their humorous story and question for Jesus were basically cynical. While they agreed to levirate marriage (Deut. 25:5), they thought resurrection was ridiculous. They probably had used the story to make fun of the Pharisees.

But Jesus did not laugh. Instead, he declared that they did not understand the Scriptures or the power of God. They thought of resurrection as a material existence after death, but Jesus interpreted it as spiritual without such an earthly relationship as marriage. Furthermore, Exodus 3:6 makes it plain, Jesus stated in verse 32, that God is the God of the living and that the patriarchs are alive. So he quoted from the Pentateuch, the part of the Bible revered by the Sadducees, to affirm the power of God in the resurrection. All this astounded the crowd.

LOVING GOD AND ONE'S NEIGHBOR (22:34-40)

When the Pharisees saw how Jesus handled the Sadducees, they decided to try again to trap him. A professional interpreter of the law asked him which was the greatest commandment. Without hesitation, Jesus quoted Deuteronomy 6:5, a part of the passage recited daily by devout Jews. Then he paired with it a part of Leviticus 19:18, a commandment not so well known.

Truths to Live By

Christians must be prepared in mind and spirit to answer their critics.—There *will* be critics—if a person is practicing the Christian way of life. They will ridicule prayer and worship; they will question the validity of the Bible; they will question Christian principles of fidelity in marriage, loyalty in business, and honesty toward government. So the Christian needs to study his Bible to be grounded in its principles. He or she needs to know how some strong Christians think and act, knowing them by either personal experience or reading. Being a Christian calls for expanding the mind as well as deepening the spirit. Goodness must be combined with clear thinking and personal concern for the critic.

Christian citizens have a responsibility both to the state and to God.—That is what Jesus was saying in Matthew 22:21. He did not pray that his followers be taken out of the world (John 17:15). He was a realist; he wanted them to stay in the world and be salt and light to it. But in the world they would have to relate to the state, and that meant obeying the laws, paying taxes, and working to improve community conditions. At the same time, Christians have another, more important relationship. Acknowledging God as Father and Giver of life, they owe first loyalty to him and his pattern of values. In some places, loyalty to God and country are in conflict, and that calls for wisdom and courage. In other places, these loyalties are so intertwined that commitment to God loses its distinctiveness. Christians must be alert at this point.

In loving God and one's neighbor we fulfill all ethical requirements for persons.—All other laws in the Bible deal with particular applications of this one. If one man loves another, he won't steal his money, wife, or good name. If a person loves God, he or she will be anxious to help the hungry people of the world because they are all his creatures. Loving persons means obeying traffic laws to share highway space and protect lives. Loving God includes missions as well as worship.

A Verse to Remember

Render therefore unto Caesar the things which are Caesar's; and unto God the things that are God's.—Matthew 22:21.

Daily Bible Readings

Mar. 9—The Priority of Faith. Matt. 21:18-22
Mar. 10—"By What Authority . . .?" Matt. 21:23-27
Mar. 11—The Priority of Deeds Over Words. Matt. 21:28-32
Mar. 12—The Stone the Builders Rejected. Matt. 21:33-44
Mar. 13—Those Who Enter the Kingdom. Matt. 22:1-14
Mar. 14—Render to God His Dues. Matt. 22:15-22
Mar. 15—Sacrificing All for Christ. Phil. 3:7-11

SIGNS OF THE END
Matthew 23:13 to 24:35

Whenever the world gets into a really bad fix, some Christians always start talking about the end of the world and the second coming. They feel that only God in some climactic way can rescue the world, and they chart the phases and even fix a date for the end. They usually get so preoccupied with working out a schedule for God that they almost stop doing the things Jesus said were most important. Many times through the centuries various groups have been led into some pitiful and hopeless positions by this emphasis on the end of the world. Most Christians have not caught this fever, either because they took the whole thing lightly or because they felt it was only one emphasis among many in the Christian faith. When held in a healthy balance, the teaching cannot be ignored, and this lesson gives real help in its understanding.

The Bible Lesson

MATTHEW 23:

37 O Jerusalem, Jerusalem, thou that killest the prophets, and stonest them which are sent unto thee, how often would I have gathered thy children together, even as a hen gathereth her chickens under her wings, and ye would not!

38 Behold, your house is left unto you desolate.

39 For I say unto you, Ye shall not see me henceforth, till ye shall say, Blessed is he that cometh in the name of the Lord.

MATTHEW 24:

1 And Jesus went out, and departed from the temple: and his disciples came to him for to shew him the buildings of the temple.

2 And Jesus said unto them, See ye not all these things? verily I say unto you, There shall not be left here one stone upon another, that shall not be thrown down.

3 And as he sat upon the mount of Olives, the disciples came unto him privately, saying, Tell us, when shall these things be? and what shall be the sign of thy coming, and of the end of the world?

4 And Jesus answered and said unto them, Take heed that no man deceive you.

121

5 For many shall come in my name, saying, I am Christ; and shall deceive many.

6 And ye shall hear of wars and rumours of wars: see that ye be not troubled: for all these things must come to pass, but the end is not yet.

7 For nation shall rise against nation, and kingdom against kingdom: and there shall be famines, and pestilences, and earthquakes, in divers places.

8 All these are the beginning of sorrows.

9 Then shall they deliver you up to be afflicted, and shall kill you: and ye shall be hated of all nations for my name's sake.

10 And then shall many be offended, and shall betray one another, and shall hate one another.

11 And many false prophets shall rise, and shall deceive many.

12 And because iniquity shall abound, the love of many shall wax cold.

13 But he that shall endure unto the end, the same shall be saved.

14 And this gospel of the kingdom shall be preached in all the world for a witness unto all nations; and then shall the end come.

The Lesson Explained

GRIEVING OVER JERUSALEM (23:37-39)

In preceding verses of this chapter Jesus said seven times, "Woe unto you, scribes and Pharisees, hypocrites!" The word *woe* here is not a curse but more a cry of anger or pity as Jesus described the self-righteousness and wrong-headedness of those accepted as religious leaders. This indictment would make his enemies even more determined to take Jesus' life.

After this bold accusation, verses 37-39 reveal the heart of Jesus—compassionate, sad, but realistic. Although Jerusalem was the center of the Jewish faith, its leaders were proud and vicious. Its people needed the love and care that Jesus could give, but most of them were so blinded with self-confidence that they rejected God's Messiah. Now there is no hope for them, said Jesus; the word *house* may refer to the city as their home or to the Temple. Soon both would be destroyed by the Roman army (A.D. 70). In his farewell sentence Jesus quoted from Psalm 118:26, which had been sung when he had ridden into Jerusalem (21:9). All who believe will ascribe that praise when he comes at last in judgment.

PREDICTING CATASTROPHES (24:1-8)

As Jesus was leaving the Temple, his disciples called his attention to the structure itself, possibly commenting on its size and beauty. But he responded with only a prediction of its complete destruction. Then after they had walked down the hill from the Temple and climbed to the Mount of Olives about two miles to the east, the disciples asked him (after others had left) about his mysterious statements. He did not give a direct answer but warned them about being deceived by imposters. In ominous or even dangerous times self-appointed messiahs could easily win followers. Josephus, the Jewish historian, mentioned them in connection with the war with Rome, A.D. 66-70. Such deceivers would point to wars and catastrophes as signs of the end time. But Jesus said they were "like the first pains of childbirth" (v. 8, TEV). They will come, "but the end is not yet." Not even the destruction of the Temple would be a sign of Christ's immediate coming.

URGING FAITHFULNESS (24:9-14)

Then Jesus turned to another condition that could be misinterpreted as a sign of the end: persecution and betrayal of believers. He predicted that some would be hated and harassed and some even killed because of his name. Persecution would cause many believers to be fearful and even betray others to save themselves. False prophets would assert themselves within the churches and would lead many astray, probably promising the imminent return of Christ and the end of the world. Although such conditions would cause many to let their Christian love (*agape*) grow cold, "he who endures to the end will be saved" (v. 13, RSV). That "enduring" was not a Stoic suffering, but Jesus saw it as active and redemptive. It included declaring the gospel throughout the world.

The good news of God was intended for "all nations," and that was a challenge to Jewish believers to share it with all Gentiles. Since the known Mediterranean world was not so large, believers then may have thought that the end was relatively near. But the "witness unto all nations" must go on while we let God decide the end.

Truths to Live By

God's love includes his judgment on those who reject it.—In God, love and justice are completely blended. He loves persons and shows it in many ways; but when they violate his laws, they must endure his judgment. On a very small scale, we see this process in the love of parents for their child.

When facing disaster, Christians must beware of leaders who have easy answers.—Of course, the easy answer refuted in this lesson is: "When the whole world gets in bad shape, the end must be around the corner." Jesus said not to accept that one. The end will come in God's good time, but beware of persons who claim to know the actual date or the inevitable conditions. But other persons with easy answers need to be questioned. Some play upon people's fears and urge them to put their trust and usually their money into the enterprises of the self-appointed messiah. At a different level, the easy-answer person may assure a bereaved father that it was God's will when his son was hit by a drunk driver. Again, in a national emergency, the easy-answer person will insist on coercion and repression.

A prime sign of the end of the age is Christian persistence in world missions.—That is what the Bold Mission Thrust is all about, trying to catch up with Jesus' expectations. He never suggested that his disciples work out a timetable for his second coming. Their job was to declare the gospel as a testimony to all nations, and many of those in the first century did just that.

A Verse to Remember

Heaven and earth shall pass away, but my words shall not pass away.—Matthew 24:35.

Daily Bible Readings

Mar. 16—The Greatest in the Kingdom. Matt. 23:1-12
Mar. 17—Blind Guides. Matt. 23:13-22
Mar. 18—Leaders Who Are Hypocrites. Matt. 23:23-32
Mar. 19—Sufferings Before the End. Matt. 24:1-14
Mar. 20—False Christs. Matt. 24:15-28
Mar. 21—The Last Days. Matt. 24:29-35
Mar. 22—Keeping the Covenant. Josh. 23:14-16

March 29, 1981

BE READY—BE FAITHFUL
Matthew 24:36 to 25:46

"Be Prepared"—that was the motto on the pin worn by second-class Scouts when I reached that rank. I had been a "tenderfoot" for some months, and the pin meant I had achieved something. But be prepared for what? Well, the Scout law and instructions at meetings helped me see that it was for almost anything that a ten-year-old boy might be able to do. It is still a good motto. All of us need to be prepared in physical strength to do our jobs. We need to be prepared in attitudes to relate helpfully with all kinds of people. Being prepared mentally means being teachable at any age and keeping our curiosity alert. In this lesson Jesus is talking about being prepared for the "grand finale"—the end of the age and his own coming. What kind of preparation does that call for? Jesus suggests some ways in the three parables of this lesson.

The Bible Lesson

MATTHEW 25:

1 Then shall the kingdom of heaven be likened unto ten virgins, which took their lamps, and went forth to meet the bridegroom.

2 And five of them were wise, and five were foolish.

3 They that were foolish took their lamps, and took no oil with them:

4 But the wise took oil in their vessels with their lamps.

5 While the bridegroom tarried, they all slumbered and slept.

6 And at midnight there was a cry made, Behold, the bridegroom cometh; go ye out to meet him.

7 Then all those virgins arose, and trimmed their lamps.

8 And the foolish said unto the wise, Give us of your oil; for our lamps are gone out.

9 But the wise answered saying, Not so; lest there be not enough for us and you: but go ye rather to them that sell, and buy for yourselves.

10 And while they went to buy, the bridegroom came; and they that were ready went in with him to the marriage: and the door was shut.

11 Afterwards came also the other virgins, saying, Lord, Lord, open to us.

12 But he answered and said, Verily I say unto you, I know you not.

13 Watch therefore, for ye know neither the day nor the hour wherein the Son of man cometh.

The Lesson Explained

NOT KNOWING THE TIME (24:42-47)

Three times in this discourse on last things Jesus told his disciples that no one knew when the Son of man would come (24:36,42; 25:13). So they should be alert and prepared. To illustrate his point, he pictured a homeowner who had been the victim of a burglar. Jesus said that if the man had known when the burglar was coming, he would have been ready for him. But since the thief won't tell his plans, the owner must be ready at all times to protect his property.

In a second parable he described a foreman or manager of an estate who was responsible for supervising work and feeding the employees. If the owner should return unexpectedly and find the manager performing his assigned tasks, he would reward him with larger responsibilities. That is being ready. On the other hand, if the owner's continued absence should make the foreman careless, the owner might surprise him. If he suddenly discovered him shirking his responsibilities and mistreating the workers, he would punish him severely. Jesus was saying to his followers that they should be ready at all times because they did not know when he would return.

WAITING FOR THE GROOM (25:1-5)

Here is a third and longer parable—and a very familiar one—about being ready for an unknown time. Although the first verse sounds like it intends a complete description of the kingdom of God, it presents only one aspect of it. But it pictures an occasion quite well-known to his hearers. The ten girls were probably friends of the bride, and they were waiting at her home or some other chosen meeting place for the groom to come for his bride. Since the wedding was at night, they needed lamps or torches to light the way of the wedding procession. Five of the young women carried extra jars of oil, but

126

the other five did not. Neither group knew how long they would have to wait, but one group was prepared for a delay. As time dragged on, they all fell asleep.

REJECTING THOSE UNPREPARED (25:6-13)

Suddenly at midnight someone yelled that the groom was coming. The girls woke up and began to trim their wicks to make them burn brighter, but the lamps of the careless ones had already gone out. When they urged the other five to share their oil, the wise ones said they did not have enough for everybody. If they shared, the procession might end up completely in the dark. Then while the unprepared ones went to buy more oil, the groom arrived and the other five went with him into the marriage feast. When the foolish ones returned and called to gain entrance, the doorkeeper or groom answered that he did not know or recognize them. That may seem heartless, but it probably reflected an acceptable practice.

Then Jesus repeated his warning about being ready because no one knows "the day nor the hour wherein the Son of man cometh." Without any sure target date, the believer can only be prepared at all times for that coming. His or her readiness is more than a pious but lazy cessation of work and witness. It is alert and redemptive involvement.

Truths to Live By

Christ's second coming is an integral part of his message.—Because some Christians resent extreme statements and overemphasis on the second coming, many tend to ignore it. But the New Testament has it in black and white, not in the actual words "second coming," but in terms of *parousia,* "the last day," "day of the Lord," and so on. The whole Bible sees history headed toward a goal which is in the mind and hand of God. That goal includes both judgment and redemption. While these go on all the time, the New Testament sees them being accomplished in a climactic way some time in the future—known only to God—and Christ would then be acclaimed King of kings.

Being ready for Christ's coming is more important than guessing when it will be.—Although that is abundantly clear from the words of Jesus himself, many people are more interested in a mystery than in everyday obedience to the Master. Others would not think of setting a date for the second coming, but they are easily preoccupied with the "signs of his coming." Thus, relating current events to various prophecies absorbs more time and concern than applying the teachings of Jesus to vexing personal and social problems. Often this preoccupation with things to come leads the unbeliever to think that Christianity has little to do or say about human problems. It frequently interferes with evangelism by giving the impression that the Christian faith is more concerned about the second coming than the first coming. Studying the Gospels will reveal the healthy balance on this subject that Jesus intended in his teachings.

Being ready means doing what Jesus commanded.—That is what Jesus complimented in the servant of 24:46. He said nothing about charts or special vigils. Since no person can know the day or the hour, the loyal believer will show his readiness in the way he lives. Obeying the Lord's commands in all his relationships, in the stewardship of time and skills, and in practicing the presence of God in prayer and Bible study—these are the ways to be ready for his coming. The very commitment to keep on believing what Jesus promised, no matter how discouraging the times may be, is another way of being ready. Still another is really depending on the power of love over hate and apathy.

A Verse to Remember

Watch therefore, for ye know neither the day nor the hour wherein the Son of man cometh.—Matthew 25:13.

Daily Bible Readings

Mar.   23—Watch and Be Ready. Matt. 24:36-44
Mar.   24—Be Faithful Servants. Matt. 24:45-51
Mar.   25—When the Bridegroom Comes. Matt. 25:1-13
Mar.   26—Talents Are to Be Used. Matt. 25:14-30
Mar.   27—Those Who Inherit the Kingdom. Matt. 25:31-40
Mar.   28—Those Who Fail to Help. Matt. 25:41-46
Mar.   29—Choosing to Serve the Lord. Josh. 24:16-24

April 5, 1981

PREPARING FOR DIFFICULT TIMES
Matthew 26

With this lesson we approach the climax of Jesus' ministry, a time of suffering and yet of victory. Lessons for February showed Jesus guiding his disciples into ways of living their new faith. Those for March focused on affirmations of the kingdom in relationships, in life's priorities, and in persistent readiness for judgment. But instead of Jesus being able to commission his disciples at that point to preach and practice his way, he had to deal with the official hostility against himself. It had been growing through the months, and his way of meeting it would mean death. God would not allow evil to overcome good, however, so these April lessons bear the general title: "Through Suffering to Victory." They lead to Easter and beyond.

The Bible Lesson

MATTHEW 26:

1 And it came to pass, when Jesus had finished all these sayings, he said unto his disciples,

2 Ye know that after two days is the feast of the passover, and the Son of man is betrayed to be crucified.

3 Then assembled together the chief priests, and the scribes, and the elders of the people, unto the palace of the high priest, who was called Caiaphas,

4 And consulted that they might take Jesus by subtilty, and kill him.

5 But they said, Not on the feast day, lest there be an uproar among the people.

6 Now when Jesus was in Bethany, in the house of Simon the leper,

7 There came unto him a woman having an alabaster box of very precious ointment, and poured it on his head, as he sat at meat.

8 But when his disciples saw it, they had indignation, saying, To what purpose is this waste?

9 For this ointment might have been sold for much, and given to the poor.

10 When Jesus understood it, he said unto them, Why trouble ye the woman? for she hath wrought a good work upon me.

11 For ye have the poor always with you; but me ye have not always.

12 For in that she hath poured this ointment on my body, she did it for my burial.

13 Verily I say unto you, Wheresoever this gospel shall be preached in the whole world, there shall also this, that this woman hath done, be told for a memorial of her.

14 Then one of the twelve, called Judas Iscariot, went unto the chief priests,

15 And said unto them, What will ye give me, and I will deliver him unto you? And they covenanted with him for thirty pieces of silver.

16 And from that time he sought opportunity to betray him.

The Lesson Explained

THINKING AHEAD OF HIS ENEMIES (26:1-5)

This first verse is a transition sentence that follows the longest of Jesus' teaching sessions in Matthew. It also rather abruptly predicts his coming death, as he had done three times earlier. Of course he did not use the first person pronoun but what seems to be his favorite self-designation: "Son of man." He would be betrayed (or delivered) for death when the Passover came. He would be "the Lamb of God," who would make the sacrifice of other lambs unnecessary in the future. Jesus knew his enemies would not be satisfied until he had been killed, but he did not seek death.

About the same time those enemies—the religious leaders—were meeting in the court of Caiaphas, the high priest. While the leading priests were usually Sadducees, the "elders of the people" were probably Pharisees. Both groups wanted to arrest Jesus without arousing the populace, and they decided that the Passover would be a bad time.

ANOINTED FOR BURIAL (26:6-13)

It was possibly that night (about two days before Passover) when Jesus and his disciples were having dinner at "the house of Simon the leper" that a woman anointed his head. Alabaster is a rather soft, marble-like stone that can be easily carved. Not only did the disciples see the act, but they caught the aroma of the ointment. Mark says that "some" were indignant (14:4) but

130

John singles out Judas Iscariot (12:4). They complained that such expensive ointment could have been sold to feed the poor instead of wasted in that display.

But Jesus did not agree—despite his concern for the poor. He did not want the woman to be embarrassed; she had shown her sincere devotion in a very generous manner.

TRAITOR AT THE TABLE (26:14-16,20-29)

No one knows why Judas Iscariot decided to hand over Jesus to his enemies, although several theories have been advanced. For some reason he volunteered to help the chief priests with their plot, and a paltry bag of silver sealed the bargain. From that time Judas looked for the right occasion.

Meanwhile Jesus sent his disciples into the city to arrange with a friend for their Passover meal. While they were eating, Jesus said that one of them would betray him to the authorities. They were shocked, but Jesus insisted that one who ate from the same bowl with him was preparing to identify him to be arrested. Then Judas asked if he were the one, and we assume that he left after Jesus' answer. As they were eating, Jesus used bread and wine to help the disciples remember that night and understand later what his death would mean. The bread represented his body, and the wine symbolized his blood that would be "shed for many for the remission of sins." It represented the new covenant between God and his new Israel. The old covenant had been memorialized in the Passover, but this one would provide a greater deliverance.

Truths to Live By

Jesus will accept whatever precious gift we offer to him.—The woman in this lesson may have sold her dowry to buy that expensive ointment to show Jesus how much she loved him. And he did not think it was foolish or wasteful. He had the grace to accept a gift in such a way as to make the giver feel good about it. Some people have trouble accepting presents. But Jesus still does it well. He accepted the skills and commitment of William Colgate and caused that soapmaker to become an effective witness and good steward of his resources. He accepted the life and limitations of Billy Sunday and helped him win many unlikely prospects to faith in Christ. He accepted the socially handicapped Mary McLeod Bethune and led her into a lifetime of improving educational opportunities for black children.

Jesus showed his followers how they should treat defectors.—Judas had been a friend, and no one knows why he turned against Jesus at the last. But Jesus did not make him a public example. Some interpreters feel that he tried until the last to save Judas from himself. Certainly he showed no fear of Judas although Jesus knew what his deed would mean. Jesus felt sorry for Judas because he knew how God's justice would deal with him. But he did not beg him to change his mind or have mercy on his victim. He faced realistically the awful decision that Judas had made and tried to get him to see it, too.

The Lord's Supper was intended to interpret Jesus' death for his followers.—Those gathered in the upper room did not know then what was in store. Immediately after the crucifixion they were too numb with grief to think of meanings. But after the resurrection the Lord's Supper became a focal point in their worship, and his words were recalled whenever it was celebrated. Death had ended the many good things he had done with his body, and it had shed his lifeblood as a sacrifice for the sins of all persons. But that was the kind of life and death to which he called his followers. It was God's way of making possible forgiveness for the repentant and eternal life for those who trusted the grace and love of God.

A Verse to Remember

O my Father, if it be possible, let this cup pass from me: nevertheless not as I will, but as thou wilt.—Matthew 26:39.

Daily Bible Readings

Mar.   30—News Difficult to Accept. Mark 8:31-37
Mar.   31—High-Level Consultation. Matt. 26:1-5
Apr.   1—Costly Devotion. Matt. 26:6-13
Apr.   2—Betrayed by a Friend. Matt. 26:14-16, 21-25
Apr.   3—The Last Supper. Matt. 26:20-29
Apr.   4—Breaking Under Pressure. Matt. 26:31-35
Apr.   5—Finding Strength Through Pressure. Matt. 26:36-46

THEY CRUCIFIED HIM

Matthew 21:1-13; 27:1-61

Through many centuries Christians in general blamed all Jews for the death of Christ, and some state churches used police power to threaten and sometimes to persecute Jewish people. But who was actually responsible for the crucifixion? Jesus seemed to judge the Pharisees more than the Sadducees because of their self-righteous demands on the people, but the Sadducees had more influence with Rome and as priestly leaders. Judas was their willing tool. Pilate could have stopped the whole thing as Roman governor. The faceless Jewish mob screamed for crucifixion, and finally Roman soldiers carried out the execution. But Jews of today are no more responsible for that death than are Gentiles. Everyone was and is responsible because Jesus died to save us all from sin and self-centeredness.

The Bible Lesson

MATTHEW 27:

33 And when they were come unto a place called Golgotha, that is to say, a place of a skull,

34 They gave him vinegar to drink mingled with gall: and when he had tasted thereof, he would not drink.

35 And they crucified him, and parted his garments, casting lots: that it might be fulfilled which was spoken by the prophet, They parted my garments among them, and upon my vesture did they cast lots.

36 And sitting down they watched him there;

37 And set up over his head his accusation written, THIS IS JESUS THE KING OF THE JEWS.

38 Then were there two thieves crucified with him, one on the right hand, and another on the left.

39 And they that passed by reviled him, wagging their heads,

40 And saying, Thou that destroyest the temple, and buildest it in three days, save thyself. If thou be the Son of God, come down from the cross.

41 Likewise also the chief priests mocking him, with the scribes and elders, said,

42 He saved others; himself he cannot save. If he be the King of Israel, let him now come down from the cross, and we will believe him.

43 He trusted in God; let him deliver him now, if he will have him; for he said, I am the Son of God.

44 The thieves also, which were crucified with him, cast the same in his teeth.

45 Now from the sixth hour there was darkness over all the land unto the ninth hour.

46 And about the ninth hour Jesus cried with a loud voice, saying, Eli, Eli, lama, sabachthani? that is to say, My God, my God, why hast thou forsaken me?

47 Some of them that stood there, when they heard that, said, This man calleth for Elias.

48 And straightway one of them ran, and took a sponge, and filled it with vinegar, and put it on a reed, and gave him to drink.

49 The rest said, Let be, let us see whether Elias will come to save him.

50 Jesus, when he had cried again with a loud voice, yielded up the ghost.

The Lesson Explained

SOLDIERS DID THEIR JOB (27:33-38)

After Jesus' arrest in Gethsemane, he was taken to the court or palace of Caiaphas, the high priest, for a preliminary hearing in the middle of the night. Two false witnesses reported what Jesus had said about the Temple, but he would not respond. When he did answer Caiaphas, the high priest claimed it was blasphemy and enough of a charge to merit death.

When morning came, the Sanhedrin convened officially to prepare their charge for Pilate. Apparently, a death sentence could not be carried out legitimately without Roman approval. Although Pilate was not convinced, he yielded to the Jewish officials to protect his position. Then the soldiers took over for a vicious lashing and some barracks cruelty. Afterward the execution squad led Jesus to a small hill probably outside the wall and crucified him. To ease his pain, they offered him a bitter drink, but Jesus refused it. Then they threw dice for his clothes, fulfilling Psalm 22:18. Over his head was nailed the charge made by the Jews. The Roman soldiers sat down to watch Jesus with a thief crucified on either side of him.

SPECTATORS RIDICULED HIM (27:39-44)

A public execution drew a large crowd, and many spectators made fun of Jesus. "Wagging their heads," they challenged him with a reported statement about the Temple and dared him to come down from the cross. Although not speaking directly to Jesus, they mocked him. How good a savior was he if he could not save himself, they asked. If he were really the King of Israel (Messiah), he could come off the cross, and they would believe him. If Jesus had been right in claiming to be God's Son, God ought to rescue him from death. Also the thieves (in Matthew's account) identified with the crowd and religious leaders in taunting Jesus.

JESUS DIED IN AGONY (27:45-50)

According to Jewish timekeeping, the first hour began at sunrise; so the sixth hour came at midday. In some way the land of Judea was darkened from noon to three o'clock. Although crucifixion was usually a slow death, Jesus died in less than a day. Perhaps the scourging had something to do with it. About mid-afternoon he called out loudly the first part of Psalm 22:1. In the noise of the crowd some were not sure what he had said, but they thought he might be calling on Elijah for help. For the sake of his Gentile readers, Matthew gave both the Hebrew and its Greek translation. We cannot know what Jesus meant in asking why God had forsaken him, but he must have been enduring intense physical pain as well as the humor despair that came with it. Perhaps one of the soldiers tried to help Jesus with a drink of sour wine, but the other people just waited to see if Elijah would "come to save him." Then suddenly giving another loud cry, Jesus bowed his head and slumped in death on the cross.

Truths to Live By

Beware of ridiculing those who suffer for their beliefs.—You could be displaying the vindictiveness of the chief priests. It is easy enough to honor pioneers and prophets of previous centuries; we have a better perspective to judge their principles and motives. But such persons in our own time are often ridiculed or even persecuted. A few years ago most white people were resenting the work of Martin Luther King, Jr., in behalf of equal rights for black people. Many also criticized the white people who took up that cause. Some were harried, beaten, and killed for their beliefs. Today people are divided on such issues as energy, nuclear power, war, and ethnic rights.

Although an ugly instrument of death, the cross has become a symbol of love and faith.—When Jesus was crucified, the cross meant death and separation. The disciples could not see beyond it; the cross was real with pain and despair. But resurrection day changed that to some extent. And as the disciples explored the meaning of the crucifixion and resurrection as the channel of salvation, believers could see the cross in a new light. Of course, sentimental and commercial people have turned it into a "good thing." But Christian believers can recognize the horrible reality of the cross and at the same time give thanks for the love of God that was expressed in the gift of his Son whose death on the cross made possible life eternal for all who believe.

The stark reality of the cross helps make Christianity a unique religion.—Most Christians do not realize how different the Jewish Old Testament and the Christian Bible are from the holy books of other religions. These two tell the history of a real people and of a real Person. Not only did that Person live the perfect life and claim to be the Son of God, but he yielded to his enemies in death. He appeared to have failed in his mission, but God raised him up. Witnesses and documents testify to all this.

A Verse to Remember

They feared greatly, saying, Truly this was the Son of God.—Matthew 27:54.

Daily Bible Readings

Apr.　6—They Praised Him. Matt. 21:1-13
Apr.　7—They Arrested Him. Matt. 26:47-56
Apr.　8—They Tried Him. Matt. 27:1-2, 11-14
Apr.　9—They Rejected Him. Matt. 27:15-25
Apr.　10—They Mocked Him. Matt. 27:27-39
Apr.　11—They Killed Him. Matt. 27:35-44
Apr.　12—"He Makes Himself an Offering for Sin." Isa. 53:7-12

VICTORY OF THE RESURRECTION
Matthew 27:62 to 28:10

A seminary graduate was telling an elderly professor some of his experiences in the pastorate. In discussing sermon themes, the young man said he had trouble with the resurrection as miracle, "I can handle the drama of Jesus' last week and the pathos of the crucifixion, but I have trouble preaching on the resurrection." In a firm but kindly manner, the professor said, "But if you don't preach the resurrection, you have no gospel." After all, it was the risen Christ who inspired first-century Christians to do what Luke tells us in the book of Acts. Without the resurrection there is no good news; it was not enough for Jesus to die as a martyr. So this lesson brings us to the peak of what is sometimes called the "Christ-event." It is the climax of God's self-revelation to mankind.

The Bible Lesson

MATTHEW 27:

62 Now the next day, that followed the day of the preparation, the chief priests and Pharisees came together unto Pilate,

63 Saying, Sir, we remember that that deceiver said, while he was yet alive, After three days I will rise again.

64 Command therefore that the sepulchre be made sure until the third day, lest his disciples come by night, and steal him away, and say unto the people, He is risen from the dead: so the last error shall be worse than the first.

65 Pilate said unto them, Ye have a watch: go your way, make it as sure as ye can.

66 So they went, and made the sepulchre sure, sealing the stone, and setting a watch.

MATTHEW 28:

1 In the end of the sabbath, as it began to dawn toward the first day of the week, came Mary Magdalene and the other Mary to see the sepulchre.

2 And, behold, there was a great earthquake: for the angel of the Lord descended from heaven, and came and rolled back the stone from the door, and sat upon it.

3 His countenance was like lightning, and his rainment white as snow:

4 And for fear of him the keepers did shake, and became as dead men.

5 And the angel answered and said unto the women, Fear not ye: for I know that ye seek Jesus, which was crucified.

6 He is not here: for he is risen, as he said. Come, see the place where the Lord lay.

7 And go quickly, and tell his disciples that he is risen from the dead; and, behold, he goeth before you into Galilee; there shall ye see him: lo, I have told you.

8 And they departed quickly from the sepulchre with fear and great joy; and did run to bring his disciples word.

9 And as they went to tell his disciples, behold, Jesus met them, saying, All hail. And they came and held him by the feet, and worshipped him.

10 Then said Jesus unto them, Be not afraid: go tell my brethren that they go into Galilee, and there shall they see me.

The Lesson Explained

MAKING USELESS PLANS (27:62-66)

The background Scripture passage for last Sunday's lesson included the remarkable things that happened at the time of Jesus' death, a reference to the women who watched "afar off," and the burial by Joseph of Arimathea. For Jesus, Joseph gave his own new tomb, a small room probably cut of a rocky hillside.

"The day of preparation" was Friday, the time for getting ready for the sabbath that began at 6 PM Friday. So the chief priests and Pharisees visited Pilate on the sabbath to ask a favor. They remembered hearing that Jesus ("that deceiver") had promised to rise after three days. Some of his disciples might try to make that promise seem to come true by stealing the body. Allowing for a claim of resurrection would be worse than letting Jesus live in the first place, with some people acknowledging him as Messiah. So they asked that the entrance to the tomb be made secure for three days. Pilate quickly agreed, and a Roman guard unit sealed the stone and set up a schedule for guard duty.

RECEIVING REMARKABLE NEWS (28:1-7)

The first phrase in this chapter is better translated: "Now after the sabbath" (RSV). Comparing the verse with other Gospels, it is clear that the women went to the tomb at early sunrise. Only Matthew mentions an earthquake, which may have occurred before the women arrived. At the same time a messenger from God had appeared like lightning, rolled back the stone, and sat upon it. All this was too much for the Roman soldiers; they quaked with fear and must have fainted. Their routine assignment had turned into a terrifying confrontation.

But the angel spoke tenderly to the two women to calm their fears. The crucified Jesus was not there but was risen—"as he said." They were invited to look at the place where he had lain. Then the angel told them to hurry to tell his disciples what had happened and that they should go to Galilee to meet the risen Lord. This would fulfill what Jesus had said in Matthew 26:32. The angel guaranteed that they would see Jesus there.

MEETING THE RISEN CHRIST (28:8-10)

So the women left hurriedly, feeling a strange mixture of fear and joy. What amazing news they had for the men in Jerusalem! But as they ran, they suddenly met Jesus himself. It was almost as though they were being rewarded for passing the "believe and obey" test. They had come to visit the tomb, perhaps to anoint the body. They were not expecting the angel's announcement, but where the Master was concerned they were willing to believe that God could do anything. Jesus' greeting was the customary one between friends, which could be translated: "Be glad" or "Peace be unto you." They recognized him instantly and showed their devotion. Although Jesus repeated the angel's command that the disciples should meet him in Galilee, he called them "my brethren." He had started his ministry in Galilee, and that was home for most of them.

Truths to Live By

The risen Christ meets ordinary people and commissions them.—A showman or politician might think of the wasted opportunity of resurrection morning. For such a great event— utterly miraculous and unique—some important people should have been the first to know, to give the risen Christ the honor he deserved. But notice whom he met first in Matthew's account. Two women who were not listed among the disciples were the first to see and believe. Jesus is still doing that, making himself known to ordinary people who believe and are willing to do his will. You may be thinking of someone in your own experience—perhaps your mother, who was not famous but responded to God as she guided her children into faith and usefulness.

In the resurrection God vindicated all that Jesus had taught and lived.—Christ's resurrection means that his teachings and pattern of life are superior to any other philosophy or system that strives for human allegiance. Of course, only believers would accept that statement. But if all of them did so, what a difference it would make in their witness and in the world.

Only in Christ's resurrection can we have salvation by his death.—His life and teachings might have won followers for many years even without his being crucified, but Jesus was more than a great teacher. He was willing to die for what he believed about God and what he wanted to accomplish for mankind. His self-sacrificial death could have appealed to many people perhaps for centuries, but Jesus was more than a noble martyr. By being victorious over death, however, he promised new life to those who believed. While we usually focus on the crucifixion as the center of God's act for our salvation, it ultimately depends on the resurrection for its power and effectiveness.

A Verse to Remember

He is not here: for he is risen, as he said.—Matthew 28:6. Jesus is neither on the cross—as the crucifix portrays—nor in the tomb; he is alive and expanding the reign of God.

Daily Bible Readings

Apr. 13—The Burial of Jesus. Matt. 27:57-61
Apr. 14—The Tomb Sealed and Guarded. Matt. 27:62-66
Apr. 15—Vainly They Watched the Tomb. Matt. 28:1-4
Apr. 16—"He Has Risen." Matt. 28:6-10
Apr. 17—Sorrow Turned to Joy. John 20:11-18
Apr. 18—"My Lord and My God." John 20:24-29
Apr. 19—Resources for Victorious Living. 1 Pet. 1:3-9

IN MISSION WITH THE VICTOR
Matthew 17:1-9; 28:11-20

On December 7 of last year we began a five-month study of the Gospel of Matthew as a guide for reviewing the life of Jesus the Christ. For each month there was a different theme as he prepared for his ministry, explained discipleship, trained the disciples for service, described the kingdom of God, and finally endured the cross and left the tomb. This Gospel emphasizes Jesus as the Messiah, refers often to the Old Testament, and stresses the kingdom as the ultimate relationship of God and persons. The writer of the Gospel never identifies himself, but Christians of the second century thought that Matthew, the disciple, had written it. We can assume that the writer was a Jewish Christian who wanted other Jews to see Jesus as their Messiah.

The Bible Lesson

MATTHEW 28:

11 Now when they were going, behold, some of the watch came into the city, and shewed unto the chief priests all the things that were done.

12 And when they were assembled with the elders, and had taken counsel, they gave large money unto the soldiers,

13 Saying, Say ye, His disciples came by night, and stole him away while we slept.

14 And if this come to the governor's ears, we will persuade him, and secure you.

15 So they took the money, and did as they were taught: and this saying is commonly reported among the Jews until this day.

16 Then the eleven disciples went away into Galilee, into a mountain where Jesus had appointed them.

17 And when they saw him, they worshipped him: but some doubted.

18 And Jesus came and spake unto them, saying, All power is given unto me in heaven and in earth.

19 Go ye therefore, and teach all nations, baptizing them in the name of the Father, and of the Son, and of the Holy Ghost:

20 Teaching them to observe all things whatsoever I have commanded you: and lo, I am with you alway, even unto the end of the world. Amen.

The Lesson Explained

A VISION OF GLORY TO COME (17:1-9)

Only six days after Peter's confession of Jesus as the Messiah, "the Son of the living God," Jesus took Peter, James, and John on a mountain hike. He seemed to feel that those three were understanding him better than the others. Matthew and Mark mention them with Jesus on several special occasions. While on the mountain a remarkable thing happened. Suddenly Jesus' face began to glow, and even his clothing became "white as light." Then before the astonished disciples two forms appeared and talked with Jesus. The disciples recognized them as Moses and Elijah. According to 2 Kings 2:11, Elijah did not die but was taken up into heaven. Deuteronomy 34:5-6 says that when Moses died, God buried him but no one knew where. Of course, Moses was the great lawgiver, and Elijah is mentioned in Malachi 4:5 as the prophet of the day of the Lord. Luke says they were talking to Jesus about his departure (9:31).

Impulsive Peter felt good about the experience and offered to provide three tents to honor and shelter Jesus and his guests. But even as he spoke, a bright cloud, like the one in the wilderness, came over them and a voice from it said, "This is my beloved Son, in whom I am well pleased; hear ye him." They were almost the same words spoken after Jesus' baptism, and they were a heavenly confirmation of Peter's recognition of Jesus' identity. Hearing the voice of God, the disciples fell to the ground, but Jesus touched and reassured them. When they looked up, only Jesus was there. As they walked down the mountain, Jesus commanded that they tell no one about the vision until after the resurrection. Mark 9:10 shows that they did not understand what he meant, but they must have recalled the experience with wonder after resurrection Sunday.

A BRIBE FOR SLEEPY SOLDIERS (28:11-15)

This incident followed immediately the Scripture story of last Sunday's lesson. While the two women were on their way to find the disciples, some of the soldiers guarding the tomb reported to the chief priests what had happened. The phrase "assembled with the elders" may mean that they called the

Sanhedrin together or conferred with certain key leaders. Whoever it was, they had access to a treasury to secure "large money." Along with the bribe, they told the soldiers what to say if anyone asked what happened. Then if the governor should hear that his soldiers had slept on the job, the Jewish leaders promised to defend them. Of course, the phrase "until this day" refers to the time the Gospel was written, perhaps sometime after A.D. 70. From two writings of about A.D. 150-165 we know that some people were still saying then that Jesus' body had been stolen by his disciples. But both Christians and Jews accepted the empty tomb as a fact.

A COMMISSION FOR ALL BELIEVERS (28:16-20)

Matthew tells of only two appearances after the resurrection, but eight others are mentioned in the other Gospels, Acts, and 1 Corinthians. This occasion in Galilee was next to the last one, and according to Paul there were more than five hundred disciples present (1 Cor. 15:6). Not all of them believed they had seen the risen Christ. But to those who believed, Jesus gave a commission—called the Great Commission here because it is longer than the others. It was a statement of his authority, an assignment of tasks, and a guarantee of support.

Despite the horror and stigma of crucifixion, the risen Christ asserted his authority in heaven and on earth. From that position he had the right to command his disciples to enlist "all nations" (Gentiles and Jews) as learners. Then after they were baptized, they should be taught all the things Jesus had taught his disciples. Thus, there would be continuity in the character and purpose of their ministry.

Truths to Live By

Although he called his disciples his brothers, Jesus was and is unique and different from mankind.—The disciples accepted him as a man first and later became convinced that he was the Son of God. The transfiguration showed his three closest friends that he was quite different from other men. Maintaining his balance is not easy in our experience. He is the Elder Brother of all believers, but he is not a "buddy." He is the great Physician and the Friend of sinners, but he is also the Son of God. We can know him personally and warmly in prayer without being chummy.

The Great Commission is broad enough for all witness and service in Christ's name.—Usually church people think of it as a text for sermons on evangelism and missions, and it is appropriate for both themes. But look at it again. It emphasizes sound Christian doctrine. It calls for an educational effort to "teach all nations." It states the content of that teaching effort as all things Jesus had commanded. That included prayer and worship, family fidelity, loving one's neighbor, readiness to forgive, creative loyalty to God's law, and many other things.

Those enlisted as Christ's followers must be taught to keep his commandments.—The believer is baptized on the basis of his or her profession of faith in Christ as Lord and Savior. But living the Christian life is no more automatic than one's becoming a good doctor just because one has been accepted by a medical college. Conversion itself means turning away from an old life; therefore, a convert must learn to walk in new ways. Beginning with personal Bible study and prayer, he or she needs some classwork in which ideas can be shared and sometimes corrected. Also, small group discussions can help a person express his own convictions. From week to week in the worship and fellowship of the church, believers can grow in appreciation of the Christian way and in commitment to practice it.

A Verse to Remember

Lo, I am with you alway, even unto the end of the world.— Matthew 28:20. Many a Christian has found in this verse enough assurance to face trouble and persecution.

Daily Bible Readings

Apr.   20—Three Disciples See Jesus' Glory. Matt. 17:1-12
Apr.   21—The Transfiguration. Luke 9:28-36
Apr.   22—The Great Commission. Matt. 28:16-20
Apr.   23—The Heart of the Good News. Mark 12:28-34
Apr.   24—Spreading False Reports. Matt. 28:11-15
Apr.   25—A Promise of Help. John 14:8-21
Apr.   26—"Be Holy ... in All Your Conduct." 1 Pet. 1:13-25

May 3, 1981

GOD'S ULTIMATE WORD

Hebrews 1:1 to 2:9

More than thirty years ago a young shepherd discovered a cave near the top of a cliff within sight of the western shore of the Dead Sea. In it he found some urns containing scrolls that turned out to be various Old Testament books. Later excavations above the cave revealed the ruins of a Hebrew community that was destroyed in A.D. 68. The people who had lived there in Qumran were a very devout and disciplined Jewish sect. Today some interpreters feel strongly that the book of Hebrews was written to show how superior Christianity was to even the best of Judaism, represented by the brave and pious people of Qumran. Since that is a possibility, the letter may have been intended for Hellenistic-Jewish Christians who needed a strong sermon on the uniqueness of Christ.

The Bible Lesson

HEBREWS 1:

1 God, who at sundry times and in divers manners spake in time past unto the father by the prophets,

2 Hath in these last days spoken unto us by his Son, whom he hath appointed heir of all things, by whom also he made the worlds;

3 Who being the brightness of his glory, and the express image of his person, and upholding all things by the word of his power, when he had by himself purged our sins, sat down on the right hand of the Majesty on high;

4 Being made so much better than the angels, as he hath by inheritance obtained a more excellent name than they.

HEBREWS 2:

1 Therefore we ought to give the more earnest heed to the things which we have heard, lest at any time we should let them slip.

2 For if the word spoken by angels was stedfast, and every transgression and disobedience received a just recompense of reward;

3 How shall we escape, if we neglect so great salvation; which at the first began to be spoken by the Lord, and was confirmed unto us by them that heard him;

4 God also bearing them witness, both with signs and wonders,

and with divers miracles, and gifts of the Holy Ghost, according to his own will?

5 For unto the angels hath he not put in subjection the world to come, whereof we speak.

6 But one in a certain place testified, saying, What is man, that thou art mindful of him? or the son of man, that thou visitest him?

7 Thou madest him a little lower than the angels: thou crownedst him with glory and honour, and didst set him over the works of thy hands:

8 Thou hast put all things in subjection under his feet. For in that he put all in subjection under him, he left nothing that is not put under him. But now we see not yet all things put under him.

The Lesson Explained

GREATER THAN THE PROPHETS (1:1-4)

In verse 1 the writer has gathered up all the work of the Hebrew prophets, who spoke at various times and in differing ways, and pushed it to one side to give him room to say how much greater Jesus was than the prophets.

Then verse 2 begins to describe Jesus' role in God's work. One translator sees in the phrase "appointed heir" the idea of Jesus' being the "predestined Lord of the universe." But at the beginning he was, to use a modern term, the "construction engineer" of creation. From start to finish he is always at the heart of God's work.

That is a great deal for a Jew to say about a being who had once been human, but he said even more in verse 3. The very radiance of God shone in Jesus, revealing "the express image of his nature." The Greek word for "image" is the source of our word *character*. Caesar's image on a coin was supposed to look exactly like the emperor. Here the word means that the Son is exactly like the Father.

Even while sustaining the universe, Jesus was willing to provide purification for our sins. Having thus accomplished God's purpose, he is now seated in the place of honor beside "the Majesty on high." Not only had his word surpassed that of the prophets; his role is far more important than that of angels.

GREATER THAN ANGELS (2:1-4)

Christ's superiority over angels was then illustrated by seven Old Testament quotations to the end of the first chapter. Finally in 1:14 the writer of Hebrews describes angels as spirits who minister to humans who are to inherit salvation. While they are messengers of salvation, only the Son could provide it.

"Therefore" in 2:1 refers to all of chapter 1 in describing the person and work of Christ. The readers of Hebrews should pay close attention to what they had heard. As second-generation Christians, they had not heard the message directly from the Lord or his first followers. The warning was against losing the reality of the Christian message. If disobeying the law given by angels brought inevitable judgment, Christians cannot escape what God has in store for those who "neglect so great salvation." The Lord—that is, Jesus—spoke of that salvation in his compassion, teachings, and death. Then those who heard and accepted it showed that it was real. At the same time God was validating their testimony by signs, marvels, and miracles, and also by distributing gifts of the Holy Spirit as he saw they were needed.

GOD'S SON AND OUR SAVIOR (2:5-9)

As messengers of God, angels had given the law to Moses and on many other occasions had demonstrated God's will among the people. But the writer of Hebrews pointed out that God chose man rather than angels to rule over "the world to come." Then he quoted three well-known verses from Psalm 8 to show the importance of mankind in God's plan. Here the Hebrew word translated "angels" really means "gods." Man was created in God's image to have fellowship with him and to do his will. But the writer of Hebrews had to admit that as yet not everything was in subjection to man.

"But we see Jesus." After all, Jesus was a man; only in that role could he suffer death for all persons. In that deed God's Son became our Savior and is now crowned with glory and honor. Here is God's revelation of himself in mercy and compassion. Neither prophets nor angels can match this disclosure and its meaning for all persons.

Truths to Live By

Christian understandings are rooted in the Old Testament.—Because the Bible is not an easy book to understand, some believers would be willing to cut out the parts they do not

147

comprehend. They would like to oversimplify Christian truth by saying the New Testament is enough. But much of the New Testament can be understood only in relation to the Old. After all, Jesus was a Jew, and the Bible he quoted was our Old Testament. His teachings were aimed in part at showing the deeper meanings of the law of Moses. The books of Matthew, Romans, and Hebrews would bewilder any reader without some knowledge of the Old Testament. Even when the Christian writers did not quote from the Old Testament, their ideas were rooted in it. God has spoken through the whole Bible.

Christ is the heart of the Christian message.—In a nation that claims to be Christian, many strange things come under that heading. Just practicing the Golden Rule is some people's idea of being Christian—or living by the Ten Commandments. Others put capitalism or "live and let live" in the Christian column. Still others feel that being neighborly and respectable and going to church is the essence of Christianity. But there is no Christianity without Christ, both as Lord and Savior. Being a Christian is a personal relationship with Jesus Christ. It begins with repentance and faith in him to handle the sin problem, and it continues through life as a person sets his values and makes his decisions by Christ's pattern.

Verses to Remember

God, who at sundry times and in divers manners spake in time past unto the fathers by the prophets, hath in these last days spoken unto us by his Son.—Hebrews 1:1-2. Now through his Spirit, God continues to speak to those who will listen.

Daily Bible Readings

Apr. 27—The Eternal God. Heb. 1:10-14
Apr. 28—God the Creator. Ps. 8
Apr. 29—God's Word Becomes Flesh. John 1:1-5, 14-18
Apr. 30—God's Son. Heb. 1:5-9
May 1—God Reveals Through His Spirit. 1 Cor. 2:6-13
May 2—The Eternal Christ. Col. 1:15-23
May 3—The Good Shepherd. John 10:1-11

PIONEER OF OUR SALVATION
Hebrews 2:10 to 4:13

Since the book of Hebrews is not addressed within itself to any person or church, some people feel that it is more like a sermon than a letter. No one knows when it was written, but since it was quoted by a writer in A.D. 95, it must have been composed sometime earlier. No one knows for whom it was intended; some scholars say Jewish Christians, and others, Gentile Christians. But everyone who reads the book with an open mind agrees that it is a little gem, in both Greek and English. Although there may be some passages in the King James Version that some readers would not want to give up, the understanding of the average person will be helped by a present-day translation. Read the whole book and then come back to concentrate on the passage for this lesson.

The Bible Lesson

HEBREWS 2:

10 For it became him, for whom are all things, and by whom are all things, in bringing many sons unto glory, to make the captain of their salvation perfect through sufferings.

11 For both he that sanctifieth and they who are sanctified are all of one: for which cause he is not ashamed to call them brethren,

12 Saying, I will declare thy name unto my brethren, in the midst of the church will I sing praise unto thee.

13 And again, I will put my trust in him. And again, Behold I and the children which God hath given me.

14 Forasmuch then as the children are partakers of flesh and blood, he also himself likewise took part of the same; that through death he might destroy him that had the power of death, that is, the devil;

15 And deliver them who through fear of death were all their lifetime subject to bondage.

16 For verily he took not on him the nature of angels; but he took on him the seed of Abraham.

17 Wherefore in all things it behoved him to be made like unto his brethren, that he might be a merciful and faithful high priest in things pertaining to God, to make reconciliation for the sins of the people.

18 For in that he himself hath suffered being tempted, he is able to succour them that are tempted.

The Lesson Explained
THE SAVIOR AND HIS BROTHERS (2:10-13)

Since no name is called in these verses until "God" appears in verse 13, we must identify the pronouns by the context. So, "him" in verse 10, refers to God, Creator of "all things" and Father of "many sons." "It was appropriate" is another way of saying "it became him" in talking about God's action to bring those sons "unto glory." He did it by completing Jesus' work through his suffering. That is the meaning of the word for "make . . . perfect." The word for "captain" can also be translated: author, leader, or pioneer. So, Jesus provided salvation and "blazed the trail."

In verse 11 the pronoun "he" refers to Jesus, and "sanctify" means to set apart or make holy. Jesus continues to set apart those who respond to the salvation he provides. He did that for the early disciples, and they all came from the same Father—he and they. Thus, he was "not ashamed to call them brethren." He identified with those whom he saved.

VICTOR OVER THE DEVIL (2:14-18)

Since those children are human and subject to human limitations, Jesus became human and was even subject to death. It was his death that set the stage for his resurrection, and God's power shown in that resurrection promised the destruction of the devil. Destroying his "power of death" would deliver believers from their lifetime fear of death. Because no religion of that time had any word of hope or comfort in the face of death, even well-educated people feared it. Jesus had submitted to human experience instead of identifying with angels.

GREATER THAN MOSES (3:1-6)

Already the writer of Hebrews has said that Jesus was greater than prophets and angels. Here he made an even more daring assertion: "My Christian brothers, who also have been called by God!" (TEV). Their Jewish background would help them appreciate the contrast he would draw. Just as Moses was faithful to the responsibility to which God had called him, so

Jesus was faithful in the task assigned him by God. The word *house* here can mean household, realm, or sphere of influence. Whoever begins and builds such a house is more significant than the house itself.

Moses was faithful within the house God had built; he led the people out of bondage, and through him the law was given. But he was a servant of God in all this. On the other hand, as God's Son, Christ was more to be honored because he was faithful "over his house." Through the ages it was the same household—the company of believers in God. Earlier they had identified Moses as leader and interpreter; but now believers were accepting Jesus in that role. But that household of God was not a matter of race or mere membership. The writer of Hebrews said, "We are his house if we keep up our courage and our confidence in what we hope for" (TEV).

Truths to Live By

Christian attitudes toward death should be different from those of unbelievers.—Of course, even believers will have some anxiety about death: How does it feel? Will they die with dignity? How will it affect loved ones? But death as the passage from this life into the unknown should not be feared. Because of Jesus' resurrection and his promise to us of life everlasting, believers ought to look forward to life after death, different from earthly existence but even more real and meaningful. With this confidence, they should be able to deal creatively with the death of loved ones. Although bereavement is a real and crushing experience, the living can keep on living beyond their sorrow, perhaps even finding some new channel for Christian service and witness. Believers can also share their faith in Christ with those who grieve without that faith, hoping to help them find a ground of hope and wholeness.

Jesus' work surpasses that of every religious genius.— Moses was indeed a remarkable leader for God's people, and even non-Jews recognize him as a deliverer and law giver. But the Jewish writer of the book of Hebrews saw in Jesus something that did not discredit Moses but just surpassed him. Jesus was the Son of God and revealed eternal truth in his teachings and self-sacrificial love in his death on the cross.

Confucius and some writers of the Hindu holy books showed wisdom and insight, but they did not match Jesus in either word or deed. Certainly, the religious leaders of the last two or three centuries have not come close to his stature. Of course, Christians affirm that his being the Son of God was the real difference. The effect of that claim as well as of his teachings and crucifixion would be more telling if his followers lived more according to his pattern.

Being Christ's brethren gives Christians remarkable opportunities.—First of all, there is the gift of salvation and eternal life. Then there is the gift of fellowship within a church. Too many people seem to play down that fact. They stress salvation as an individual experience—and it is—but they do not seem to see the challenge and privilege of church membership. Although it will not *save* anyone, it is the school and family in which believers learn Christian truth and practice Christian behavior. Also, as Christ's brethren, believers have the privilege of telling others what fellowship with him might mean to them. This is no posture of pride or judgment but a sharing with those in need. Along with witnessing, believers have the opportunity of serving and helping others in material ways. In fact, Jesus said that doing so "to one of the least of these my brethren" was positive evidence of a real commitment to him.

A Verse to Live By

For in that he himself hath suffered being tempted, he is able to succour them that are tempted.—Hebrews 2:18.

Daily Bible Readings

May   4—Sending of the Son. John 3:16-21
May   5—Salvation Through Jesus Christ. 2 Tim. 2:8-13
May   6—"Salvation Is at Hand." Ps. 85:7-13
May   7—"The Day of Salvation." 2 Cor. 6:1-10
May   8—"No Longer Strangers." Eph. 3:11-22
May   9—"Salvation Belongs to . . . the Lamb." Rev. 7:9-11
May   10—"I Am the Bread of Life." John 6:35-41,44-45

OUR GREAT HIGH PRIEST
Hebrews 4:14 to 7:28

Most people today think of a priest as a person who officiates in worship and represents the high church leaders in the local congregation. In early Hebrew days the priest was the intermediary for God and people. Since he was human, he represented the worshipers before God; and since he was consecrated by God for his work, he interpreted God to the people. God was too holy to be approached by ordinary human beings. Only the priest could sacrifice animals and pronounce cleansing on the people. Above the other priests was the high priest who was anointed with holy oil. Originally he was appointed for life, but in New Testament times the office was filled by Roman rulers as they wished. But the role of high priest was still one of honor and power, and that is the background for the theme of this lesson.

The Bible Lesson

HEBREWS 4:

14 Seeing then that we have a great high priest, that is passed into the heavens, Jesus the Son of God, let us hold fast our profession.

15 For we have not an high priest which cannot be touched with the feeling of our infirmities; but was in all points tempted like as we are, yet without sin.

16 Let us therefore come boldly unto the throne of grace, that we may obtain mercy, and find grace to help in time of need.

HEBREWS 5:

1 For every high priest taken from among men is ordained for men in things pertaining to God, that he may offer both gifts and sacrifices for sins:

2 Who can have compassion on the ignorant, and on them that are out of the way; for that he himself also is compassed with infirmity.

3 And by reason hereof he ought, as for the people, so also for himself, to offer for sins.

4 And no man taketh this honour unto himself, but he that is called of God, as was Aaron.

153

5 So also Christ glorified not himself to be made an high priest; but he that said unto him, Thou art my Son, to-day have I begotten thee.

6 As he saith also in another place, Thou art a priest for ever after the order of Melchisedec.

7 Who in the days of his flesh, when he had offered up prayers and supplications with strong crying and tears unto him that was able to save him from death, and was heard in that he feared;

8 Though he were a Son, yet learned he obedience by the things which he suffered;

9 And being made perfect, he became the author of eternal salvation unto all them that obey him;

10 Called of God an high priest after the order of Melchisedec.

The Lesson Explained

HIS COMPASSION MAKES US BOLD (4:14-16)

Throughout Jewish history the high priest had always been a prominent leader, and when they were subjugated by foreign nations, the high priest was considered the head of the state. Devout Jews, of course, were more impressed with his religious role than with his political one. On the annual Day of Atonement the high priest—and he alone—would enter the holy of holies of the Temple and sprinkle the blood of sin offerings on the mercy seat to atone for his own and the people's sin. It was an awesome task. The author of Hebrews had this in mind when he wrote these verses.

HE WAS APPOINTED BY GOD (5:1-6)

This idea in Hebrews that Jesus was the great High Priest is the basic theme of the book from 4:14 through 10:22. The writer knew that for his Jewish readers he was making a strong case. The high priest was the mediator of atonement for the people; he could enter into the very presence of God. Yet he was one of the people, selected by God for his special role. Therefore, he ought to understand the problems of the people. Historically, he had not sought the office, although in recent decades the position had become a political plum.

Even as Aaron had been chosen by God, so Christ was appointed by the One who said, "Thou art my Son," and "Thou art a priest for ever," quoting verses from Psalms 2 and 110. Thus the writers of Hebrews showed his familiarity with Jesus' interpretation of himself based on Old Testament writings. (See Luke 24:44-45.) But his real purpose was to stress God's selection of Jesus as High Priest. Although he had been rejected by earthly priests, Jesus was God's choice.

HE PROVIDED SALVATION FOR ALL (5:7-10)

Why was Melchisedec brought into a discussion of the Jewish priesthood? Mentioned in Genesis 14:18 as "priest of the most high God," he lived centuries before Aaron. He was also king of Salem, but we do not know how he was appointed a priest. Thus, in a sense, the priesthood of Melchisedec was superior to the Aaronic line and a foregleam of the uniqueness of Jesus.

Far more important, however, are the ways in which Jesus qualified himself to be the great High Priest. Evidently referring to the Gethsemane experience, the writer of Hebrews described Jesus as praying "with loud cries and tears" (RSV). He believed that God could help him, and because God wanted his will to be done, he responded. Again, Jesus was prepared for his work as High Priest when he learned obedience through suffering. Although he was God's Son, he needed the experience of obedience in the flesh regardless of cost to achieve his goal ("being made perfect") of providing salvation for all who obey him. Referring again to the Melchisedec verse, the writer seems to be concluding a brief explanation of that reference as it applied to Christ. Because Christ is the source and giver of salvation—not just the mediator—he is far above any priest of the Levitical line.

Truths to Live By

Seeing Jesus aright includes both his humanity and his deity.—Because the New Testament emphasizes the deity of Christ shown in his miracles and resurrection, many present-day believers are defensive on that point. They sometimes overstate their case as they overlook New Testament evidence of his humanity—hunger, fatigue, praying, suffering, and death. Others deny the deity while stressing his humanity. Because no one has been able to describe the mystery of his personality, these two factors remain in tension while we strive to comprehend Jesus. Because he is the Son of God, we shall never be able to define him, but that does not prevent our obeying and worshiping him. Following the judgment of ancient councils, we can do no better than say he was truly God and truly man.

The believer need not fear to confess his sins to God in Christ.—Our age is characterized by an almost chummy familiarity with God; the sense of awe in his presence has worn thin. For many disobeying his law brings no guilt feelings. At the other extreme, some do not know what to do with their guilt feelings; just confessing to a friend or counselor does not satisfy. Somehow they feel that things must be set right at a higher level. But how can one confess prejudice, envy, greed, and infidelity to God? These are problems for people who never run afoul of the law. Because Jesus was "tempted like as we are, yet without sin," and because he has compassion on both the ignorant and the sophisticated, he will always receive our confession and help us profit from his forgiveness.

While Jesus holds onto us, we must hold onto him.—The New Testament is clear as to the power of God to save the believer now and into eternity, but the believer must trust and obey. He must respond to God's offer in order to receive salvation in the first place; and having received it, he will keep on trusting and obeying throughout life. In John's Gospel Jesus described his disciples as branches that must keep on abiding in the vine.

A Verse to Remember

Let us therefore come boldly unto the throne of grace, that we may obtain mercy, and find grace to help in time of need.—Hebrews 4:16.

Daily Bible Readings

May 11—The Source of Eternal Salvation. Heb. 5:7-14
May 12—"Offer Right Sacrifices." Ps. 4
May 13—"Offer Spiritual Sacrifices." 1 Pet. 2:1-10
May 14—"A Living Sacrifice." Rom. 12:1-8
May 15—The Sacrificial Love. John 15:12-17
May 16—The Priest Who Offered Himself. Heb. 7:23-28
May 17—"The Spirit of Truth." John 14:15-24

MEDIATOR OF A NEW COVENANT
Hebrews 8–9

Two families had been at odds for a dozen years. They lived in the same general section of a small town and were members of the same church. Only the older people could remember what the problem had been, but members of those two families would not speak to one another. The new pastor listened and watched, but he refused to discuss the problem with other members of the church. He knew the risks involved in trying to be a peacemaker, but he also knew that such a condition should not continue in a church. So, he decided to talk with members of both families and try to bring them together. At first he was rebuffed and accused of meddling, and one family stopped its church gifts. But after many conversations, the older members agreed to talk together with the pastor. He led them gently to face up to their misunderstandings and hear God's Word on forgiveness and love. Finally on a Sunday morning they told the whole church family how much they appreciated their pastor as a mediator.

The Bible Lesson

HEBREWS 9:
11 But Christ being come an high priest of good things to come, by a greater and more perfect tabernacle, not made with hands, that is to say, not of this building;

12 Neither by the blood of goats and calves, but by his own blood he entered in once into the holy place, having obtained eternal redemption for us.

13 For if the blood of bulls and of goats, and the ashes of an heifer sprinkling the unclean, sanctifieth to the purifying of the flesh:

14 How much more shall the blood of Christ, who through the eternal Spirit offered himself without spot to God, purge your conscience from dead works to serve the living God?

15 And for this cause he is the mediator of the new testament, that by means of death, for the redemption of the transgressions that were under the first testament, they which are called might receive the promise of eternal inheritance.

24 For Christ is not entered into the holy places made with hands, which are the figures of the true; but into heaven itself, now to appear in the presence of God for us:

25 Nor yet that he should offer himself often, as the high priest entereth into the holy place every year with blood of others;

26 For then must he often have suffered since the foundation of the world: but now once in the end of the world hath he appeared to put away sin by the sacrifice of himself.

27 And as it is appointed unto men once to die, but after this the judgment:

28 So Christ was once offered to bear the sins of many; and unto them that look for him shall he appear the second time without sin unto salvation.

The Lesson Explained

GOD PROMISED A NEW COVENANT (8:1-8)

Here is a very obvious summary and transition verse. The writer wanted his readers to understand what he had been saying and be ready for the next point. The word that is translated "the sum" can also mean "main point." In Christ, he said, we have the High Priest (described in previous chapters) who has finished his sacrificial task and has taken the place of honor beside "the Majesty in the heavens." There he ministers in a sanctuary made by God rather than men, but without earthly sacrifices to offer. Instead, he is "the mediator of a better covenant." That covenant idea stretched from Genesis throughout the Old Testament. (Recall our study for September to November.) It pictured the Lord (Yahweh) offering his Chosen People a covenant relationship of blessing based on faith and obedience. But the people often violated the covenant.

Finally, with Jerusalem and the Temple in ruins and the people in captivity, Jeremiah had promised that the Lord would make a new covenant with his people (31:31-34). That is the passage the writer of Hebrews quoted in 8:8-12. The main problem of the first covenant was the disobedience of the people. The new covenant would be based on God's grace rather than law, and Christ was its mediator.

CHRIST HIMSELF THE SACRIFICE (9:11-15)

The first ten verses of this chapter return to the tabernacle and worship patterns related to that first covenant, preparing to contrast it with the new one. And the contrast begins with verse 11. Instead of the earthly holy of holies in the Temple, Christ had entered the tabernacle of heaven. Instead of offering the blood of animals, he had secured redemption "by his own blood.

So Christ was both the mediator of the new covenant and the sacrifice needed for the mediation. Verse 15 uses "testament" to translate the word for covenant, probably because the writer was bringing up the idea of the will of a dead person. By the death of Christ, those who respond to God's call are delivered from guilt that accumulated under the first covenant and receive the eternal inheritance promised in the new covenant or will. Of course, that is eternal life.

RETURN OF THE MEDIATOR (9:24-28)

Here the writer returned to this idea in verse 11 of Christ as High Priest entering, not a handmade sanctuary, but heaven itself. There in the presence of God he continues to witness in our behalf. Furthermore, in contrast to the annual visit of the earthly high priest into the holiest place of the Temple, Christ needed to offer himself as the sacrifice only once. In verse 26 the phrase "the end of the world" means end of the age. Christ's life and death did signify the end of one age and the beginning of another, for his death defeated the sin principle once for all.

But that was not all; something else will happen. Just as surely as death must come to every person, he said, so must judgment follow death. In a similar way, Christ died once "to bear the sins of many," but he will "appear the second time." This is a very clear statement about the second coming. But when he comes again, it will not be "to deal with sin but to save those who are eagerly waiting for him" (RSV). Here "salvation" means the completion of his whole saving ministry.

Truths to Live By

The Christian gospel is superior to Old Testament insights.—That is the major point made by the book of Hebrews. It shows appreciation for the Hebrew faith and Scripture, but it warns Jewish believers about going back instead of going forward with Christ. Although many Christians seem willing to almost ignore the Old Testament, some others lean in another direction. They are intrigued by the symbolism of the tabernacle, predictions of the prophets, and certain emphases in the law. Following interpreters with intricate charts, they memorize details but often miss the major teachings of the Bible.

Christ's death makes believers right in God's sight.—That is the essence of justification. Although many have tried to explain how it works, it really is beyond our comprehension. Most of the theories are based on analogies and comparisons, with one appealing to this theologian and another appealing to that. But the idea itself is stated many times in the New Testament. God sent his Son to die that those who believe might have forgiveness and eternal life. Believers are not just called righteous; they are made righteous (not perfect) by the death of Christ and the work of the Spirit. He is the Mediator between proud and fearful persons and the loving Father.

As the resurrection vindicated Christ before his enemies, his second coming will vindicate the faith of his followers.—The writer of Hebrews said that Christ would come again, not to deal with sin but to complete the salvation of believers. Of course believers are already saved unto eternal life, but Christ's return will say to the whole world: "What God began in Jesus he has now brought to final judgment and victory." Those who trust him then will rejoice in his coming, but those who fear or resent him will be undone.

A Verse to Remember

He is the mediator of the new testament, that by means of death, . . . they which are called might receive the promise of eternal inheritance.—Hebrews 9:15.

Daily Bible Readings

May 18—"Mindful of His Covenant." Ps. 105:1-11
May 19—"End of the Law." Rom. 10:1-11
May 20—"The Law Was Our Custodian." Gal. 3:23-29
May 21—"A New Covenant." Heb. 8:6-13
May 22—"Ministers of a New Covenant." 2 Cor. 3:1-6
May 23—Blood of the New Covenant. 1 Cor. 11:23-26
May 24—"Lord of the Church." Eph. 1:15-23

PERFECTER OF OUR FAITH
Hebrews 10–13

Among Christians one of the favorite chapters in the New Testament is Hebrews 11—the faith chapter. Beginning with a description of faith, it recalls great men and women of faith, from Abel to David. It is a gallery of great Jews, and except for verses 26 and 39-40 and the fact that it says nothing about the law, it could also be a favorite chapter of Jews. Each hero in his or her time believed and acted on the revelation received from God, usually at some serious risk. But God always vindicated their thrust of faith, even in the nameless summary in verses 35-38. Through the centuries many had believed that God would achieve his purpose in their nation. But in the last verse the writer of Hebrews said that the faith of these notables could not be complete without the fulfillment of the messianic promise in the believers he represented.

The Bible Lesson

HEBREWS 12:

1 Wherefore seeing we also are compassed about with so great a cloud of witnesses, let us lay aside every weight, and the sin which doth so easily beset us, and let us run with patience the race that is set before us,

2 Looking unto Jesus the author and finisher of our faith; who for the joy that was set before him endured the cross, despising the shame, and is set down at the right hand of the throne of God.

3 For consider him that endured such contradiction of sinners against himself, lest ye be wearied and faint in your minds.

4 Ye have not yet resisted unto blood, striving against sin.

5 And ye have forgotten the exhortation which speaketh unto you as unto children, My son, despise not thou the chastening of the Lord, nor faith when thou art rebuked of him:

6 For whom the Lord loveth he chasteneth, and scourgeth every son whom he receiveth.

7 If ye endure chastening, God dealeth with you as with sons; for what son is he whom the father chasteneth not?

8 But if ye be without chastisement, whereof all are partakers, then are ye bastards, and not sons.

9 Furthermore we have had fathers of our flesh which corrected us, and we gave them reverence: shall we not much rather be in subjection unto the Father of spirits, and live?

10 For they verily for a few days chastened us after their own pleasure; but he for our profit, that we might be partakers of his holiness.

11 Now no chastening for the present seemeth to be joyous, but grievous; nevertheless afterward it yieldeth the peaceable fruit of righteousness unto them which are exercised thereby.

12 Wherefore lift up the hands which hang down, and the feeble knees;

13 And make straight paths for your feet, lest that which is lame be turned out of the way; but let it rather be healed.

The Lesson Explained

THE CHRISTIAN'S RACE (12:1-4)

As he ended his tribute to the heroes of faith in chapter 11, the writer was reminded of an athletic contest. When they had finished their own events, those heroes became spectators to see what modern runners might do. Perhaps he saw the life of faith as a kind of relay race, with one generation handing off the baton to the next. No individual runner could go the whole course, but each one contributed to the success of the team.

To "run" at his best, the Christian must get rid of anything that would limit his effort, including any sin that might, like a flowing garment, entangle his feet. "Patience" is a mild translation of a Greek word that also means determination and endurance. Since the course may be long and difficult, the runner needs to "pace" himself—know what he can do and then do it without worrying about the other runners.

But the real secret of success in the Christian's race of life is the believer's concentration on Jesus. Perhaps the writer was thinking of him as the coach or teacher; he is the pioneer and completer of faith. One translation says that faith depends on him "from beginning to end" (TEV). And the reason for his unique role is the way he dealt with the cross and now has a place of heavenly honor. When you compare your sufferings with the hostility he endured, the writer said, you discover fresh courage. After all, his readers had not yet been required to shed blood in facing opposition.

THE FATHER'S DISCIPLINE (12:5-11)

To help his readers understand the trials they faced for the faith, the writer quoted Proverbs 3:11-12 and Job 5:17. They describe God's chastening of those he loves. The Greek word for "chasten" here means to train a child, including physical punishment for misbehavior. Believers at that time were being persecuted or threatened; so the writer of Hebrews interpreted their suffering as within the permissive will of God. Their experiences were being used by God to practice their courage, purge their resentment, and deepen their love of others. The very fact that they were suffering proved that they were God's sons. That principle holds true even on the human level; the illegitimate child would probably not receive the father's care. Discipline rather than indulgence reveal the loving father.

The phrase "after their own pleasure" in verse 10 means "as they saw fit"; good parents intend discipline for the child's benefit. But the discipline of God will lead to sharing in his holy character. However painful it may be at the time, God's discipline will yield the serenity of a righteous life.

THE CHURCH'S NEEDS (12:12-16)

From his general discussion of the rigorous training which Christians were enduring, the writer then made some specific applications. In verse 12 he almost quoted Isaiah 35:3 in urging his readers to "condition" themselves for the race of life. Hands and knees must be strong and supple. Listless hands must be raised for work; stiffened knees must be exercised.

Perhaps still thinking of the athletic contest, the writer urged believers to "chase after" peace and holiness. That kind of peace is not mere inactivity but peaceful relationships. That kind of holiness is not the goal of the self-righteous; it is the commitment that yearns for a closer fellowship with God. At the same time believers must be concerned that no brother or sister in the faith fails to respond to God's grace.

Truths to Live By

Faith is commitment proved in action.—Some popular evangelism has given the impression that having faith is walking down the aisle of a church and saying the right words to the preacher. But in Hebrews we see that faith is far more. It is

163

believing God—his offer of salvation, his loving forgiveness, his challenge to new life—and then risking everything to live by that belief.

The Christian endures suffering because he can see meaning in it.—The P. O. W. who believed that God cared about what was happening to him was fortified against pain and boredom. The widow who is grateful to God for her marriage memories and believes she can witness to him even in bereavement will be led through her grief to new life. The man whose job is phased out but still believes that God has work for him to do will endure retraining and find a new channel for his skills. Seeing one's life in God's framework makes the difference.

A Christian's faith is enriched by its heritage.—A father's faith cannot save his son; each person must have his own relationship with God in Christ. But the faith of men and women of earlier generations can enrich our own. Paul's interpretation of the worldwide intention of Christ will keep us from being provincial and narrow. Martin Luther's daring use of the Bible against a rich and powerful hierarchy brought freedom and variety into Christian experience. Luther Rice gave up his desire to be a missionary so he could solicit funds at home to support the Judsons and others who were witnessing abroad. These and many others can enrich our Christian knowledge and spur us to Christian service.

Verses to Remember

Let us run with patience the race that is set before us, Looking unto Jesus the author and finisher of our faith.—Hebrews 12:1-2.

Daily Bible Readings

May 25—"Eyewitnesses of His Majesty." 2 Pet. 1:3-7, 16-19
May 26—"Every Knee Should Bow." Phil. 2:1-11
May 27—Reconciled Through Christ. 2 Cor. 5:17-21
May 28—"He Who Promised Is Faithful." Heb. 10:19-25
May 29—The Unchanging Christ. Heb. 13:7-8, 18-21
May 30—"Dying in Faith." Heb. 11:13-16
May 31—"Keeping Them in Thy Name." John 17:1-11

For the first time in many years we will spend a whole quarter on the book of Deuteronomy. Although it may be unfamiliar to most Christians, it is quoted more than eighty times in the New Testament. Jesus used it often, especially in dealing with the Tempter during the wilderness experience. To be sure, it is somewhat repetitious in reviewing Israel's early history, but it was addressed to the rank and file of the people of Israel for their understanding of and commitment to God. As such, it can speak to believers of our day, both Jew and Christian. It is concerned for the community of faith, for the worship of Yahweh, and for the faithfulness of the people. As you study these lessons, read the text in a present-day translation for a fresh look at the book of Deuteronomy.

The Bible Lesson

2 KINGS 23:

1 And the king sent, and they gathered unto him all the elders of Judah and of Jerusalem.

2 And the king went up into the house of the Lord, and all the men of Judah and all the inhabitants of Jerusalem with him, and the priests, and the prophets, and all the people, both small and great: and he read in their ears all the words of the book of the covenant which was found in the house of the Lord.

DEUTERONOMY 10:

12 And now, Israel, what doth the Lord thy God require of thee, but to fear the Lord thy God, to walk in all his ways, and to love him, and to serve the Lord thy God with all thy heart and with all thy soul,

13 To keep the commandments of the Lord, and his statutes, which I command thee this day for thy good?

14 Behold, the heaven and the heaven of heavens is the Lord's thy God, the earth also, with all that therein is.

15 Only the Lord had a delight in thy fathers to love them, and he chose their seed after them, even you above all people, as it is this day.

16 Circumcise therefore the foreskin of your heart, and be no more stiffnecked.

17 For the Lord your God is God of gods, and Lord of lords, a

great God, a mighty, and a terrible, which regardeth not persons, nor taketh reward:

18 He doth execute the judgment of the fatherless and widow, and loveth the stranger, in giving him food and raiment.

19 Love ye therefore the stranger: for ye were strangers in the land of Egypt.

20 Thou shalt fear the Lord thy God; him shalt thou serve, and to him thou shalt cleave, and swear by his name.

21 He is thy praise, and he is thy God, that hath done for thee these great and terrible things, which thine eyes have seen.

22 Thy fathers went down into Egypt with threescore and ten persons; and now the Lord thy God hath made thee as the stars of heaven for multitude.

DEUTERONOMY 11:

1 Therefore thou shalt love the Lord thy God, and keep his charge, and his statutes, and his judgments, and his commandments, alway.

The Lesson Explained

A BOOK IS FOUND IN THE TEMPLE (2 Kings 23:1-2)

Most scholars feel that the scroll Hilkiah found when the Temple was being cleaned and refurbished in King Josiah's time was part or all of Deuteronomy. Second Kings 23:2 calls it "the book of the covenant," and Deuteronomy 29:9 refers to "the words of this covenant.

Manasseh had ruled Judah for fifty-five years, imitating "the abominations of the heathen" (2 Kings 21:2), even setting up Baal altars in the Temple. His son Amon was just as bad but was assassinated after only a two-year reign. Then eight-year-old Josiah came to the throne with a different attitude toward Yahweh worship. When he was eighteen, he ordered the cleaning of the Temple, and in that process the "book of the covenant" was discovered. Josiah was much disturbed when it was read to him because he knew how much the kings and people had forsaken the ways of God. Calling all the people together, he read "all the words of the book of covenant." After he committed himself to God, and the people agreed with him, Josiah began a thorough reform of the nation.

A STANDARD FOR GOD'S PEOPLE (Deut. 10:12-19)

The book of Deuteronomy appears to be a collection of Moses' speeches, including some retelling of Israel's history, some restating of the law of God, and some sermons about worship and right living. The passage for this lesson is part of one of those sermons. Verse 12 may remind us of Micah 6:8, but it is different. The people were urged to fear the Lord, walk in his ways, love and serve him, and keep his commandments. If their lives could be patterned after that standard, they would meet the requirement of the covenant.

Because Yahweh was superior to all gods, he did not play favorites or accept bribes. He was interested in justice for orphans and widows and strangers. Therefore, his chosen people must love the stranger because they "were strangers in the land of Egypt." Their standard was based on the character of God.

A GOD TO WORSHIP AND OBEY (Deut. 10:20 to 11:1)

Really these two passages cannot be divided easily. Both sets of verses called on the people to worship and obey the Lord, but verses 18-19 do stress right human behavior toward others. That was based on the kind of God they worshiped; they were to be like him. No matter how many gods others might worship, his people should serve Yahweh, cling to him, and make their vows in his name. Remembering all that he had done for them should confirm their devotion. They should show their love for the Lord by being faithful to the covenant and obeying all his laws always. Worship and obedience always go together in the Old Testament.

Truths to Live By

Studying God's Word from some new perspective is almost like rediscovering it.—Some of the older Israelites may have remembered "the book of the covenant," but they saw it in a new light after nearly sixty years of Baal worship through the land. Adults may recall the Bible stories they heard as children, but when they read the Bible with a teacher who understands its languages and history, it is almost like seeing it for the first time. Other adults may remember long and tiresome Bible sermons in their childhood, but a neighborhood Bible class can open it up as a personal message with practical help for everyday living. Or an individual with a present-day translation can find a Bible he never knew existed. No one can ever outgrow the Bible.

Worshiping and loving God is closely related to obeying him in behalf of others.—Some Christians seem to feel that their religion is somehow separated from everyday life. They worship and love God on Sunday; then on the other days of the week they deal with the real problems of life. Of course, the Bible does not teach this; it always puts together loving God and loving persons. That love is not just a warm feeling toward friends; it is unselfish concern for the welfare of others—as much for them as for oneself. The God of the Bible is not pleased with worship—elaborate or simple—that is not matched with compassion and generosity toward others.

God deals with each generation in its own time.—He is the God of the centuries—even of eternity. He cannot be restricted to biblical history. He spoke to his people through Moses during the deliverance from Egypt. Hundreds of years later he spoke again through the "book of the covenant" to a misguided nation and an eager young king. He still speaks to those who will hear, who want guidance and support. Today he calls for integrity in government and old-fashioned honesty in the home. He weighs nations in his balance of justice, but he also judges persons who are proud and wasteful. While no other books of the Bible are being written today, God is speaking through those who are working for righteousness, justice, and kindness.

A Verse to Remember

Therefore thou shalt love the Lord thy God, and keep his charge, and his statutes, and his judgments, and his commandments, alway.—Deuteronomy 11:1.

Daily Bible Readings

June   1—Finding the Book of Law. 2 Kings 22:3-10
June   2—Huldah Prophesies. 2 Kings 22:11-20
June   3—Renewing the Covenant. 2 Kings 23:1-3,21-22
June   4—The Wrath of the Lord. 2 Kings 23:24-30
June   5—Stone Tables for the Ark. Deut. 10:1-5
June   6—God of Love and Justice. Deut. 10:12-22
June   7—Coming of the Spirit. Acts 2:1-13

CLAIMING GOD'S PROMISE
Deuteronomy 1

A news release of September 1979, from the Lutheran World Federation carried a lengthy report from Dr. Andrew Hsiao, president of the Lutheran Seminary in Hong Kong, about his three-week trip into China to visit family members and other Christians. He talked freely to many of them and concluded that Christian faith is not dead in China. But he found many problems and obstacles. Although he feels that the time is not right for a vigorous mission campaign, he heard many believers say, "Pray for us." Many years ago Christians of various denominations responded to a promise from God when they began sharing the gospel with the Chinese people. Thousands responded with faith, but they have suffered under Communist pressures. Now after thirty years we learn that the church in China is not dead, and God's promise is still good.

The Bible Lesson

DEUTERONOMY 1:

19 And when we departed from Horeb, we went through all that great terrible wilderness, which ye saw by the way of the mountain of the Amorites, as the Lord our God commanded us; and we came to Kadesh-barnea.

20 And I said unto you, Ye are come unto the mountain of the Amorites, which the Lord our God doth give unto us.

21 Behold, the Lord thy God hath set the land before thee: go up and possess it, as the Lord God of thy fathers hath said unto thee; fear not, neither be discouraged.

22 And ye came near unto me every one of you, and said, We will send men before us, and they shall search us out the land, and bring us word again by what way we must go up, and into what cities we shall come.

23 And the saying pleased me well: and I took twelve men of you, one of a tribe:

24 And they turned and went up into the mountain, and came unto the valley of Eshcol, and searched it out.

25 And they took of the fruit of the land in their hands, and brought it down unto us, and brought us word again, and said, It is a good land which the Lord our God doth give us.

26 Notwithstanding ye would not go up, but rebelled against the commandment of the Lord your God.

. . . .

29 Then I said unto you, Dread not, neither be afraid of them.
30 The Lord your God which goeth before you, he shall fight for you, according to all that he did for you in Egypt before your eyes;
31 And in the wilderness, where thou hast seen how that the Lord thy God bare thee, as a man doth bear his son, in all the way that ye went, until ye came into this place.

The Lesson Explained

REJECTING THE SCOUTS' REPORT (1:19-26)

The setting is suggested in verse 1; Moses had led the people to a plain east of the Jordan River, and the sermons of the book were to prepare them in spirit for the invasion. Verse 19 begins a condensed review of the journey from Mount Sinai (Horeb) to the first possible entry into the Promised Land at Kadesh-barnea. Moses reminded the people that although the Lord had promised them a homeland, they must do their part by taking it. But when he had said they must fight for it with God promising a victory, they had requested that some scouts be sent to find trails and decide on the first objectives. Moses had agreed and selected one man from each tribe. When they returned, they brought samples of the fruit they saw growing and said it was "a good land which the Lord our God doth give us."

This account does not include as much as Numbers 13:26-33. While all twelve men said the land was rich, ten of them were fearful because of the walled cities and warlike people. The people accepted that majority report and refused to invade Canaan. Numbers 14 gives a graphic account of what followed.

URGING THE PEOPLE TO ACT (1:29-33)

Moses did not remind the people of all that took place then, especially how he had pled with the Lord to give them another chance. He had tried to stiffen their courage. After all, the Lord had promised to fight for them, just as he had done in the marvelous deliverance from Egypt. Of course, they had to do their part: believe and act. Moses reminded them that Yahweh had cared for them in the wilderness like a father would carry his son. He had guided them in a cloud by day and had found good camping sites and protected them by a pillar of fire at night. That was the Lord who had offered to lead them successfully into Canaan. But even in the light of all that evidence, they "did not believe the Lord." They distrusted him and chose to act by their own wisdom. In a sense, they rejected him at that point, and Moses was helpless.

JUDGING FEARFUL UNBELIEVERS (1:34-39)

But the Lord did not overlook the rejection of the people. Moses reminded them of his final judgment: that not one of the men who had mistrusted him would live to "see that good land." Only two men living at that time would be allowed to enter Canaan, even Moses himself was to be forbidden. (See Num. 20:7-12.) Caleb, one of the twelve scouts, would have an inheritance "because he hath wholly followed the Lord." Also, Joshua, another of the scouts, would go in "for he shall cause Israel to inherit it." He would lead the invasion.

Then Moses reminded the people that God had something else to say. If that generation would not trust him, he had another plan. The children who were not old enough to know right from wrong when their fathers rejected the Lord would possess the land. The very ones whom those men feared would be killed beyond Kadesh-barnea would be the soldiers who would capture the land a generation later. Thus Moses reminded the people of the reason for their forty years of wandering in the wilderness, moving from one pastureland to another, and failing to have both faith and courage to take what God had promised to them.

Truths to Live By

Many of God's promises depend on our willingness to act.—The very promise of salvation cannot be fulfilled without our responding in faith. As with the Hebrews, God's promise to give us a victorious life cannot be fulfilled if we don't get involved in living. That includes setting goals, making plans to reach them, and exerting real effort to achieve. God's promise to comfort us in sorrow assumes that we will not wallow in self-pity but make an effort to appreciate the past and look beyond the present.

Fears must be weighed against knowledge and faith.— Everyone is fearful at sometime or another. Fear is an inherent part of our human makeup, and some fears are needed and healthy: the fear of a hot stove, a naked power line, a mad dog, and a dread disease. Other fears are natural but can be overcome. I did not learn to drive a car until I was in my late thirties, and I still remember taking the road test for that driver's license. It was a stick-shift Chevy and a bit old. But I had a good instructor, and several friends had ridden with me for practice. The time finally came when they all said I was ready. They gave me faith in myself, even for parallel parking. It doesn't sound like much of a venture now, but fear could have kept me out of the driver's seat.

When one generation rejects God's promise, he just waits for the next one.—When the Hebrews refused to enter Canaan at first, they were really questioning God's honesty and power. So they were not ready to be used by him. But he had promised the patriarchs and the nation he led out of Egypt that they would have a homeland, and he would not go back on that promise. When the men who came out of Egypt showed that they really did not trust him, the Lord said he could wait for another generation. He is still looking for heroes—hardworking believers—to end war, to feed the hungry, to heal the sick, and above all, to win the lost.

A Verse to Remember

Behold, the Lord thy God hath set the land before thee: go up and possess it, as the Lord God of thy fathers hath said unto thee.—Deuteronomy 1:21.

Daily Bible Readings

June   8—Moses Speaks in the Wilderness. Deut. 1:3-9
June   9—Moses Speaks About Judges. Deut. 1:9-18
June   10—Moses Speaks About the Spies. Deut. 1:19-25
June   11—Moses Speaks of God's Care. Deut. 1:26-33
June   12—Moses Speaks of God's Denial. Deut. 1:34-40
June   13—Moses Speaks of Disobedience. Deut. 1:41-46
June   14—Do What Is Right. 2 Cor. 13:5-13

June 21, 1981
RECALLING GOD'S ACTION
Deuteronomy 3:18 to 4:14

Two teenage boys, both active church members, went to their pastor with a question that had bothered them. "Of course, it has some great stories about God and his people," they said, "but is the Old Testament so important to Christians today?" Patiently, he replied, "Well, let's see what we can find." Then followed a half hour of his listing Old Testament ideas that were projected into the New, and Old Testament principles that were fulfilled in the teachings of Jesus. Instead of reprimanding them for such a wrongheaded view, the pastor let the Bible speak for itself. Although the boys were not completely convinced at the time, they were helped to have open minds and eventually both became enthusiastic teachers of God's Word.

The Bible Lesson

DEUTERONOMY 4:

1 Now therefore hearken, O Israel, unto the statutes and unto the judgments, which I teach you, for to do them, that ye may live, and go in and possess the land which the Lord God of your fathers giveth you.

2 Ye shall not add unto the word which I command you, neither shall ye diminish ought from it, that ye may keep the commandments of the Lord your God which I command you.

. . . .

5 Behold, I have taught you statutes and judgments, even as the Lord my God commanded me, that ye should do so in the land whither ye go to possess it.

6 Keep therefore and do them; for this is your wisdom and your understanding in the sight of the nations, which shall hear all these statutes, and say, Surely this great nation is a wise and understanding people.

7 For what nation is there so great, who hath God so nigh unto them, as the Lord our God is in all things that we call upon him for?

8 And what nation is there so great, that hath statutes and judgments so righteous as all this law, which I set before you this day?

9 Only take heed to thyself, and keep thy soul diligently, lest

thou forget the things which thine eyes have seen, and lest they depart from thy heart all the days of thy life: but teach them thy sons, and thy sons' sons;

10 Specially the day that thou stoodest before the Lord thy God in Horeb, when the Lord said unto me, Gather me the people together, and I will make them hear my words, that they may learn to fear me all the days that they shall live upon the earth, and that they may teach their children.

The Lesson Explained
AFTER THE FIRST VICTORIES (3:18-22)

The narrative part of Deuteronomy began in last Sunday's lesson with Moses reminding the people of what had happened when their fathers had mistrusted God and feared to enter the Promised Land at Kadesh-barnea. After forty years as nomads they finally turned northward, east of the Dead Sea. With the Lord's help, they quickly conquered two kingdoms, and the land was divided among the tribes of Reuben, Gad, and half of Manasseh.

But Moses recalled in verse 18 that he had charged the fighting men of those tribes that their work was not over. They would leave their families in the various captured cities and join the warriors of the other tribes when they went across the Jordan River to possess the land. So, all twelve tribes would cooperate in the invasion. Although the land was given by God, they still must possess it.

TO OBEY THE WHOLE LAW (4:1-2,5-8)

In this chapter Moses moved from narrative into his first sermon on the First Commandment. And since the Ten Commandments are the heart of the covenant between Yahweh and his people, it was intended to strengthen the people's commitment to that covenant. The statutes and judgments in verse 1 probably include both the Decalogue and other requirements about worship and everyday life. The people needed to listen to Moses' instruction and interpretation and then to obey the whole law so they could live and possess the land that the Lord had promised to give them. Verse 2 underscores the wholeness of the law when it forbids adding anything or taking anything away from the law as Moses was teaching it.

In verses 5-8 Moses stressed the influence of the children of Israel on other nations as they obeyed the law of God. As they would make their home in Canaan, their neighbors would be watching to see what kind of people they were. Living by God's law would win for the Israelites a reputation of wisdom and understanding. Then in verses 7-8 Moses asked a rhetorical question that pointed up the nearness of the Lord and the righteousness of his law. Although he referred to Israel as a great nation, his real point was the superiority of the Lord.

TO REMEMBER AND TEACH (4:9-10)

But Moses hastened to add that the possible reputation of Israel in its new homeland would not come about automatically. "Be on your guard! Make certain that you do not forget, as long as you live, what you have seen with your own eyes" (TEV). Reciting the law as a child would not be enough; it must become the heart of daily life through the adult years. Never should the people think they had outgrown it.

The real test of its continuing forcefulness would be in how it was passed on from one generation to another. Fathers and mothers must see to it that their children learned the law as they were able. Even grandparents should do their part in teaching the law so that the chain of knowledge would not be broken.

Truths to Live By

Today's adults are largely responsible for preparing tomorrow's citizens.—Of course parents are the first line of that continuing activity. Their shaping of personality and character begins as soon as the baby is born—really, even before. A basic need of the infant is to feel loved and wanted. Failure at this point may contribute to a poor self-image on the part of the child that can warp personality throughout life. But other adults do their part also. Teachers can spur curiosity and show appreciation for even little achievements that will encourage a youngster to tackle bigger jobs. Scout leaders and club sponsors can help children relate to the adult world outside the home as well as learn skills that the home may not be able to teach. Church workers have a similar opportunity. If all these constructive helpers do not do their part, the rest of the world will exercise its influence for evil.

God's principles for living are applicable in every generation.—The instructions for building the tabernacle and guiding worship were intended for a certain period in Israel's life. But the Ten Commandments were the pattern for all believers in relation to God and one another. They were given to the Hebrews for all mankind. Jesus came not to set that law aside but to fulfill it. In every culture and nation these principles would bless all men, women, and children. They reveal a God who is great enough for the needs of all races and times. Of course each generation makes its own interpretations.

Teaching God's way is done by action and attitude as well as by words.—Having ready answers to religious questions is no guarantee that a person is a Christain or acts like one. So, memorizing a catechism may fool the instructor, but the real test comes in making moral and ethical decisions. This is where the unconscious example of parents, teachers, and preachers will show up. The father who is generous and fair in dealing with others is making an invaluable contribution to his growing son and/or daughter. The mother who is less concerned for a spic-and-span house than for the well-rounded growth of her children is reflecting God's pattern of values.

A Verse to Remember

Only take heed to thyself, and keep thy soul diligently, lest thou forget the things which thine eyes have seen, and lest they depart from thy heart all the days of thy life: but teach them thy sons, and thy sons' sons.—Deuteronomy 4:9.

Daily Bible Readings

June   15—Pass Through Esau's Territory. Deut. 2:1-8
June   16—A Hardened Spirit Brings Defeat. Deut. 2:24-31
June   17—God Fights for You. Deut. 3:18-22
June   18—Look But Don't Cross. Deut. 3:23-28
June   19—Keep God's Statutes and Ordinances. Deut. 4:1-8
June   20—Teach ... God's Commands. Deut. 4:9-14
June   21—Faith in the Promise. Rom. 4:13-25

EXPERIENCING GOD'S PRESENCE
Deuteronomy 4:15-49

Throughout this month we have been getting into the message of the book of Deuteronomy; so this lesson concludes what might be called a unit on "Foundations for Faith." The whole book deals with the covenant between the Lord and his people Israel. In Moses' day it proclaimed and described that covenant. In Josiah's time it was used to call for a renewal covenant (see lesson for June 7). So through these first four chapters we are examining the background of that relationship in God's promise to the patriarchs, the deliverance from Egypt, and the adventures in the wilderness. As the people were being prepared to enter the Promised Land, they would review the contents of the covenant. But before that they must sense again the unique presence of the Lord.

The Bible Lesson

DEUTERONOMY 4:

32 For ask now of the days that are past, which were before thee, since the day that God created man upon the earth, and ask from the one side of heaven unto the other, whether there hath been any such thing as this great thing is, or hath been heard like it?

33 Did ever people hear the voice of God speaking out of the midst of the fire, as thou hast heard, and live?

34 Or hath God assayed to go and take him a nation from the midst of another nation, by temptations, by signs, and by wonders, and by war, and by a mighty hand, and by a stretched out arm, and by great terrors, according to all that the Lord your God did for you in Egypt before your eyes?

35 Unto thee it was shewed, that thou mightest know that the Lord he is God; there is none else beside him.

36 Out of heaven he made thee to hear his voice, that he might instruct thee: and upon earth he shewed thee his great fire; and thou heardest his words out of the midst of the fire.

37 And because he loved thy fathers, therefore he chose their seed after them, and brought thee out in his sight with his mighty power out of Egypt;

38 To drive out nations from before thee greater and mightier than thou art, to bring thee in, to give thee their land for an inheritance, as it is this day.

39 Know therefore this day, and consider it in thine heart, that the Lord he is God in heaven above, and upon the earth beneath: there is none else.

40 Thou shalt keep therefore his statutes, and his commandments, which I command thee this day, that it may go well with thee, and that thou mayest prolong thy days upon the earth, which the Lord thy God giveth thee, for ever.

The Lesson Explained

A WARNING AGAINST IDOLATRY (4:25-31)

The use of "when" in verse 25 makes the following description sound like a prediction rather than a conditional promise of punishment *if* the people forsook their God. The verse pictures a nation that would become large and forgetful of God and his gift of their homeland. Worshiping idols and doing evil in God's sight were closely related. Loyalty to any god meant adopting his morality and ethnics. Those conditions would surely bring the Lord's judgment. They would lose their homeland and be scattered among the nations. There they could worship all kinds of wooden and stone images, thus condemning themselves to worship something less than human.

A UNIQUE REVELATION (4:32-36)

Verse 7 of this chapter had already asked: "What great nation is there that has a god so near to it as the Lord our God is to us, whenever we call upon him" (RSV). Here Moses asked a similar question. If you search early history beginning with the creation and look from one horizon to the other, has any nation ever heard the voice of God out of fire as you have heard and still lived? Of course, that was a reference to the awesome confrontation at Sinai. Often in the Old Testament fire is seen as a channel or symbol of God's presence. Being close enough to God to hear him speak may have seemed to violate his sanctity, for which death could have been the punishment.

Then came a second question in verse 34, and it should begin: "Has any god ever attempted to . . . take a nation for himself from the midst of another nation?" (RSV). Moses was calling attention to the unique action of the Lord in selecting Israel for his purpose and dramatically leading the people out of Egypt. Nothing like that had happened before. Combining the voice from heaven, the fire on the mountain, and the words that were said, the people ought to recognize that the God who called himself Yahweh (the Lord) was the one and only God. They had experienced his very presence.

GOD OF HEAVEN AND EARTH (4:37-40)

Of course it all dated back to the Lord's love of Abraham, Isaac, and Jacob; that was the reason he chose their descendants and delivered them from Egyptian bondage. Already he had given them victories over two kings, and he would lead them against others that were "greater and mightier" than Israel to provide a homeland for them. This should be enough to convince them that the Lord (Yahweh) is the God of heaven and earth; "there is no other god" (TEV). All kinds of deities were being worshiped by nations and tribes of that time: gods of storm, fire, mountains, and fertility. But the Lord was the Creator of all these and ruled the whole world.

For this reason, Moses continued, the people should obey all the Lord's laws as given through their leader. If they did, things would go well for them and their descendants, and they would "continue to live in the land that the Lord" (TEV) was giving them forever. Then in the next chapter of Deuteronomy Moses restated the Ten Commandments, the heart of the covenant.

Truths to Live By

The sense of God's presence can give comfort and moral courage.—People express this conviction when they are sitting in a family waiting room during critical surgery on a loved one. They also declare it in bereavement when talking with friends at a funeral home. Missionaries have affirmed it when enduring some natural catastrophe or cruel actions by unbelievers. Some persons in public life are strengthened by a sense of God's presence when they take a conscientious but unpopular position in the city council or legislature. A sense of his presence has enabled college students to give a thoughtful and wholesome reaction to campus gods of sex, drugs, and hopelessness. Even in the routines of everyday life the sense of his presence can sharpen the enjoyment of natural beauty and the appreciation of friendships.

Believing in God's purpose for one's life can provide zest and endurance.—This can account at least in part for the persistence of the children of Israel through centuries of stress and opposition. Although they adopted often the gods and life patterns of their neighbors, some prophet or king would remind them of God's purpose in the covenant. That sense of purpose has helped them endure recurring waves of antisemitism through the centuries of the Christian era. That sense of purpose can make a difference in any individual's life. It gave Viktor Frankl what he needed to endure a concentration camp in World War II. It gave Martin Luther King the assurance that his cause would eventually overcome. It has given many a young person the patience and enthusiasm in arduous years of preparation for a career in some kind of service to others.

The Lord of the Bible is the one true God.—The word *god* may refer to any deity, but the God of the Old Testament called himself "Yahweh," and that word is usually translated "the Lord" in the King James Version. It was Yahweh (the Lord) who gave Moses the Ten Commandments; it was the Lord God who moved the prophets to declare both judgment and possible forgiveness. It was the Lord who revealed himself finally in Jesus—in his teachings, life, and death. Christians proclaim him as the Son of God and the Lord of life. Thus, the revelation of the one true God continues through both the Old and New Testaments.

A Verse to Remember

Thou wilt show me the path of life: in thy presence is fulness of joy.—Psalm 16:11.

Daily Bible Readings

June   22—The Lord's Name Proclaimed. Ex. 34:1-10
June   23—The Glory of God's Presence. Ex. 34:29-35
June   24—God Is a Jealous God. Deut. 4:15-24
June   25—God Is a Merciful God. Deut. 4:25-31
June   26—God of Heaven and Earth. Deut. 4:32-40
June   27—Summary of Moses' Speech. Deut. 4:41-49
June   28—Return and Be Revived. Hos. 6:1-6

July 5, 1981
TEN COMMANDMENTS
Deuteronomy 5

Last fall we had a three-month study of "God's Covenant with His People," beginning in Genesis and ending in Revelation. The idea of "covenant" is very important in the Bible, picturing God making a covenant with his chosen people. He promised them a homeland and success as a nation; they promised to worship him instead of other gods and to obey his commandments. This book of Deuteronomy was written to remind the people of that covenant. The Ten Commandments were the heart of the covenant requirements. So, Moses needed to review them with the people as they were preparing to enter the Promised Land.

The Bible Lesson

DEUTERONOMY 5:

6 I am the Lord thy God, which brought thee out of the land of Egypt, from the house of bondage.

7 Thou shalt have none other gods before me.

8 Thou shalt not make thee any graven image, or any likeness of any thing that is in heaven above, or that is in the earth beneath, or that is in the waters beneath the earth.

. . . .

11 Thou shalt not take the name of the Lord thy God in vain: for the Lord will not hold him guiltless that taketh his name in vain.

12 Keep the sabbath day to sanctify it, as the Lord thy God hath commanded thee.

13 Six days shalt thou labour, and do all thy work:

14 But the seventh day is the sabbath of the Lord thy God: in it thou shalt not do any work, thou, nor thy son, nor thy daughter, nor thy manservant, nor thy maidservant, nor thine ox, nor thine ass, nor any of thy cattle, nor thy stranger that is within thy gates; that thy manservant and thy maidservant may rest as well as thou.

15 And remember that thou wast a servant in the land of Egypt, and that the Lord thy God brought thee out thence through a mighty hand and by a stretched out arm: and therefore the Lord thy God commanded thee to keep the sabbath day.

16 Honour thy father and thy mother, as the Lord thy God hath commanded thee; that thy days may be prolonged, and that it may go well with thee, in the land which the Lord thy God giveth thee.

181

17 Thou shalt not kill.

18 Neither shalt thou commit adultery.

19 Neither shalt thou steal.

20 Neither shalt thou bear false witness against thy neighbour.

21 Neither shalt thou desire thy neighbour's wife, neither shalt thou covet thy neighbour's house, his field, or his manservant, or his maidservant, his ox, or his ass, or any thing that is thy neighbour's.

The Lesson Explained

GOD'S FIRST COMMAND (5:6-8)

Moses reminded the people of the drama at Horeb (Sinai) when the Lord had made the covenant with them. Verses 3-4 are difficult to interpret but may mean that the covenant was "not only" with the fathers but also with their direct descendants. Certainly that generation needed to feel a direct involvement.

In a time and place of many gods, the Lord (Yahweh) identified himself as the God of Israel, the one who worked through Moses to deliver his people from slavery in Egypt. They must not confuse him with some Egyptian or Canaanite deity. Because he had done so much for the children of Israel, he expected their undivided loyalty. Verse 7 does not teach monotheism, that there is only one God. It assumes that other nations were worshiping other gods, but it requires Israel's complete devotion. The Lord would not tolerate their giving reverence to the sun, the storm god, or any other earthly power.

Furthermore, the children of Israel were not to make any images to represent the deities of their neighbors. Since the Lord had created the world, all the things and forces in it were far less than the Creator—therefore not worthy of worship. That included men, animals, heavenly bodies, and sea monsters. The Lord's first command was the basis for all the others.

LAWS REFLECTING GOD'S NATURE (5:11-15)

The Lord had revealed his name to Moses at the burning bush, and that name in Hebrew was Yahweh, which is translated in the King James and many other versions as "the Lord." That name must not be misused, this Third Commandment declares. For instance, if it is used in a solemn promise or oath,

Points
for
Emphasis

A Pocket Commentary
International Bible Lessons for
Christian Teaching
Uniform Series

1980-81

Sixty-fourth Annual Volume

William J. Fallis

BROADMAN PRESS
Nashville, Tennessee

4214-54
ISBN: 0-8054-1454-1
The Outlines of the International Sunday School Lessons,
Uniform Series, are copyrighted by the Committee on the
Uniform Series, and are used by permission.

Dewey Decimal Classification: 268.61
Subject headings: SUNDAY SCHOOL LESSONS—COMMENTARIES

Library of Congress Catalog Card Number: 35—3640
Printed in the United States of America

Foreword

Last year was the 400th anniversary of the Kralice Bible. Although it was originally called the "Czech Bible," it is better known by the name of the town in Moravia where it was first printed. The first volume, containing the Pentateuch, appeared in 1579, and the sixth volume presented the New Testament in 1594. This translation is still used and admired by many non-Catholics in Czechoslovakia. But a new translation from an interdenominational team of linguists was published in 1979 with the United Bible Societies furnishing the paper for the first 60,000 copies.

Also in 1979 the Cuban government approved the purchase and importing of 10,000 copies of a new translation of the Bible entitled *Dios Habla Hoy* ("God Speaks Today"). The Ecumenical Council of Cuba chose this United Bible Societies' product because its Catholic and Protestant translators used everyday Spanish.

From August, 1979, to the end of the year the United Bible Societies sponsored a Bible reading radio program that could be heard in mainland China. Called "The Most Popular Book in English," the program offered Bible readings in both English and Chinese with the most difficult words explained. Of course, it appealed to people wishing to learn English, but the UBS Asia Pacific center in Hong Kong received a number of letters from listeners requesting more information about Christianity and the Bible. Enquirers were sent copies of the Chinese New Reader Scripture Portions that are used on the program.

All around the world people are still reading the Bible or are discovering it for the first time. Its message still arouses curiosity, speaks to deep life needs, and portrays the love of God in Christ that promises freedom, forgiveness, and eternal life. Unfortunately, some people—even church people—take it for granted in countries where it is easily available. Perhaps they don't know it well enough to appreciate it, don't know more than a few of its stories and memorable verses.

The primary purpose of *Points for Emphasis* is to help people at all levels to catch the lively spirit of the Bible and to find in it guidance for life in the 1980's.

Although the Bible is far too long to be studied thoroughly in only 52 sessions, one of its basic themes can be followed for three months from Genesis to Revelation. That is what we have in "God's Covenant with His People" from September through November. Various aspects of the covenant are examined in the Old Testament, and then the November lessons show it fulfilled in Jesus Christ.

In December we begin a 21-session study of "The Gospel of Matthew" to see the life of Christ from that Gospel's point of view. Without attempting to deal with every event or teaching, this course depicts Jesus as the Messiah (Christ) who fulfilled Old Testament promises and then selected and trained his disciples for service in the Kingdom of God. Of course this study closes with the resurrection and the Great Commission.

Five lessons in May focus on the book of Hebrews, urging believers to move toward maturity in Christ.

Summer Bible study will be devoted to the book of Deuteronomy, emphasizing again the covenant theme. Although this book is seldom studied as a whole, some of it shows up in the New Testament, revealing its influence on early believers.

If the treatment of the text in *Points* seems too brief, by all means look for more help in commentaries on Bible books. After all, one interpreter may only whet your appetitite for life-changing truths. That is what the Bible is about.

WILLIAM J. FALLIS

Broadman Books to Enrich Your Study

September—November
Layman's Bible Book Commentary: Genesis; Exodus; Mark; Acts; 2 Corinthians, Galatians, Ephesians

December—February
Good News from Matthew   Tolbert
The Broadman Bible Commentary, Volume 8,
   "Matthew"   Stagg

March—May
How to Follow Jesus (Hebrews)   Hobbs
The Broadman Bible Commentary, Volume 12,
   "Hebrews"   Trentham

June—August
These Ten Words   Honeycutt
The Broadman Bible Commentary, Volume 2,
   "Matthew"   Watts

Abbreviations and Translations

Contents

THIRD QUARTER The Gospel of Matthew

Unit IV: Affirmations of the Kingdom

Unit V: Through Suffering to Victory

The Book of Hebrews

FOURTH QUARTER The Book of Deuteronomy

Unit I: Foundations for Faith

Unit II: Laws to Live By

Unit III: Covenant Renewal

the person must live up to the promise. The name must not be used as a mere instrument of fear or personal gain.

The Lord has also chosen a day—the seventh in the week—to be set apart for rest. In Exodus 20:11 the reason given for santifying the sabbath was that the Lord had rested from creation on the seventh day. Here it was based on the Lord's deliverance of the people from slavery.

LAWS FOR HUMAN RELATIONSHIPS (5:16-21)

After the Lord, a person's next duty would be to his parents. In the large family setting of that day sons and daughters continued under their authority for a long time. As they would honor their parents, they could expect a long and orderly experience in their new homeland.

Because God had created all life, his people must not take the life of others by design or accident. The word probably did not then include killing in war or in legal punishment.

Verse 18 refers to the violation of another's marriage and was addressed primarily to men. But it must be interpreted today in several ways to protect marriage in our society.

The law against stealing recognizes the right of private property. As those wilderness wanderers claimed new land and established homes, they would have no right to take anything that rightfully belonged to another.

The Ninth Commandment deals with stealing a person's reputation by giving untruthful testimony against him in court. Two lying witnesses could pervert justice and ruin a life.

The last Commandment goes further, in a sense, than the others; it forbids desiring for oneself anything that belongs to one's neighbor—wife, house, field, even his animals. It focuses on greed that could lead to murder, adultery, or stealing.

Truths to Live By

Taking the Ten Commandments seriously must begin with accepting God as the Lord of life.—That is the reason the First Commandment says: "Thou shalt have none other gods before me." The whole thing begins with a commitment of self to God. Some people say piously that the Ten Commandments are religion enough for them. They probably mean that they don't kill, steal, or ignore their parents. But they forget about the first four requirements for total allegiance to God and the revering of his name and day. The Decalogue is not just a moral code; it is a pattern for religious living. On the other hand, some people would never think of violating the First Commandment in a religious sense or of worshiping idols, but they let money, social pressures, or a desire for power influence decisions in their relationships. So, something else takes God's place for them.

Interpreted honestly, the last six commandments cover most human relationships.—Honoring one's parents can include concern for their welfare, respect for their dignity (especially in old age), and determination to protect the family name. The law against killing speaks to the drunk driver and also the careless one; it includes the manufacturer who produces shoddy and dangerous products; it also points to the drug pusher as well as the supplier. Stealing can be done in violent ways, but it can also be done in quiet and respectable ways. A collegian can steal the answers for an exam; a businessman can turn in a fraudulent tax return and thus steal from the government. A person can use credit cards to buy clothes, cars, and property of all kinds with no intention of paying the bill.

A Verse to Remember

Ye shall walk in all the ways which the Lord your God hath commanded you, that ye may live, and that it may be well with you, and that ye may prolong your days in the land which ye shall possess.—Deuteronomy 5:33.

Daily Bible Readings

June   29—Laws About God. Deut. 5:1-15
June   30—Laws About Others. Deut. 5:16-21
July   1—The Voice of God. Deut. 5:22-27
July   2—Obey God's Laws. Deut. 5:28-33
July   3—God's Perfect Law. Ps. 19:7-14
July   4—"How I Love Thy Law!" Ps. 119:97-104
July   5—Love Fulfills the Law. Rom. 13:8-10

July 12, 1981
GOD'S WORDS IN OUR HEARTS
Deuteronomy 6:1-15

"My conscience is captive to the Word of God!" They were the words of Martin Luther in April 1521, when he was being tried for heresy as the Reformation was getting started. Instead of accepting traditional pronouncements of Roman Catholic authorities, he had found both truth and freedom as he studied God's Word for himself. Not only has God's Word been a corrective for false and shallow religion, it continues to be a channel for new life when it gets into people's hearts. That was Moses' hope when he preached to the Israelites before they entered Canaan. The Bible still makes a difference—a big difference—when men and women let it into their hearts.

The Bible Lesson

DEUTERONOMY 6:

4 Hear, O Israel: The Lord our God is one Lord:

5 And thou shalt love the Lord thy God with all thine heart, and with all thy soul, and with all thy might.

6 And these words, which I command thee this day, shall be in thine heart:

7 And thou shalt teach them diligently unto thy children, and shalt talk of them when thou sittest in thine house, and when thou walkest by the way, and when thou liest down, and when thou risest up.

8 And thou shalt bind them for a sign upon thine hand, and they shall be as frontlets between thine eyes.

9 And thou shalt write them upon the posts of thy house, and on thy gates.

10 And it shall be, when the Lord thy God shall have brought thee into the land which he sware unto thy fathers, to Abraham, to Isaac, and to Jacob, to give the great and goodly cities, which thou buildest not,

11 And houses full of all good things, which thou filledst not, and wells digged, which thou diggedst not, vineyards and olive trees, which thou plantedst not: when thou shalt have eaten and be full;

12 Then beware lest thou forget the Lord, which brought thee forth out of the land of Egypt, from the house of bondage.

13 Thou shalt fear the Lord thy God, and serve him, and shalt swear by his name.

14 Ye shall not go after other gods, of the gods of the people which are round about you;

15 (For the Lord thy God is a jealous God among you) lest the anger of the Lord thy God be kindled against thee, and destroy thee from off the face of the earth.

The Lesson Explained

WAYS FOR KEEPING GOD'S WORDS (6:4-9)

In Hebrew the first word in verse 4 is *shema* with emphasis on the last syllable, and that is what Jews today call this passage from Deuteronomy. Every Jewish child memorizes it, and the synagogue service is opened with its recitation. It is a call to worship and a testimony of faith. Verse 4 affirms Israel's conviction that Yahweh (the Lord)—their God—was unique. He was and is *one* God, independent of all other so-called gods and consistent in worship and moral requirements.

Because of his uniqueness and his having chosen Israel for his purposes, the Lord had the right to command that his people love him completely. This love was more than mere affection; it included loyalty and obedience and therefore could be commanded. When a man asked Jesus about the "great commandment," he quoted this verse and added one from Leviticus (Matt. 22:34). Heart, soul, and might represent the whole personality.

On this basis, Moses could require that the laws of the covenant should be constantly in their minds. That is the meaning of "in thine heart." To achieve that goal, the people must teach the truths of God to their children, clearly and persistently. They should discuss them in all the activities of daily life; thus, they would permeate and influence all aspects of life. Whether verses 8-9 were to be taken literally we do not know. Orthodox Jews have done so through the centuries. Moses could have meant that the people should do whatever was needed to keep the truths of the Lord before their minds and make them visible as a witness to their neighbors.

WARNING THOSE WHO MIGHT FORGET (6:10-12)

In these verses we see the realism of Moses; he had learned a great deal about the multitude he had led through the wilderness. He may have remembered how easily they had become discouraged, how easily they had thought of other gods. Here he looks beyond the conquest of Canaan to the time when the people would be enjoying all the things the Lord had provided. Houses, wells, and vineyards could make people comfortable and self-satisfied. Instead of nomads, they would be land-owners and farmers. Then they must not forget that it was the Lord who delivered them from Egypt and had given them the land promised to their grandfathers. Forgetting the Lord meant more than a lapse of memory; it meant rejecting the covenant and refusing to love the Lord. They would be spurning the One who had made them into a nation and given them a purpose in the world.

GOD WOULD JUDGE AND PUNISH (6:13-15)

If the children of Israel should "forget the Lord," he would not forget them. Along with their love they should also "fear the Lord." He was not to be trifled with. Their relationship with him was serious, and he expected them to serve him and make their serious vows in his name. They must not imitate their new neighbors by worshiping or sacrificing to their tribal deities. The Lord did not accept them as gods, as rivals for the loyalty of his chosen people. If they should insult him by dallying with those artificial gods, the Lord would judge and punish them. That was the other side of his nature: love paired with justice. Accepting his gracious gifts of deliverance from Egypt and a homeland in Canaan obligated them to loyalty in worship and obedience to the Lord. Otherwise, they knew what to expect.

Truths to Live By

Religious experience and understanding must begin in the home.—That is where God told the ancient Hebrew to begin, and the present-day Jew still follows that pattern with amazing success. Many, if not most, Jewish young people seem to have an assured knowledge of their faith and a commitment to its practice that many Protestant parents would desire for their own children. Christian fathers and mothers—both—need to feel comfortable in discussing Christian truth in the home and guide their children in and toward the faith as they grow. Of course, the individual child must make his or her own decision concerning Christ, but parents should not depend upon the church to do all the teaching and guiding.

Real religion is based on personal experience rather than form and rituals.—Binding fragments of the law on their arms or writing it on doorposts did not prove that ancient Hebrews had real religion. These were to be only surface reminders. The real thing was their commitment to the Lord as the delivering God. Regular attendance at Christian worship can screen the hypocrite or refresh the true believer. Even tithing might be a cover for a selfish or self-righteous person, or it could be a generous response of a family with really limited means. The difference is the relationship of all those persons with God in Christ. Living in faith and by God's words in the heart will lead to the transformed life that helps to transform others.

Self-sufficiency is both false and dangerous.—There is no such thing as a self-made man or woman. To be sure, some persons face more obstacles in life with less help than others. But everyone has had some kind of boost, some gift, some encouragement at the right time that helped them to achieve. It would have been easy—and it was—for the Hebrews to forget all the Lord had done for them after they were "at ease in Zion." Moses told them that would be dangerous. In their conceit they would overlook their weaknesses. Such self-sufficiency would bring the Lord's destroying judgment.

Verses to Remember

The Lord our God is one Lord: And thou shalt love the Lord thy God with all thine heart, and with all thy soul, and with all thy might.—Deuteronomy 6:4-5.

Daily Bible Readings

July   6—Remember God's Commands. Deut. 6:1-9
July   7—Remember God's Goodness. Deut. 6:10-15
July   8—"Teach Me ... Thy Statutes." Ps. 119:33-40
July   9—Trust God's Word. Ps. 119:41-48
July   10—"Incline My Heart to Thy Testimonies."
              Ps. 119:57-64
July   11—"I Delight in Thy Law." Ps. 119:65-72
July   12—"The Joy of My Heart." Ps. 119:105-112

GOD CHOSE ISRAEL
Deuteronomy 6:16 to 7:26; 9:4-5

These lessons for July make up the second unit of the quarter and are entitled "Laws to Live By." In the ancient covenant pattern of the Hittites as well as the Hebrews there was always a list of specific requirements. The Hittite covenants were between the major ruler and his vassal kingdoms. Covenant in the Old Testament was between Yahweh and his chosen people. His requirements—primarily the Ten Commandments—were intended to shape twelve tribes of former slaves into one nation that worshiped one God and practiced a responsible ethic. After their mixed history in Egypt, the people had many things to learn in order to show other nations what Yahweh was like. So, the laws were not arbitrary; they were essential to God's purpose in choosing Israel.

The Bible Lesson

DEUTERONOMY 6:

20 And when thy son asketh thee in time to come, saying, What mean the testimonies, and the statutes, and the judgments, which the Lord our God hath commanded you?

21 Then shalt thou say unto thy son, We were Pharaoh's bondmen in Egypt; and the Lord brought us out of Egypt with a mighty hand:

22 And the Lord shewed signs and wonders, great and sore, upon Egypt, upon Pharaoh, and upon all his household, before our eyes:

23 And he brought us out from thence, that he might bring us in, to give us the land which he sware unto our fathers.

24 And the Lord commanded us to do all these statutes, to fear the Lord our God, for our good always, that he might preserve us alive, as it is at this day.

25 And it shall be our righteousness, if we observe to do all these commandments before the Lord our God, as he hath commanded us.

DEUTERONOMY 7:

6 For thou art an holy people unto the Lord thy God: the Lord thy God hath chosen thee to be a special people unto himself, above all people that are upon the face of the earth.

7 The Lord did not set his love upon you, nor choose you, because ye were more in number than any people; for ye were the fewest of all people:

8 But because the Lord loved you, and because he would keep the oath which he had sworn unto your fathers, hath the Lord brought you out with a mighty hand, and redeemed you out of the house of bondmen, from the hand of Pharaoh king of Egypt.

9 Know therefore that the Lord thy God, he is God, the faithful God, which keepeth covenant and mercy with them that love him and keep his commandments to a thousand generations;

10 And repayeth them that hate him to their face, to destroy them: he will not be slack to him that hateth him, he will repay him to his face.

11 Thou shalt therefore keep the commandments, and the statutes, and the judgments, which I command thee this day, to do them.

The Lesson Explained

ANSWERING THE SON'S QUESTION (6:20-25)

Verse 20 foresees a possible incident while the parents—probably the father—would be following the instruction of Moses in verse 7. The son is pictured as listening to the recitation of the Commandments; then he asks an honest question of his parent: What do they mean? This question is still raised in Jewish family worship. Between the lines it reveals a wholesome relationship between the child and his father.

SETTING THE NATION APART (7:6-8)

Chapter 7 turns to the practical matters of how Israel would interpret the First Commandment in dealing with the nations they would meet in and around Canaan. It calls for radical treatment of both the people and their religion. To avoid identifying the Lord with other gods and combining one religion with another, the Israelites were to destroy any person or thing that might lead them astray.

And the reason appears in verse 6: they had been set apart (the meaning of "holy") by the Lord for his own purpose. He had selected them to "be a special people unto himself." Lest they be proud of that action, Moses reminded them that they had not been chosen because they were great in numbers. Instead, they "were the smallest nation on earth" (TEV). So, their favored role had nothing to do with their merits. It was God's doing altogether. It came because of his love for Israel and his faithfulness to their ancestors. That love could not be earned or deserved; it was the Lord's initiative of goodwill.

REQUIRING THE PEOPLE'S LOYALTY (7:9-11)

Here Moses returned to the essence of the First Commandment. In a world of many gods the Israelites must realize that Yahweh (the Lord) is God—not one of several but the only one. He can be depended on because he is faithful. He could not be bribed or cajoled, nor would he go back on his word. "He will keep his covenant and show his constant love to a thousand generations of those who love him and obey his commands" (TEV). He was not like the idols of the neighboring nations; his support would always be available and his pattern for living would never change. At the same time, he would not hesitate to judge and punish those who turned against him. His love was paired with righteousness; it was not just a mushy emotion. Therefore, Moses called on the people who had accepted God's covenant to live by its requirements in loyalty to the loving God.

Truths to Live By

Parents should be prepared to answer their children's religious questions.—That could be a big order because youngsters can ask hard questions. But fathers and mothers may need to ask some questions on their own to find out what a child really wants to know. In a little dialogue both the question and the possible answer can be more sharply focused. Of course, most questions must be answered at the child's level of understanding. But that does not mean that answers can be untrue because the child would not comprehend a profound truth. Answers should always be true, but they need not tell everything. The young child probably will be unable to understand an abstract idea; so the answer may need to be in terms of everyday experience. But parents need a continuing study of the Bible and some opportunity to discuss their religious ideas with other adults if they are to be ready for their children's questions.

God's choice of any nation brings more responsibility than

191

privilege.—That was surely true of Israel. Moses repeatedly told them of God's grace and generosity in selecting them, but just as often he told them of God's commandments and his expectation that the nation obey them. Their obedience would be a witness for Yahweh to the surrounding nations. But especially after their exile did Israel seem to feel that their privilege was more important than their duty to be God's witness. We do not know what other nations may have been in the focus of God's will for a special purpose. Many Americans have felt that we were given remarkable resources for a special purpose. If so, have we measured up to the purpose while wasting natural resources and despising our spiritual heritage?

Proclaiming one's faith includes being faithful to God's commands.—So, the evangelistic worker must not look down on others because of their color, education, or social standing. A church that seeks the lost must also help the hungry, the sick, and the imprisoned. The pastor or Bible teacher who decries Bible ignorance of so many church people must also show the relevance of the Bible in family life, in business, and in politics. The pastor and church staff that will do anything to increase church membership must also guide their members into a loving and maturing fellowship that helps individuals stand on their own feet in the faith.

A Verse to Remember

For thou art an holy people unto the Lord thy God: the Lord thy God hath chosen thee to be a special people unto himself.—Deuteronomy 7:6.

Daily Bible Readings

July 13—A People Holy to the Lord. Deut. 6:16-25
July 14—Chosen in Love. Deut. 7:1-11
July 15—Chosen for Blessing. Deut. 7:12-16
July 16—The Lord Is in Your Midst. Deut. 7:17-26; 9:4-5
July 17—"Fear Not, I Will Help You." Isa. 41:8-13
July 18—We Are the Lord's. Isa. 44:1-5
July 19—A Prayer for God's Chosen People. Neh. 1

COMMITMENT IN WORSHIP
Deuteronomy 12:1 to 14:29

A very popular book of ten years ago on the renewal of the church had only a few paragraphs on congregational worship. While it seemed to take worship for granted, it emphasized evangelism and social action through small groups. Several times it referred to church worship as the "preaching service," which needed improving. That may be a failure of many churches; instead of worship, they have preaching services. Instead of planning a gathering of the church that focuses on God in Christ, too many churches just have preaching. Certainly, the preaching of the Word is vitally important, but the whole experience of the hour should help worshipers be aware of God—in wonder, praise, confession, prayer, and fresh commitment. Without that the church cannot do much in real evangelism or ministry.

The Bible Lesson

DEUTERONOMY 12:

5 But unto the place which the Lord your God shall choose out of all your tribes to put his name there, even unto his habitation shall ye seek, and thither thou shalt come:

6 And thither ye shall bring your burnt offerings, and your sacrifices, and your tithes, and heave offerings of your hand, and your vows, and your freewill offerings, and the firstlings of your herds and of your flocks:

7 And there ye shall eat before the Lord your God, and ye shall rejoice in all that ye put your hand unto, ye and your households, wherein the Lord thy God hath blessed thee.

8 Ye shall not do after all the things that we do here this day, every man whatsoever is right in his own eyes.

9 For ye are not as yet come to the rest and to the inheritance, which the Lord your God giveth you.

10 But when ye go over Jordan, and dwell in the land which the Lord your God giveth you to inherit, and when he giveth you rest from all your enemies round about, so that ye dwell in safety;

11 Then there shall be a place which the Lord your God shall choose to cause his name to dwell there; thither shall ye bring all that I command you; your burnt offerings, and your sacrifices, your

tithes, and the heave offering of your hand, and all your choice vows which ye vow unto the Lord:

12 And ye shall rejoice before the Lord your God, ye, and your sons, and your daughters, and your menservants, and your maidservants, and the Levite that is within your gates; forasmuch as he hath no part nor inheritance with you.

DEUTERONOMY 14:

27 And the Levite that is within thy gates; thou shalt not forsake him; for he hath no part nor inheritance with thee.

28 At the end of three years thou shalt bring forth all the tithe of thine increase the same year, and shalt lay it up within thy gates:

29 And the Levite, (because he hath no part nor inheritance with thee,) and the stranger, and the fatherless, and the widow, which are within thy gates, shall come, and shall eat and be satisfied; that the Lord thy God may bless thee, in all the work of thine hand which thou doest.

The Lesson Explained

ONE PLACE TO WORSHIP ONE GOD (12:2-7)

Chapters 12—26 constitute the legal section of the book of Deuteronomy, but the laws are presented in a sermonic style. After all, the purpose of the book was to interpret the covenant to the people generally; so it is preaching that teaches.

This passage begins with instructions on how to deal with the religions of the Canaanites. They were to be given no quarter; every shrine, altar, and idol must be destroyed. Even their names must be obliterated.

Of course, the people would not act that way toward the Lord (v. 4). When they were all settled, he would select a place that would bear his name and represent his presence. To that place they would bring their various offerings and sacrifices, and they would banquet together in his presence to celebrate his goodness and achievements. Having a central place for worship should foster unity among the people and nourish them in the true faith.

A PLACE OF SACRIFICE AND JOY (12:8-12)

This passage is largely a repetition of the previous verses. Moses said in verse 8, however, that the people would not do in their homeland what they had been accustomed to doing while on their way. Instead of setting up here and there a holy place to the Lord, they would have then one place chosen by the Lord for their worship. That would be after they had conquered the land and received their inheritance. When they could live there in safety, they would all gather at one place before the Lord.

The Lord would not be housed in the tabernacle (or much later, the Temple), but "his name" would "dwell there." Using his name in many worship practices there would be like recognizing his presence in the place. Five kinds of these practices are mentioned in verse 11, they are described fully in Exodus, Leviticus, and Numbers. They dealt with forgiveness, commitment, and restitution. Verse 12 can be paired with verse 7, specifying that all household members should take part in a happy festal meal in the Lord's presence. Remembering his holiness, their worship should be solemn; but they must also rejoice in his goodness.

A PLAN FOR THOSE IN NEED (14:27-29)

Verse 12 in the previous passage commanded that any Levites who might be in the towns should be included in the feast. Because the tribe of Levi had been given by the Lord responsibility for the care, maintenance, and protection of the sanctuary, it received no section of the land as an inheritance. Instead, the various tribes allowed the Levites residence in forty-eight cities throughout the country. Having no land to provide their living, the Levites looked to the other tribes for food. That is the background for verse 27. Every three years the other people were to use one tenth of their income (produce or money) to supply the needs of the Levites. Also included in that arrangement were others who were disadvantaged: orphans, strangers, and widows. So, the tithe that was dedicated to the Lord as an act of worship was channeled to meet human need.

Truths to Live By

Christian public worship is a celebration of God's greatness and love.—Often it does not impress people that way; some worship services are too cold and formal to be a celebration. On the other hand, some are so noisy and person-centered that God seems to have been overlooked. A service need not appear to be a pep rally to prove it is a celebration. God's greatness and love can be celebrated in Bible reading, congregational singing, fervent prayer, and effective preaching. The really important thing about worship is its purpose and direction. All that is done in the service—prayer, singing, silence, giving, preaching—must be offered to God, the Father of our Lord Jesus Christ.

All members of the church need to worship together regularly.—The years of togetherness in the family usually forge strong relationships between parents and children and between brothers and sisters. Somewhat the same thing is true in the church. In worship, its members share their praise and needs with the Father. Together they are confronted by his truth and offer their gifts and lives in Christ's service. Personal worship brings its own distinctive blessings, but worshiping with other Christians stretches horizons and deepens appreciations as no other experience can do. And all members need it. Those who say they don't may be reacting to poorly planned worship services, or they may be snobbish or afraid to risk hearing God's call in a real worship experience.

Worshiping God includes giving money to help others.— Our lesson makes that quite clear. If it was true for the Jews of old, certainly it is true for the Christian who promises his *all* for Christ. The church itself—meaning all the members—deserves the money to pay its bills and carry on its cooperative work. Some of that work will be caring for disadvantaged people as well as sharing the gospel at home and abroad.

A Verse to Remember

Ye shall rejoice in all that ye put your hand unto, ye and your households, wherein the Lord thy God hath blessed thee.—Deuteronomy 12:7.

Daily Bible Readings

July 20—A Place to Worship God. Deut. 12:1-14
July 21—Do Not Go After Other Gods. Deut. 13:1-5
July 22—Give a Tithe to God. Deut. 14:22-29
July 23—"Worship and Bow Down." Ps. 95:1-7
July 24—"Declare His Glory." Ps. 96
July 25—"The Lord Reigns." Ps. 99
July 26—True Worship. Amos 5:18-24

GOD DESIRES JUSTICE
Deuteronomy 16:18 to 17:20; 24:1-22

Since we have no record of general moral and ethical conditions among the children of Israel while in Egypt, we must read between the lines of later writings. If there had been no problems among the people, the law would not have said as much as it did about right living. But as God brought them out of bondage, he provided a standard for them to live by as they carried his name among unbelievers. So, the Ten Commandments deal with basics: killing, lying, stealing, coveting, and violating a marriage. On that foundation other principles and precepts were given to guide the people as they grew into nationhood. Because the Lord is just, he required his people to be just—and still does.

The Bible Lesson

DEUTERONOMY 16:

18 Judges and officers shalt thou make thee in all thy gates, which the Lord thy God giveth thee, throughout thy tribes: and they shall judge the people with just judgment.

19 Thou shalt not wrest judgment; thou shalt not respect persons, neither take a gift: for a gift doth blind the eyes of the wise, and pervert the words of the righteous.

20 That which is altogether just shalt thou follow, that thou mayest live, and inherit the land which the Lord thy God giveth thee.

DEUTERONOMY 24:

10 When thou dost lend thy brother any thing, thou shalt not go into his house to fetch his pledge.

11 Thou shalt stand abroad, and the man to whom thou dost lend shall bring out the pledge abroad unto thee.

12 And if the man be poor, thou shalt not sleep with his pledge:

13 In any case thou shalt deliver him the pledge again when the sun goeth down, that he may sleep in his own raiment, and bless thee: and it shall be righteousness unto thee before the Lord thy God.

14 Thou shalt not oppress an hired servant that is poor and needy, whether he be of thy brethren, or of thy strangers that are in thy land within thy gates:

15 At his day thou shalt give him his hire, neither shall the sun go

197

down upon it; for he is poor, and setteth his heart upon it: lest he cry against thee unto the Lord, and it be sin unto thee.

. . . .

17 Thou shalt not pervert the judgment of the stranger, nor of the fatherless; nor take a widow's raiment to pledge.

18 But thou shalt remember that thou wast a bondman in Egypt, and the Lord thy God redeemed thee thence: therefore I command thee to do this thing.

19 When thou cuttest down thine harvest in thy field, and hast forgot a sheaf in the field, thou shalt not go again to fetch it: it shall be for the stranger, for the fatherless, and for the widow: that the Lord thy God may bless thee in all the work of thine hands.

The Lesson Explained

IMPARTIAL JUDGES (16:18-20)

The judges mentioned here were probably the older men who had won the confidence of the people for knowing the law and wisely interpreting it. They were different from those described in the book of Judges, most of whom were leaders because of their special gifts for crucial times in Israel's history. Each town probably had several older men who sat in the open place (square or market) before the gate to hear complaints and make decisions. They were expected to be fair in listening to both sides and give a verdict reflecting an impartial application of the law. They would not twist or pervert the law to favor a prominent citizen over against a small farmer. Nor would they do the opposite just to be nice to the disadvantaged.

CONSIDERATE LENDERS (24:10-15)

Verses 10-13 picture a simple transaction between a person who needed a tool or some money on a short-term loan and another who could help him. The lender must not invade the man's home to get collateral—perhaps his cloak. He must wait outside until the borrower brought the "pledge." And if the borrower be a poor man, the lender should not keep his cloak overnight because he would have no cover against the cool night. Requiring collateral was not forbidden, but lenders in their fortunate position should not take advantage of those who had to borrow.

In the same way, an employer—farmer, builder, or shopkeeper—should not take advantage of his employee. He probably had to "hire out" because his crop failed or he had lost

198

his land. So he worked by the day to feed his family that night. Whether he was another Israelite or an alien, he should be paid his wage at the end of the day because he was depending on it as his livelihood. Not being fair to a day laborer would be counted by God as a sin.

HONEST AND KIND CITIZENS (24:17-22)

Previously, Moses had described justice as mostly in relationships of fellow Israelites. In these verses he focused on the disadvantaged people. Evidently at that time each husband and father would be given some land as his part of his tribe's inheritance. With it he would provide food and clothing for his family. Thus, if he died, his widow and orphans would have no—or at least, limited—means of support. Of course, a non-Israelite, having no land to claim, would have to "hire out" for his living.

How easy it would have been to take advantage of these people! But Moses declared: "You shall not pervert the justice due" them (RSV), After all, the Israelites had been slaves once and should sympathize with persons in real trouble. They should practice the kind of mercy and kindness the Lord had shown in delivering them from slavery. One way was in leaving some of their harvest in the fields for the widows, orphans, and strangers. If the farmer had forgotten a sheaf of grain, he should not go back for it. After he gathered olives and grapes, he should not go back to get the very last of the fruit that might have been overlooked.

Truths to Live By

Americans have the privilege and responsibility of choosing honest civil leaders.—Very few nations in the world's history have had that privilege. Most of them have endured rulers who won their positions by cruel force; many only inherited their thrones. Sheriffs, judges, and regional governors got their jobs by favoritism, bribery, or chance. Do we realize how privileged we are? We can vote for persons we think can do the right job, and if they prove untrustworthy, we can vote them out of office. If we really want good government, that privilege is a responsibility. Even if judges are not elected in some states, they can be recalled by serious, popular demand.

All persons need to practice justice and thoughtfulness

toward others.—Justice is not a responsibility of judges only. Do you supervise a group at the office or shop? Do you perform some volunteer service for a community agency? In either role you are probably dealing with persons of varying culture and ability. Is it hard not to play favorites with persons of your own race, religion, or social level? Or again, do you really know enough about the public schools in your community to criticize the teachers and complain against equal education for all children? If your church is helping a family that just doesn't seem able to "get on its feet," have you tried to understand the basic problem before labeling the father as a ne'er-do-well? You need not know a lot about the law to practice real justice.

Respect and concern for others is basic to Christian love.—Some people talk about Christian love as though it were some high-flown emotion that only pious persons could understand. But basically it begins with accepting other people as they are and respecting them as persons. That is where good race relations must begin: black with white as well as white with black. That is the first thing that everybody wants: to be respected as a person. A person is more than a statistic, a client, a thing. After seeing others as persons—persons for whom Christ died—even average Christians can have concern and begin to practice Christian love.

A Verse to Remember

That which is altogether just shalt thou follow, that thou mayest live, and inherit the land which the Lord thy God giveth thee.—Deuteronomy 16:20.

Daily Bible Readings

July   27—Provisions for Justice. Deut. 16:18 to 17:1
July   28—Bases for Determining Justice. Deut. 17:2-13
July   29—Kings Must Be Just. Deut. 17:14-20
July   30—Justice Tempered with Mercy. Deut. 24:6-7,10-22
July   31—Praise for God's Justice and Righteousness.
            Ps. 89:14-18
Aug.   1—Justice and the Messianic King. Isa. 9:2-7
Aug.   2—The Rule of the Messiah. Isa. 11:1-9

August 9, 1981
THE BASIS OF COVENANT RENEWAL
Deuteronomy 29:1-15

On the Fourth of July or at some other time when you have
had opportunity to repeat the pledge of allegiance to the flag,
have you felt a sort of reaffirmation of your commitment to
your country? Or maybe at a wedding when you've heard
another couple recite their vows, you have remembered the
day you were married and promised to be and do all those
things. A little like covenant renewal? No, because it takes two
persons to make a covenant—at least two—and two to renew it.
You cannot renew a covenant by yourself. When the Israelites
went through covenant renewal, they were not alone. They
were confronting the Lord and responding to him. That was
dramatically true when this book of Deuteronomy was used by
Josiah to call his kingdom back to Yahweh, his worship and his
way.

The Bible Lesson

DEUTERONOMY 29:

2 And Moses called unto all Israel, and said unto them, Ye have
seen all that the Lord did before your eyes in the land of Egypt unto
Pharaoh, and unto all his servants, and unto all his land;

3 The great temptations which thine eyes have seen, the signs,
and those great miracles:

4 Yet the Lord hath not given you a heart to perceive, and eyes
to see, and ears to hear, unto this day.

5 And I have led you forty years in the wilderness: your clothes
are not waxen old upon you, and thy shoe is not waxen old upon thy
foot.

6 Ye have not eaten bread, neither have ye drunk wine or strong
drink: that ye might know that I am the Lord your God.

7 And when ye came unto this place, Sihon the king of
Heshbon, and Og the king of Bashan, came out against us unto
battle, and we smote them:

8 And we took their land, and gave it for an inheritance unto the
Reubenites, and to the Gadites, and to the half tribe of Manasseh.

9 Keep therefore the words of this covenant, and do them, that
ye may prosper in all that ye do.

10 Ye stand this day all of you before the Lord your God; your

captains of your tribes, your elders, and your officers, with all the men of Israel,

11 Your little ones, your wives, and thy stranger that is in thy camp, from the hewer of thy wood unto the drawer of thy water:

12 That thou shouldest enter into covenant with the Lord thy God, and into his oath, which the Lord thy God maketh with thee this day:

13 That he may establish thee to day for a people unto himself, and that he may be unto thee a God, as he hath said unto thee, and as he hath sworn unto thy fathers, to Abraham, to Isaac, and to Jacob.

14 Neither with you only do I make this covenant and this oath;

15 But with him that standeth here with us this day before the Lord our God, and also with him that is not here with us this day.

The Lesson Explained

UNDERSTANDING PAST EVENTS (29:2-15)

The book of Deuteronomy consists of three collections of speeches or sermons by Moses, and the third one begins with these verses. Verse 1 is a sort of editorial sentence to show the reader where the new section begins. It refers to the covenant the Lord had made with the people "in Horeb" (Sinai) a generation earlier. Now that covenant was being renewed in Moab before the people started their conquest of Canaan.

Moses spoke to the people as though they had been present at the dramatic deliverance from Egypt, and of course those who were children and young people then had seen it. In verse 3 the word translated "temptations" should be "trials." Although they had seen or had heard vivid accounts from their elders, they had not understood what all those things meant. Those miracles were more than just a show of the Lord's power. Now they would learn in the covenant that he was the Lord their God. Furthermore, he had cared for them along the wilderness way with enough clothing and food. Those gifts too should convince them that their protecting God was the Lord.

REMEMBERING FIRST VICTORIES (29:7-9)

Moses said little here about those first victories because he had already told the full story in 2:24 to 3:11. As Israel had approached Canaan from the south, Moses had requested permission to pass through Heshbon peacefully, but Sihon the king refused. When he led his army against Israel, the Lord promised victory to his people. In much the same way, Israel dealt with Og of Bashan farther north. In both cases the Lord promised victory, and the people first realized what "holy war" meant: utterly destroying the enemy and appropriating all their property.

Then Moses told the people what they should have learned from those first victories. So long as they carefully obeyed the covenant, they would "prosper" in all that they did.

COVENANTING ACROSS THE YEARS (29:10-15)

This passage describes the actual making of the covenant. Moses surveyed the people, possibly ranked before him in the order of their social standing. "The men of Israel" were the responsible ones—before the Lord and in battle. But wives, children, and the aliens who did the menial tasks were also witnesses. As they stood that day before the Lord, they were ready to respond to the covenant that he offered to them. It had two purposes: first, that they might be confirmed as the nation he had chosen for his special intention, and second, that the Lord might be acknowledged as their God.

This covenant was based on the promises made to Abraham, Isaac, and Jacob centuries before. As it looked backward, the covenant also looked forward. It included more than just those who were present at the time. It was a covenant made with the nation of Israel, and it extended in blessing and responsibility to coming generations of that nation.

Truths to Live By

A real relationship with God always leads to growth in understanding.—That does not mean that a devout Christian is bound to understand all mysteries. What kind of God would he be if mere human beings could comprehend all he knows? No, we won't ever know it all. But that does not keep us from growing in understanding from wherever we are to another level. As the source of all truth, God wants his children to have a balanced view of truth, depending on their needs and abilities. "Understanding" is more than factual knowledge; it includes the appreciation of persons and the ability to grasp relationships of facts and persons. Growth in understanding requires giving up some ideas and making room for new ones, and God is at work in that process.

A believer can be strengthened as he or she identifies with the believing community.—The Roman Catholic Church has emphasized that salvation comes only through the Church. Other Christians have insisted that salvation is a relationship between God in Christ and the individual. Some who hold the latter view have played down the church so much that some believers don't see its importance. But Jesus founded the church and has made it serve and grow through his Spirit. The individual believer needs its supporting fellowship in time of trouble and as he gives up worldly ways for the pattern of Christ. He or she needs the church also to provide worship opportunities and channels for service and witness. As part of the family of God, the local church offers shelter, companionship, and challenge. Being able to love one another in the church proves that we are disciples of Christ.

God will respond when believers renew their covenant with him.—Along with the Bible's picture of his righteousness is also the story of the father of the prodigal son. That does not mean that God ignores their past whenever his children get into trouble. Our asking to renew the covenant must include true repentance—a radical about face in ways of thinking and living. On that basis, God is always ready to forgive. If we accept his forgiveness and are able to forgive ourselves, our covenant with the Father is renewed.

A Verse to Remember

The eternal God is thy refuge, and underneath are the everlasting arms.—Deuteronomy 33:27.

Daily Bible Readings

Aug. 3—The Covenant with Abraham. Gen. 17:1-8
Aug. 4—Covenants and Holiness. Ex. 19:1-6
Aug. 5—Conditions of Covenants. Ex. 19:7-14
Aug. 6—The Ten Commandments. Ex. 20:1-8,12-17
Aug. 7—The Covenant at Shechem. Josh. 24:1-3,14-15
Aug. 8—The Covenant at Moab. Deut. 29:1-15
Aug. 9—The New Covenant. Jer. 31:31-37

REPENTANCE AND RESTORATION
Deuteronomy 29:16-28; 30:1-10

When the famous psychiatrist, Karl Menninger, reflected on all the aggression, anxiety, and self-centeredness he had met in his patients and in himself, he asked a question and made it the title of his book published in 1973: *What Ever Became of Sin?* Preachers, doctors, lawyers, and almost everybody had called sin something else to avoid assigning blame. But Dr. Menninger argued that people must be led to accept "personal responsibility for all human acts, good and bad." Then, and only then, could they recognize the need and possibility of forgiveness, the kind that acts to heal and help.

The Bible Lesson

DEUTERONOMY 30:

1 And it shall come to pass, when all these things are come upon thee, the blessing and the curse, which I have set before thee, and thou shalt call them to mind among all the nations, whither the Lord thy God hath driven thee,

2 And shalt return unto the Lord thy God, and shalt obey his voice according to all that I command thee this day, thou and thy children, with all thine heart, and with all thy soul;

3 That then the Lord thy God will turn thy captivity, and have compassion upon thee, and will return and gather thee from all the nations, whither the Lord thy God hath scattered thee.

4 And if any of thine be driven out unto the outmost parts of heaven, from thence will the Lord thy God gather thee, and from thence will he fetch thee:

5 And the Lord thy God will bring thee into the land which thy fathers possessed, and thou shalt possess it; and he will do thee good, and multiply thee above thy fathers.

6 And the Lord thy God will circumcise thine heart, and the heart of thy seed, to love the Lord thy God with all thine heart, and with all thy soul, that thou mayest live.

7 And the Lord thy God will put all these curses upon thine enemies, and on them that hate thee, which persecuted thee.

8 And thou shalt return and obey the voice of the Lord, and do all his commandments which I command thee this day.

9 And the Lord thy God will make thee plenteous in every work of thine hand, in the fruit of thy body, and in the fruit of thy cattle,

and in the fruit of thy land, for good: for the Lord will again rejoice over thee for good, as he rejoiced over thy fathers:

10 If thou shalt hearken unto the voice of the Lord thy God, to keep his commandments and his statutes which are written in this book of the law, and if thou turn unto the Lord thy God with all thine heart, and with all thy soul.

The Lesson Explained

THE SCANDAL OF DISOBEDIENCE (29:21-28)

Both passages for this lesson seem to reflect ideas much later than the time of Moses, even in the time of the Exile. Some interpreters say that reveals Moses' greatness as a prophet. Others say that the writer of Deuteronomy used Mosaic material but lived centuries later, either fearing an impending captivity or actually enduring the Exile. The message is the same either way. God would both punish and forgive.

Verse 18 points to the man, woman, family, or tribe that might forsake the Lord for other gods and a pagan way of living. Then verses 21-23 describe the desolation promised in the covenant curses that would come upon that person or group. The uninhabited land would suffer from plagues, sicknesses, burning, and barrenness. Neighboring nations would ask why the Lord did all that to his own people. Moses suggested what the answer would be: "They violated their covenant with the Lord and went after other gods. Because of his righteousness, he had to bring judgment on them."

THE EFFECT OF REPENTANCE (30:1-5)

But Moses looked beyond the beginning of the ordeal. Some day the people would come to the time when they could remember the blessing as well as the curse in the covenant. Their bitterness would be matched with their recollection of the Lord's goodness. And then they would turn again to him, willing to "obey his voice" as it had first offered the covenant. When they made a new commitment to him with all their heart and soul, the Lord would show his mercy by ending their captivity. However far they may have been scattered, the Lord would bring them back. He did the scattering in the first place; he could find and restore them, even those in the farthest reaches of the horizon. Once again, their goal would be "the land which thy fathers possessed." This promise probably meant much more to the people of the Exile than to those preparing to enter Canaan for the first time. The Lord still planned to do them good—on the basis of their repentance.

THE BENEFITS OF NEW LOYALTY (30:6-10)

In Genesis 17:10 when God was making a covenant with Abraham, he declared that circumcision would be the physical token of that covenant. But when the Israelites violated their covenant, they showed that the fleshly reminder had not been adequate. So here in verse 6 the Lord would drastically change their hearts so that they would love him wholeheartedly. The curses of the covenant would be redirected from them to their enemies, a just repayment for their hatred and persecution.

Freed of the effect of the covenant curses, Israel would, with its changed heart, obey all the Lord's commandments. And that would open the way for his blessings to flow again. The people would prosper in every way: large families, increased flocks and herds, and good crops. Moses said that the Lord "will be as glad to make you prosperous as he was to make your ancestors prosperous" (TEV). But immediately he reminded them in verse 10 of the condition of that promise. The original covenant was still in effect; the Lord had promised much, but he expected much as well. Their turning to the Lord must be completely sincere, and they must agree to keep all his commandments.

Truths to Live By

Remorse is a state of mind; repentance is a pattern for action.—The child who gets caught doing something forbidden is embarrassed and resentful. Nobody likes to get caught. But even if he does not get caught, he may be "caught" by conscience and have the same feelings. But it does not mean that he would not do the same thing again. Remorse is unpleasant inside, but it does not necessarily change anything. That is as true of adults as it is of children—maybe more so. But repentance is something else. It means to turn around and go in the opposite direction. It includes remorse but goes further. Repentance admits the wrong, seeks forgiveness, and resolves never to make that mistake again. That is the reason Dr. Menninger believes that accepting personal responsibility is at least part of the key to our moral and ethical dilemma.

Rejecting God means rejecting the highest and best that has been revealed to humankind.—Of course, for people who think that the God of the Bible is only one of several deities, rejecting him is not all that serious. But if we accept him as Creator and Sustainer of the universe and the Father of our Lord Jesus Christ, then his law *is* the last word and his standard of values does meet all needs. So, the Israelites were not just snubbing a "god" who had picked them as his favorite nation. They were scorning complete righteousness and perfect love. That is still going on among people who have heard the message of the Bible and even some who once said they accepted it. Many may be handicapped by the distorted view of God that some believers project. But the God and Father of Jesus Christ comes through clearly enough, especially in the New Testament.

God's forgiveness includes the requirement of future obedience.—That is the way he put it to the Israelites; he would not let them mock him with pious pretense. Those who follow him in the name of Christ are also committed by profession of faith and in the symbol of baptism to continuing loyalty and obedience. A real believer would not do any less although he or she might be occasionally selfish and even rebellious. But the direction or thrust of life for them must continue "unto the measure of the stature of the fulness of Christ" (Eph. 4:13).

A Verse to Remember

Obey the voice of the Lord, and do all his commandments which I command thee this day.—Deuteronomy 30:8.

Daily Bible Readings

Aug. 10—The Results of Breaking Covenants. Deut. 29:16-28
Aug. 11—Restoration After Repentance. Deut. 30:1-10
Aug. 12—Repentance in Josiah's Time. 2 Kings 23:1-5
Aug. 13—"Return to the LORD." Joel 2:10-14
Aug. 14—"Pardon My Guilt." Ps. 25:8-21
Aug. 15—"Why Will You Die?" Ezek. 33:10-16
Aug. 16—Welcome for the Prodigal. Luke 15:11-24

August 23, 1981
CHOICE AND ITS CONSEQUENCES
Deuteronomy 30:11-20

Because of his confessed involvement in the Watergate scandal as the so-called "hatchet man," Charles W. Colson had a hard time convincing even some of his friends that he had been "born again." But in his book with that title he reveals himself before and after that experience. He tells of the choices he had made that finally helped bring him into the White House staff. In five years they also led him into the morass that seemed to end with President Nixon's resignation. Those choices were centered in pride, ambition, and hero-worship. But he made another choice in 1974 that changed the direction of his life even though he had to serve a prison sentence. That decision was to offer himself to Christ for forgiveness and a new life—one dedicated to helping people in prison get ready for living creatively outside. Choices do have consequences.

The Bible Lesson

DEUTERONOMY 30:

11 For this commandment which I command thee this day, it is not hidden from thee, neither is it far off.

12 It is not in heaven, that thou shouldest say, Who shall go up for us to heaven, and bring it unto us, that we may hear it, and do it?

13 Neither is it beyond the sea, that thou shouldest say, Who shall go over the sea for us, and bring it unto us, that we may hear it, and do it?

14 But the word is very nigh unto thee, in thy mouth, and in thy heart, that thou mayest do it.

15 See, I have set before thee this day life and good, and death and evil;

16 In that I command thee this day to love the Lord thy God, to walk in his ways, and to keep his commandments and his statutes and his judgments, that thou mayest live and multiply: and the Lord thy God shall bless thee in the land whither thou goest to possess it.

17 But if thine heart turn away, so that thou wilt not hear, but shalt be drawn away, and worship other gods, and serve them;

18 I denounce unto you this day, that ye shall surely perish, and that ye shall not prolong your days upon the land, whither thou passest over Jordan to go to possess it.

209

19 I call heaven and earth to record this day against you, that I have set before you life and death, blessing and cursing: therefore choose life, that both thou and thy seed may live:

20 That thou mayest love the Lord thy God, and that thou mayest obey his voice, and that thou mayest cleave unto him: for he is thy life, and the length of thy days: that thou mayest dwell in the land which the Lord sware unto thy fathers, to Abraham, to Isaac, and to Jacob, to give them.

The Lesson Explained

NEARER THAN THEY WOULD ADMIT (30:11-14)

Of course "this commandment" is the same one that has been emphasized through most of Deuteronomy—the First Commandment. After all, it is the keystone of the whole arch. Worshiping only the Lord would make the people deaf to heathen religions, and would establish the highest standard of personal values.

Moses told the people that this law or teaching was not away over their heads, faraway in the sky. It was not so high that it was removed from human experience, something that only God could contemplate. They need not ask for some super-person to bring it down to their level. Nor was it a pattern of living known by some distant nation requiring a foreign emissary to come and interpret it. The people should not play "dumb" or act humbly ignorant. The word—the first of the "ten words" as the Decalogue was called—was very near them. They had memorized and could recite it. Many had made a heart commitment to it, and all at one time had promised to live by it. So, they had no reason not to do it.

SIMPLE ENOUGH IN ITS ESSENCE (30:15-18)

In the remaining verses of the lesson Moses reviewed in summary fashion the contrasting factors in the ancient covenant: blessing and curse. If his people would love and obey the Lord their God, he would enrich and give them long life in the homeland he had promised. But if they should ever spurn him and his ways for "an affair" with the gods who are only idols, they would perish and lose their inheritance.

So Moses said that the issue was simple: either "life and good" or "death and evil." And the response was not just a matter of commitment, a promise; it was lifetime obedience that the Lord was seeking. A nation of slaves he had led out of Egypt, a people who often scorned their earthly leader, Moses. A loose confederation of nomadic tribes who needed to learn cooperation were being challenged to stand together as God's chosen and responsible people. They were not confronted by an abstract philosophical system or involved formulas of occultism. Moses made the choice as clear as possible: life or death; good or evil.

BLESSING THEM AND THEIRS (30:19-20)

The first part of verse 19 repeats the alternatives in the decision that Moses called on the people to make. Then he revealed that he was not neutral. After all, they were his people, and the Lord was his God. So, he urged them to "choose life." Of course he was not talking about mere physical existence, the challenge that lay before them of taking over the Promised Land and making it a home for themselves. Life for him meant loving the Lord and obeying his voice; for "he is thy life, and the length of thy days." Paul said something like that many years later about himself and Christ. Israel was intended to be a demonstration of the Lord's purposes before the other peoples of the world. Living in loyalty to him would be a blessing for themselves and for their children.

Truths to Live By

God's pattern for human living is understandable and practical.—"Thou shalt not kill." If everyone lived by this Commandment, no one need fear drunk drivers, drug pushers, ambitious and unreasonable bosses, or even war. "Do for others what you want them to do for you" (Matt. 7:12, TEV). You want to be accepted as a person with certain rights; so treat all others that same way. That would take care of dishonesty and race prejudice, and a raft of other problems. "If any man would come after me, let him deny himself and take up his cross and follow me" (Mark 8:34, RSV).

The decision to follow Christ influences the Christian's daily choices.—When you accepted him as Lord and Savior, you may have been thinking more about salvation from hell and to everlasting life. But accepting him as Lord included accepting his ideas of right and wrong, his methods of dealing with others, and his view of God as Father. So the next day after you became a Christian, you probably had to decide: how to deal with someone of another race, whether to give more than your quarter-a-Sunday for the Lord's work, when you would give up smoking for the sake of your family, how you would show concern for world peace when the "club" swung into its customary round of platitudes. Some have argued that the decision for Christ even affected their choice of ties. Far more important would be the choice of friends, candidates, and heroes.

The choices made by adults often influence those made by children and youth.—Of course that is true in the family circle, even more than many parents like to admit. It is true that some things are inherited, and a parental pair cannot prevent their showing up in their offspring. But many more things are learned—learned when Father and Mother don't know they are doing the teaching. Together they can teach unconsciously that marriage is not worth the effort—little affection, constant nagging, petty quarrels, wasteful living. Together they can teach that sharing the home with friends brings happiness, that trusting one another helps everybody be dependable, that talking freely about one's faith makes Christian living a satisfying venture in togetherness. In every case, some choices influence other choices.

A Verse to Remember

I have set before you life and death, blessing and cursing: therefore choose life.—Deuteronomy 30:19.

Daily Bible Readings

Aug. 17—The Religious Union of Twelve. Josh. 24:1-7
Aug. 18—Israel Possesses the Promised Land. Josh. 24:8-13
Aug. 19—Choose Life or Death. Josh. 24:14-18
Aug. 20—Witness Your Own Choice. Josh. 24:20-25
Aug. 21—Here I Raise My Ebenezer. Josh. 24:25-31
Aug. 22—Choose to Delight in the Law. Ps. 1
Aug. 23—Pray for an Understanding Mind. 1 Kings 3:5-14

When we began our three-month study of Deuteronomy, we noted its use by King Josiah in 621 B.C. in calling his kingdom of Judah back to a renewal of their covenant with Yahweh, the Lord. We noted also that it is organized primarily as three sermons or addresses of Moses while the children of Israel were encamped east of the Jordan River before being mobilized for their invasion of Canaan. Those addresses appear in 1:6 to 4:43; 4:44 to 28:68; and 29:1 to 30:20. So this lesson comes from the closing section of miscellaneous writings, some by Moses and some by another writer or editor. Since it is primarily a book of teaching about the law intended for the rank and file of the people, we can understand its frequent use in the New Testament to interpret God's word and will to the people of that day.

The Bible Lesson

DEUTERONOMY 30:

1 Give ear, O ye heavens, and I will speak; and hear, O earth, the words of my mouth.

2 My doctrine shall drop as the rain, my speech shall distil as the dew, as the small rain upon the tender herb, and as the showers upon the grass:

3 Because I will publish the name of the Lord: ascribe ye greatness unto our God.

4 He is the Rock, his work is perfect: for all his ways are judgment: A God of truth and without iniquity, just and right is he.

5 They have corrupted themselves, their spot is not the spot of his children: they are a perverse and crooked generation.

6 Do ye thus requite the Lord, O foolish people and unwise? is not he thy father that hath bought thee? hath he not made thee, and established thee?

7 Remember the days of old, consider the years of many generations: ask thy father, and ye will shew thee; thy elders, and they will tell thee.

8 When the Most High divided to the nations their inheritance, when he separated the sons of Adam, he set the bounds of the people according to the number of the children of Israel.

9 For the Lord's portion is his people; Jacob is the lot of his inheritance.

The Lesson Explained

PROCLAIMING GOD'S GREATNESS (32:1-3)

Chapter 31 tells the background of this "song." When Moses and Joshua "presented themselves in the tent of meeting" (v. 14, RSV), the Lord appeared in a cloud and talked with Moses. He said that after Moses' death, the people would eventually forsake him for other gods. Thus, Moses was to write a song and teach it to the people so "it will stand as evidence against them" (v. 21, TEV) when they had forsaken the Lord. Moses obeyed, but before the writer got to the song, he told some other things in 31:23-30.

The song begins with 32:1, and unless you use a present-day translation, you will not see it as poetry. Biblical poetry is different from ours. Although it did not rhyme, it does have rhythm in the Hebrew and also parallelism in thought, which shows up in the repetitions of verse 2.

REBUKING DISLOYAL CHILDREN (32:4-6)

How did he describe the Lord? As "the Rock," and he repeated that figure in verses 15, 18, and 30. Contrary to sand and crumbling shale, this Rock was massive and immovable. With that figure, Moses paid tribute to God's dependability over and against the idols of Canaan and the fickleness of the people. *Today's English Version* translates the rest of that verse: "perfect and just in all his ways;/Your God is faithful and true,/he does what is right and fair." That is both praise and interpretation of God's character.

Then the next two verses accuse the people of disloyalty as the prophets would speak many years later. Verse 5 is hard to translate, but it may mean that the people in their repudiation of God were no longer worthy to be called his children. They had become deceitful and twisted. Then Moses asked how they could so repay the Lord for his good treatment of them. He had been like a father in delivering them from Egypt and making a nation from a mob of slaves. This indictment is developed further in later verses of the chapter. It would be applicable on many occasions through their history.

RECALLING THE LORD'S CHOICE (32:7-9)

These verses are not easy to interpret, but basically they

214

point again to God's choice of Israel from among other nations. First, the people were to remember what they had heard from the past, and if they were hazy about happenings of many years ago, they should ask their fathers and elders. Older people could be depended on for that information.

Evidently, what would be told begins with verses 8-9. They seem to picture a time before Abraham or perhaps the heavenly action before the covenant was offered to Abraham. Verse 8 may be telling of the heavenly council in which "the Most High" was assigning homelands to the various nations as they began separating into groupings (after Babel?). At the same time, each nation became the responsibility of a member of that council, or "he assigned to each nation a god" (TEV). Whatever verse 8 means, we are on sure ground with verse 9. For himself, the Lord chose Jacob and his descendants who were the children of Israel. So, the Lord's choice is seen from a different perspective.

Truths to Live By

God's greatness is seen in his justice and fidelity.—Both the words and tune of the hymn "How Great Thou Art" focus our minds first on the majesty and marvels of creation. Then they remind us of God's love and mercy in sending Christ for our salvation. In somewhat the same way, today's lesson points to other aspects of God's greatness. His justice is seen in his laws, the balanced pattern for righteous living. They are fair to rich and poor, learned and ignorant; and they are concerned with animals and natural resources as well as with mankind. His justice is also seen in the way so-called natural law operates in energy and electronics and in the physical well being of animals and humans. God's fidelity also shows up in those areas. But men and women are aware of it mostly in experiences of physical and spiritual strain when they turn to God in prayer for insight and endurance.

Our witness about God needs more comfort and sincerity than pious judgment.—That is at least part of the meaning of 32:2. The "small rain" was intended for refreshment and nourishment of growing plants. The gully-washer may bring lots of water, but its force may flood the plants away or beat them down to the ground. Instead of declaring only or primarily the message of God's judgment against sin, Christians must share with unbelievers his offer of love and forgiveness. Many, if not most, people already know they are having problems with life. Sometimes they don't realize that they are longing for understanding and acceptance until someone offers it in the spirit of Christ. The difference in our witness about God may be the difference between bread and a stone—in the way we do it.

God's dependability is shown in the lives of those who trust him.—Corrie ten Boom has given a remarkable testimony from her ordeal during World War II. Chester Swor has battled several handicaps but has shared most effectively his Christian faith with thousands of students and young people. Clarence Jordan was not appreciated by many of his own people, but he persevered in showing how the Christian spirit should deal with race prejudice. Everley Hayes has used her nursing skills and learned two languages within the complex tensions of the Far East for more than thirty years to fulfill Christ's commission to minister to people who hurt.

A Verse to Remember

Happy art thou, O Israel: who is like unto thee, O people saved by the Lord.—Deuteronomy 33:29.

Daily Bible Readings

Aug. 24—Living the Blameless Life. Ps. 119:1-8
Aug. 25—Keeping Your Life Clean. Ps. 119:9-16
Aug. 26—Finding Delight in God's Law. Ps. 119:17-24
Aug. 27—Restoring One's Life. Ps. 119:25-32
Aug. 28—Trust in the Lord. Ps. 146
Aug. 29—Sing Praises Unto God. Ps. 119:169-176
Aug. 30—"The Steadfast Love of the LORD." Ps. 103:6-18

Lessons
for
SEPTEMBER, OCTOBER, NOVEMBER, 1981

Great Passages of the Bible

September 1981

God and His Creation

Sept. 6—In the Beginning
  Basic Passage: Genesis 1:1 to 2:3
  Focal Passages: Genesis 1:1-3,5,14-15,20,26-27
Sept. 13—Our Shepherd God
  Basic Passage: Psalm 23
  Focal Passage: Psalm 23
Sept. 20—Our Place in God's Will
  Basic Passage: Ecclesiastes 3:1-15
  Focal Passage: Ecclesiastes 3:1-15
Sept. 27—The Everlasting God
  Basic Passage: Isaiah 40
  Focal Passage: Isaiah 40:21-23,25-31

October 1981

God's Love and Mercy

Oct. 4—God's Offer of Mercy to All
  Basic Passage: Isaiah 55
  Focal Passage: Isaiah 55:1-9
Oct. 11—The New Covenant
  Basic Passage: Jeremiah 30—31
  Focal Passage: Jeremiah 31:27-34
Oct. 18—What the Lord Requires
  Basic Passage: Micah 6
  Focal Passages: Micah 6:3-4,7-13
Oct. 25—God So Loved the World
  Basic Passage: John 3
  Focal Passages: John 3:3,6-21

November 1981

The Christian Life

Nov. 1—Jesus Prays for His Church
  Basic Passage: John 17
  Focal Passages: John 17:1-6,20-26
Nov. 8—Life in the Spirit
  Basic Passage: Romans 8
  Focal Passages: Romans 8:12-17,28,35-39
Nov. 15—A More Excellent Way
  Basic Passage: 1 Corinthians 12—13
  Focal Passages: 1 Corinthians 12:27 to 13:13
Nov. 22—Growing in Christ
  Basic Passage: Ephesians 4
  Focal Passage: Ephesians 4:1-16
Nov. 29—Love One Another
  Basic Passage: 1 John 4
  Focal Passage: 1 John 4:7-11

DECEMBER 1981, JANUARY, FEBRUARY 1982

The Person and Work of Jesus

MARCH, APRIL, MAY 1982

The Person and Work of Jesus (continued)
The Book of Revelation

JUNE, JULY, AUGUST 1982

New Testament Personalities